# NEYMAR

MATT AND TOM OLDFIELD

ULTIMATE
FOOTBALL HEROES

# NEYMAR

FROM THE PLAYGROUND
TO THE PITCH

DINO

First published by Dino Books in 2017,
an imprint of Bonnier Books UK,
4th Floor, Victoria House, Bloomsbury Square, London, WC1B 4DA
Owned by Bonnier Books,
Sveavägen 56, Stockholm, Sweden

@UFHbooks
@footieheroesbks
www.heroesfootball.com
www.bonnierbooks.co.uk

Text © Matt Oldfield 2022
The right of Matt Oldfield to be identified as the author of this work has been
asserted by him in accordance with the Copyright, Designs and Patents Act 1988.

Design by www.envydesign.co.uk

Paperback ISBN: 978 1 78606 404 2
E-book ISBN: 978 1 78946 111 4

British Library cataloguing-in-publication data:
A catalogue record for this book is available from the British Library.

Printed and bound in Great Britain by Clays Ltd, Elcograf S.p.A.

17

*For Noah and the future Oldfields to come*
*Looking forward to reading this book together*

## ULTIMATE FOOTBALL HEROES

Matt Oldfield is an accomplished writer and the editor-in-chief of football review site Of Pitch & Page. Tom Oldfield is a freelance sports writer and the author of biographies on Cristiano Ronaldo, Arsène Wenger and Rafael Nadal.

Cover illustration by Dan Leydon.
To learn more about Dan visit danleydon.com
To purchase his artwork visit etsy.com/shop/footynews
Or just follow him on Twitter @danleydon

# TABLE OF CONTENTS

ACKNOWLEDGEMENTS . . . . . . . . . . . . . . . . . . . . . . . . . . . . 9

CHAPTER 1 – OLYMPIC GOLD . . . . . . . . . . . . . . . . . . . . . 11

CHAPTER 2 – A LUCKY ESCAPE . . . . . . . . . . . . . . . . . . . 17

CHAPTER 3 – RUNNING AROUND . . . . . . . . . . . . . . . . . 22

CHAPTER 4 – FUTSAL VS STREET FOOTBALL . . . . . . . . . . 28

CHAPTER 5 – ON THE BEACH . . . . . . . . . . . . . . . . . . . . . 34

CHAPTER 6 – GREAT TIMES AT GREMETAL . . . . . . . . . . . 40

CHAPTER 7 – SCOUTED BY SANTOS . . . . . . . . . . . . . . . . 46

CHAPTER 8 – FINDING SPACE TO SHINE . . . . . . . . . . . . . 51

CHAPTER 9 – THE BOY WHO TURNED DOWN REAL MADRID . 57

CHAPTER 10 – WELCOME TO THE FIRST TEAM . . . . . . . . . 62

CHAPTER 11 – **THE FUTURE OF BRAZIL** . . . . . . . . . . . . . . 68

CHAPTER 12 – **FAME AND GLORY** . . . . . . . . . . . . . . . . . . 73

CHAPTER 13 – **UPS AND DOWNS** . . . . . . . . . . . . . . . . . . . 82

CHAPTER 14 – **FOLLOWING IN THE FOOTSTEPS OF 'THE KING'** . . . . . . . . . . . . . . . . . . . . . . . 90

CHAPTER 15 – **MEETING MESSI** . . . . . . . . . . . . . . . . . . . 96

CHAPTER 16 – **THE HAT-TRICK** . . . . . . . . . . . . . . . . . . . 102

CHAPTER 17 – **BARCELONA** . . . . . . . . . . . . . . . . . . . . . . 109

CHAPTER 18 – **CONFEDERATIONS CUP** . . . . . . . . . . . . . . 115

CHAPTER 19 – **NEW START IN SPAIN** . . . . . . . . . . . . . . . 122

CHAPTER 20 – **WORLD CUP 2014** . . . . . . . . . . . . . . . . . 129

CHAPTER 21 – **THE TREBLE** . . . . . . . . . . . . . . . . . . . . . 137

CHAPTER 22 – **MSN** . . . . . . . . . . . . . . . . . . . . . . . . . . . . 145

CHAPTER 23 – **BRAZILIAN SUCCESS** . . . . . . . . . . . . . . . 153

# ACKNOWLEDGEMENTS

First of all, I'd like to thank John Blake Publishing –
and particularly my editor James Hodgkinson – for
giving me the opportunity to work on these books
and for supporting me throughout. Writing stories for
the next generation of football fans is both an honour
and a pleasure.

I wouldn't be doing this if it wasn't for Tom. I owe
him so much and I'm very grateful for his belief in
me as an author. I feel like Robin setting out on a
solo career after a great partnership with Batman. I
hope I do him (Tom, not Batman) justice with these
new books.

Next up, I want to thank my friends for keeping

me sane during long hours in front of the laptop. Pang, Will, Mills, Doug, John, Charlie – the laughs and the cups of coffee are always appreciated.

I've already thanked my brother but I'm also very grateful to the rest of my family, especially Melissa, Noah and of course Mum and Dad. To my parents, I owe my biggest passions: football and books. They're a real inspiration for everything I do.

Finally, I couldn't have done this without Iona's encouragement and understanding during long, work-filled weekends. Much love to you.

## CHAPTER 1

# OLYMPIC GOLD

'We have to win!' Neymar Jr told his teammates. He normally liked to laugh and dance before a match but not this time. He was captain and this was serious. 'Let's get revenge for the 2014 World Cup!'

Neymar Jr was the only member of Brazil's 2016 Olympic squad who had also been there for that awful night in Belo Horizonte two years earlier. When Germany thrashed Brazil 7–1 in the semi-finals on home soil, the whole nation was left heartbroken. Football was their greatest passion.

But it hurt Neymar Jr more than most because he was injured for that game and couldn't be the national hero that they needed. This time, though, as they faced Germany once again, he was fit and raring to go.

'Germany better watch out!' his strike partner, Gabriel Jesus cheered.

After a long season at Barcelona, Neymar Jr had taken a little while to find his form at the Olympics. As the one of the oldest players in the squad, his teammates depended on him. It was a lot of responsibility and after three matches, Neymar Jr hadn't scored a single goal.

'Don't worry,' the coach Rogério Micale told him. 'That was your warm-up; now we need you at your best in these next big games!'

Neymar Jr scored one against Colombia in the quarter-finals, then two against Honduras in the semi-finals. He had rediscovered his *ginga* rhythm, his Brazilian flair, just in time.

'That means you should score a hat-trick in the final!' his teammate Marquinhos joked.

'No pressure, then!' Neymar Jr replied with a smile on his face.

He led the players out on to the pitch to face

Germany at the Maracanã Stadium in Rio de
Janeiro. Nearly 60,000 Brazilians had come to
cheer on their country, wearing the famous yellow
shirt and waving yellow-and-green flags. They were
ready for a party, and the noise and colour were
incredible.

Neymar Jr stood with his hand on his heart and
sang the national anthem loudly. He was so proud to
represent his nation and he was one win away from
making everyone very happy. He couldn't wait.

Midway through the first half, Brazil won a free-
kick just outside the penalty area. It was a perfect
opportunity for Neymar Jr. He placed the ball down,
stepped back and took a long, deep breath. Then he
curled the ball powerfully towards the top corner.
It was too quick and high for the goalkeeper to
save. The shot hit the underside of the crossbar and
bounced down into the back of the net.

*Goooooooooooooooaaaaaaaaaaaaaaaaaaallllllllllllllllll
llllllllll!!!!!!!!!!!!!!!!!!!*

Neymar Jr had always dreamed of scoring amazing
goals in international finals. Now it was a reality

and he would never forget the moment. All of his teammates ran over and jumped on him.

'You did it!' Gabriel shouted.

After the celebrations, Neymar Jr told the others to calm down and focus. 'We haven't won this yet – concentrate!'

Brazil defended well but after sixty minutes, Germany equalised. Neymar Jr had more work to do. He dribbled past one defender and then dropped in a clever Cruyff Turn to wrong-foot a second. It was magical skill and the crowd loved it. He now had the space to shoot. The ball swerved past the goalkeeper's outstretched arm but just wide of the post.

'So close!' Neymar Jr said to himself, putting his hands on his head.

Brazil attacked again and again but they couldn't find a winning goal, even after thirty minutes of extra-time. Now it would go to penalties.

'I'll take the last one,' Neymar Jr told Micale. He was determined to be the national hero this time.

After eight penalties, it was 4–4. When Brazil's goalkeeper Weverton saved the ninth spot-kick,

Neymar Jr had his golden chance. He walked from the halfway line towards the penalty spot with thousands of fans cheering his name.

He picked up the ball, kissed it and put it back down. As he waited for the referee's whistle, he tried to slow his heartbeat. If he was too excited, he might kick it over the bar. He needed to be his normal, cool self.

As he ran up, he slowed down to try to make the German goalkeeper move early. The keeper dived low to the right and Neymar Jr put his shot high and to the left. As the ball went in, Neymar burst into tears of joy. He had led his country all the way to the Olympic Gold Medal for the first time ever. As he fell to his knees and thanked God, the other Brazil players ran to hug their hero.

'You always said that we could do it!' his teammate Luan shouted. 'Now it's carnival time!'

As Neymar Jr got back on his feet, he listened to the incredible noise of the Maracanã crowd. It was the best thing he had ever heard.

'Imagine what the atmosphere would have been

like if we'd made it to the World Cup final and won it in 2014!' Neymar Jr thought to himself, but it was time to forget about the pains of the past and move forward. Thanks to him, his country was back at the top of world football again.

'Thank you!' the coach Micale said to him, giving him the biggest hug of all.

He was still only twenty-four but Neymar Jr had already been Brazil's number one superstar for years. There was so much pressure on him but he refused to let his country down, even after moving to Spain to play for Barcelona.

Neymar Jr had Brazil to thank for everything: the love of his family and friends; the support of his coaches at Portuguesa Santista and Santos; and above all, the amazing skills that he had first developed in street football, beach football and *futsal* matches in São Paulo.

## CHAPTER 2

# A LUCKY ESCAPE

'Nadine, don't forget Junior's blanket!' Neymar
Senior called into the house. They were driving to
Santos to visit some relatives and they needed to
keep their newborn son warm. In his baby seat,
Neymar Jr giggled and wiggled his toes.

'I'm still not sure about that name,' Nadine
muttered as she wrapped the blanket tightly around
her son. She still hadn't forgiven her husband. 'Why
didn't you just go with Mateus like I asked you to? I
thought you liked that name too! It's much nicer.'

'You'll learn to love this name, I promise!' Neymar
Sr replied. Like father, like son.

As he got into the car, he groaned. Neymar Sr's

body hurt more and more after every match that he played for União FC in the third division of the São Paulo league. He was getting older and now that he had a child to look after, he was always tired. Football was the first love of his life and he worked hard to earn enough money for his family. But perhaps his dad, Ilzemar, was right. Was it time to finally give up on his dream and find a proper job with a better wage?

In the passenger seat, Nadine turned to check on her little boy – he was fast asleep. 'He looks so peaceful,' she said lovingly. 'Please drive carefully! The roads are wet today.'

The journey down the mountain from Mogi das Cruzes was always dangerous. The roads were narrow and winding, with blind bends everywhere. Also, Brazilians weren't known as the safest drivers in the world. Neymar Sr wasn't going to take any risks with their tiny and precious new arrival.

But as they turned a corner, a car came towards them at high speed. 'Watch out!' Nadine shouted. Neymar Sr swerved to the left to try to avoid it but there wasn't enough time. There was a loud crashing sound and then everything went black for a minute. Once the shock had worn off, the pain was unbearable.

'Nadine, are you okay?' Neymar Sr called out. It felt like he had broken every bone in his body.

'Yes,' she managed to reply eventually. 'But what about Junior?'

Slowly, they turned around to look – the back seat was empty. 'Where is he?!' Nadine shouted, panicking.

Neymar Sr tried to stay calm but the possibilities were terrible. The car was right on the edge of a cliff – what if their son had been thrown out of the car? He prayed to God to protect Neymar Jr. When he tried to escape from the car to check, he couldn't move.

'We're going to get you both out of there!' a voice shouted from outside. Fortunately, people who had seen the accident had stopped to help them.

'Our son was in the car too but we can't find him!' Neymar Sr cried out.

The helpers forced the back door open and soon

there was very good news. 'He's here!' someone cheered. Neymar Jr had fallen into the footwell under the front seat.

'Is he alive?' Nadine asked, fearing the answer. If they had all survived the crash, it would be a miracle.

'Yes!' a woman replied, showing her the baby in her arms. He had some cuts and bruises but his eyes were open and Neymar Jr began to cry. Tears of relief rolled down Nadine's cheeks. She was so happy to see her son's little face.

'What about my husband?' she asked next.

The ambulance rushed Neymar Sr straight to the hospital. His injuries were very serious and it took a long time for them to heal. When Neymar Jr came to visit, with a small bandage tied around his head, and saw his dad surrounded by all the big medical machines, he burst into tears.

'Don't worry, Junior – I'm just lucky to be alive!' Neymar Sr reassured him, holding his hand. 'I'll be better soon and then we'll able to play together again.'

When Neymar Jr was one year old, his dad was finally able to hold him in his arms again. It was a beautiful moment after so many months of waiting.

'My golden child,' Neymar Sr said, kissing his son's forehead. 'You're going to grow up and do something very special – I'm sure of it!'

As one football career faded out, another was about to begin.

**CHAPTER 3**

# RUNNING AROUND

'Junior, please sit still for one minute!' Nadine begged. She was trying to feed him but he preferred to be moving at all times, and kept wriggling around in his chair. 'Fine,' she said, 'once you've had a few more vegetables, you can go back to your games!'

Neymar Jr was only three years old, and so too young to go out playing in the neighbourhood with the other local boys. For now, their house had to be his playground. He climbed all over the furniture and ran from room to room, knocking into anything that got in his way.

'Careful, Junior!' his dad shouted. 'We can't afford to replace all the things that you break.'

Neymar Sr was working three jobs at the
same time but it wasn't making them rich at all.
Sometimes they couldn't pay the electricity bill and
so the family had to live by candlelight. In the semi-
darkness, Neymar Jr's running around was even
more dangerous.

'What are we going to do?' Nadine asked her
husband. She was pregnant again and they needed to
think about the future of their family.

'We'll have to move in with my parents for now,'
Neymar Sr replied. 'It's not perfect but we can save
up money for a home of our own.'

In his grandparents' house, Neymar Jr shared a
bedroom with his parents and soon with his baby
sister Rafaela too. It was very cramped but that didn't
stop the young boy's games. He only needed a tiny
bit of space and his imagination.

'We're under attack!' he shouted. 'Go Go Power
Rangers, it's time to fight back!'

Neymar Jr's games changed when he was given his
first football. Suddenly, it was his favourite toy and
he took it everywhere with him. When his parents

were in the kitchen, Neymar Jr turned the bedroom into an obstacle course. He started at the door and dribbled as fast as he could between the mattress and the wardrobe. When Rafaela and his cousins were around, he made them play too.

'Leave us alone – we're playing our own game!' his sister complained.

'You don't have to do anything – just stand still,' he told her. 'You're the goalpost!'

Sometimes Neymar Jr was the striker. He dribbled around one cousin and then another before kicking his little football as hard as he could. As it flew between Rafaela and another cousin, he celebrated wildly with his shirt over his head.

'And Neymarzinho scores another brilliant goal!'

Sometimes he was the goalkeeper, making incredible saves by diving across the mattress. And sometimes he just practised his technique, kicking the ball against the wall again and again, first with his right foot and then with his left foot.

Neymar Sr was very pleased with his son's progress. When he passed him the ball, he didn't pick it up and run away with it like most toddlers. Instead, he kicked it straight back with a strong and accurate pass. Neymar Jr's little face looked so serious.

'He's going to be a top footballer – I know it already!' Neymar Sr told his wife excitedly.

But Nadine wasn't so impressed. 'Junior's got too much energy to be stuck in here all day,' she said. 'If he breaks one more vase, I'm going to scream!'

'Okay, I'll take him to my beach football match this weekend,' Neymar Sr told her. 'He can run around while I play and people will keep an eye on him. I'll make sure he's exhausted by the time we come back!'

Neymar Jr loved being outside in the sunshine but the football match was really boring to watch. His dad had made him leave his football in the car and so he switched to Plan B: running *without* the ball. There weren't many spectators in the stand and so Neymar Jr could run up and down the big steps and then along each row. There was plenty of space for adventures.

Amongst the spectators was Betinho, a local youth coach and scout. He had brought his young son along to watch the game but, like Neymar Jr, the boy quickly got bored and went off to explore.

'Where is my son? I must keep an eye on him!' Betinho remembered when the game stopped because of an injury. As he turned and looked across the stand, he spotted another skinny little boy running around.

'He's got a nice style,' Betinho said to himself. He had been scouting young footballers for years and so he knew exactly what to look for. Skilful Brazilians moved in a special, natural way that combined balance with agility and rhythm. They looked like they were dancing as they dribbled past defenders.

'I'd like to see that kid running with a football!' Betinho thought. So he asked a friend, 'Who is that boy?'

'That's Junior, son of Neymar Sr,' the friend replied, pointing down at the winger on the pitch.

When the match finished, Betinho went to speak to the boy's dad. 'Well played today. I saw your son

up in the crowd. Is he playing for a team yet?'
he asked.

'Not yet,' Neymar Sr replied. 'He's still only five
years old. Isn't that too young?'

'You're never too young to start playing football!'
Betinho argued with a smile on his face. 'Can I please
train your son? He'll love it and you never know – we
might have a world champion right here!'

## CHAPTER 4

# FUTSAL VS STREET FOOTBALL

'Here you go,' Betinho said, passing a football to Neymar Jr. 'Let's see if I was right about you!'

Neymar Jr controlled it with his left foot, flicked it to his right foot and then passed it back. He hadn't done anything particularly special yet but Betinho was already excited. Eight years earlier, he had discovered a brilliant young player called Robinho and he was getting that special feeling again.

'Okay, let's see you dribble. Try to get past me!'

Neymar Jr ran forward at speed – this was his favourite game. As he got near to Betinho, he pretended to go left but did a step over and went right.

The youth coach was too amazed to move. 'Wow, yes you've got *ginga!*'

Neymar Jr looked confused. 'What's that?'

'It's Brazilian flair,' Betinho explained. 'You can't teach *ginga* – it's a natural style that makes us the best footballers in the world! Do you like dancing to samba music?'

Neymar Jr nodded.

'I thought so! It's the same thing really – when you take that rhythm and movement and you put it on the football pitch, it's magical!'

Betinho took his new star for a trial at Clube de Regatas Tumiaru, the local *futsal* club where he coached. *Futsal* was a five-a-side indoor sport that many young Brazilians played before moving on to football. The ball was smaller and heavier and the hard court wasn't so large, so players needed great close control and clever skills.

'We know that you've got the technique but it's time for you to learn about the other areas of the game,' Betinho told Neymar Jr beforehand. 'Things like teamwork, stamina, strength and tactics are just as important.'

Neymar Jr listened to every word of advice because he wanted to get better and better. In the passing and dribbling practices, he was focused and precise. He didn't do anything wrong but nor did he do anything exceptional. He was saving that for the match at the end.

When the coach blew the whistle to start, all of Neymar Jr's teammates chased after the ball. It was chaos in the middle of the court as nine kids battled each other.

'I'm in space!' Neymar Jr called from out on the wing.

When his team won possession, they passed to him, and he dribbled forward and scored easily.

'I've been trying to get them to spread out like that for months!' one of the other coaches said with a smile. 'He's a smart kid.'

'I didn't even tell him to do that,' Betinho replied. 'He's a thinker!'

As his opponents passed the ball to each other,

Neymar Jr was already running to where he thought their next pass might go. And once he won the ball back, he never lost it. He dribbled whenever he could but if he couldn't, he made sure that he gave it to his teammates.

'Excellent, Junior!' the coach shouted, clapping loudly.

The other team soon realised how good Neymar Jr was and they tried to double-mark him. But he hypnotised them with his quick feet every time.

'I've never seen a kid that good,' the other coach admitted.

'Robinho was very good but I think Junior might be even better!' Betinho predicted.

When the session finished, the boys got changed and left, one by one, until only one remained: Neymar Jr.

'Come on, your dad will be waiting for you at home,' Betinho called to the boy but he was in his own world, gliding past imaginary defenders and shooting past an imaginary goalkeeper. 'The goal will still be here next time, I promise!'

Neymar Jr took one last shot and followed Betinho to the car. He was pleased with his first practice. There was still a lot of work to do but it felt good to play for a proper club.

'How was it?' his dad asked him as he ran inside for dinner.

'Awesome!' he replied with a huge grin on his face.

'That kid might be a football genius one day!' Betinho had told Neymar Sr as they said goodbye.

From that first day onwards, Neymar Jr was the star of the team. He scored lots of great goals as Tumiaru won every local tournament and trophy. The club were so desperate to keep him that they started sending food baskets to his house.

'Good boy, you're already earning a wage for the family!' Neymar Sr joked.

Betinho's only problem was actually finding his protégé. Neymar Jr was always playing football but where? As soon as school finished each day, he rushed outside to play football with his friends. The streets were always full of cars and bikes but they used whatever space they could find.

Neymar Jr loved the noisy atmosphere: the people chatting, the car horns sounding, the Brazilian hip-hop music blaring. It gave him the extra energy he needed to show off his full range of tricks and flicks. That was what street football was all about. They often played barefoot with a deflated ball and the contest was simple: who could do the coolest bit of skill?

'Is Junior at home?' Betinho asked, when he came to pick Neymar Jr up for training at Tumiaru.

Nadine shook her head. 'No, sorry, he's still out playing.'

Betinho drove slowly through the streets looking for him. Eventually, he spotted Neymar Jr. A crowd of people were standing around, cheering loudly as the others tried to get the ball off him. He was a born entertainer.

'Junior!' Betinho shouted through the car window. 'Come on, you're late!'

Neymar Jr rolled the ball off his neck and back down on to his foot. Then he flicked it up into his arms and sprinted to the car.

'I'll be back after training!' he called to his friends.

## CHAPTER 5

# ON THE BEACH

'That's it!' Neymar Sr encouraged his son. It was a very warm afternoon in São Paulo and for once, he had a day off from work. That meant only one thing: football practice. 'And if you want to kick it really hard, use the top of your foot. Yes, just like that!'

As the football flew through the air, Neymar Jr chased after it across the hot sand. If it went in the sea, the ball might drift away. That would be a disaster.

'Don't step on a jellyfish!' his dad joked.

Neymar Sr had built a new home for his family in Praia Grande, an area with a long coastline of beautiful beaches. In the evenings and at the weekends, thousands of Brazilians came down there to play volleyball and football.

'If you can play well here,' he told his son, 'you'll be unbelievable on the pitch at Santos!'

Neymar Jr loved playing beach football because it was a real test of his technique. He also played *futsal* but he preferred playing outside with the sun, sea and sand.

'Slow down, Junior – you don't want to injure yourself!'

Balance was very important in beach football because the surface wasn't smooth and flat like grass. It was lumpy and covered in obstacles like shells and litter. If you took one wrong step, you could easily twist your ankle. Luckily, Neymar Jr was a natural, just like Betinho had predicted.

Neymar Jr could dribble really fast with either foot and he could shift his body to either side in an instant to escape a tackle. He was only seven years old, and yet Neymar Sr was already finding it difficult to get the ball off him.

'You dance like a Brazilian!' his dad laughed.

Thanks to all the hours spent practising in the bedroom at his grandparents' house, Neymar Jr didn't panic when there wasn't much space around him. Instead, he was calm and creative, and improvised something special.

'Yes, you're certainly going to be a star one day!' his dad told him.

But Neymar Jr was impatient. He was ready for the next challenge – trying out his skills in proper beach football matches. That was the best way to keep learning.

'Dad, can we ask to join in?' he said, pointing to the people playing nearby.

Neymar Sr was worried. There were a few kids playing in the game but none were as young and skinny as his son. What if he got badly hurt? Some of the adults looked very strong but at least he would be there to protect Neymar Jr.

'Okay, but first I need to give you two more lessons,' he said.

His son rolled his eyes. 'Not more lessons – I want to *play!*'

Neymar Sr ignored him. 'Lesson One: Don't be a show-off. If you're going to dribble with the ball, do it to create a goal. If you try to do lots of tricks and don't pass the ball, your teammates will be angry and your opponents will tackle you even harder.'

His son nodded.

'And Lesson Two: Work hard. Always keep moving to find space away from the defenders. Make life difficult for them. When you stand still, it's easy to mark you.'

Neymar Jr nodded again. 'Now can we play?'

At first, Neymar Sr felt nervous every time his son touched the ball. But soon, he relaxed and enjoyed himself because Neymar Jr was playing very well. He had listened carefully to all of his dad's advice. He ran and ran to help his team and when they attacked, he was fearless against players twice his size. He dribbled down the wing and if he couldn't get past the defender, he looked up for the pass, rather than being selfish.

'Wow, your son is brilliant,' one of the adults said to Neymar Sr. 'His ball skills are better than mine!'

'Thanks,' he replied proudly. And to himself, he muttered, 'He's got two good coaches!'

Neymar Jr's team won and as father and son walked home together, the boy talked happily about the match.

'Did you see it when I flicked it round the fat guy and then crossed the ball for Jorge to score?'

His dad nodded.

'Did you see the tackle I did on the midfielder? I was so quick that he didn't even see me coming!'

His dad nodded.

'And did you see the goal I scored at the end? The goalkeeper didn't think I had the power to kick it that hard!'

Neymar Sr smiled; he could remember being just as excited about football when he was younger. 'Junior, of course I saw it – I was playing in the match too!'

Neymar Jr couldn't wait to share his stories with Nadine and Rafaela at dinner.

'Mum, I had so much fun!' he began, wolfing down the rice and beans on his plate. Twenty minutes later, he was only halfway through his story of the match.

'This is so boring!' Rafaela moaned, pretending to yawn.

'Yes, can we skip to the end now please?' Nadine asked nicely. 'Otherwise, we might be here all night! Did you win?'

'Of course!' Neymar Jr cheered with a mouth full of food.

'That's disgusting!' Rafaela said, but they all laughed.

When Neymar Sr went to say goodnight to his son, he was lying in bed surrounded by round objects. There was barely room for his little body. Some kids slept with animal soft toys next to them, but Neymar Jr chose footballs.

'Well played today,' Neymar Sr said, kissing him on the forehead. 'We'll work on a few more things next weekend – there's always room for improvement!'

## CHAPTER 6

# GREAT TIMES AT GREMETAL

'I've got a new coaching job at Gremetal,' Betinho told Neymar Sr one day, 'and I really want Junior to come with me. What do you think?'

'I think it's a very good idea,' Neymar Sr replied immediately. He trusted Betinho with his son's future and he knew that Gremetal was a great *futsal* club that looked after its young players.

'Great to see you!' Luiz Ricardo shouted, giving Neymar Jr a high-five. They knew each other well from their street football games in Praia Grande. 'Guys, this is Junior. Just wait until you see him play – he's incredible. We're going to win everything now that he's here!'

Luiz was right. Once Neymar Jr arrived, the Gremetal Under-11s were unbeatable. He was their youngest player but he was so brilliant that he quickly became one of the leaders. He even made matching white headbands for his teammates.

'We all look like Karate Kids now!' he laughed.

The other players were good but Neymar Jr was in a league of his own. He started every attack and he was there at the end too, either with a shot or a cross. Despite all his skills, he wasn't a selfish player. As long the team won, he didn't mind who scored.

'We win together!' Gremetal cheered before each match.

As Neymar Jr ran towards goal, defenders knew what was going to happen but there was nothing that they could do to stop it. Even fouling didn't work because they couldn't get close enough to kick him. He was just too quick, too skilful, too clever – too good. Betinho's job was easy and his instructions were simple: 'Just play your natural game'.

Neymar Jr was the king of the *futsal* court and as

he got older, more and more scouts came to watch him play.

'Please don't leave us, Junior!' Luiz said as the team relaxed after yet another victory. They were enjoying their success and they didn't want it to end.

Neymar Jr smiled. 'Don't be silly, the only place I'm going to is Dudu's house!'

Dudu, Luiz, Michael and Neymar Jr usually spent their whole weekends together. They worked hard and they played hard too. When they weren't playing football together for Gremetal, they were often playing football against each other in the street. The two-vs-two matches were very competitive.

'Okay, I'm playing with Junior this time,' Luiz said before anyone else could beat him to it. 'It's my turn!'

Whoever played with Neymar Jr almost always won; it was as simple as that. After about thirty seconds, Dudu and Michael stopped marking Luiz and both focused on the danger boy.

'Michael, if you tackle him from the left, I'll tackle him from the right,' Dudu suggested. 'Don't let him escape!'

But Neymar Jr spun around on the ball, did a couple of step overs and played a perfect pass to Luiz. 1–0!

Fifteen minutes later, it was 3–3. 'Next goal wins!' Luiz shouted.

Neymar Jr shielded the ball from Dudu and looked for a path to goal. He rolled the ball from right to left, as if to pass to Luiz. As Michael ran to block it, Neymar Jr flicked the ball behind him instead and tried to turn. Dudu stuck out his leg and tripped him up.

'Foul!' Luiz shouted. 'You can't do that!'

Dudu shrugged dramatically like the professionals. 'I didn't touch him – he just fell!'

As the others fought over whether it was a penalty or not, Neymar Jr got up and wiped his bleeding knee. He had an idea.

'Okay, if I can kick the ball from here into that bin over there, we win. If I can't, we keep playing.'

Michael nodded. 'That sounds fair, but you only get one go!'

The bin was at least twenty yards away but

Neymar Jr had been practising his long-range passing. This was the ultimate test. He chipped the ball carefully and it floated through the air. He'd got the distance just right but would it land neatly inside or bounce off the edge? The ball rolled around the rim and dropped in.

'Yes!' Luiz shouted, giving Neymar Jr a big hug. 'That was amazing!'

Michael was disappointed to lose but he patted his opponent on the back. 'I've got no idea how you do stuff like that. I'm just glad you're on my team for Gremetal!'

'What time do you guys have to be home?' Dudu asked. 'Have we got time for a quick game of FIFA?'

There was always time to play PlayStation. They had changed the names of four top players so that 'Junior', 'Dudu', 'Michael' and 'Luiz' were teammates for the Brazilian national team. Neymar Jr was allowed to be his hero – the best player in the world, Ronaldo.

'It's only fair,' Dudu had decided after listening to the arguments. 'Junior is the best player here!'

Ronaldo was a striker at Italian club Inter Milan and Neymar Jr loved to watch him glide past defenders to score great goals. He was always looking for new tricks to learn. The boys took it in turns to lead their nation to 2002 World Cup glory.

'How amazing would it be if this was real life?' Luiz said as they watched the players lift the golden trophy. 'Imagine how cool it would be to play for Brazil!'

For most of them, that was just a fantasy. But for Neymar Jr, it was a genuine possibility. He was still only eleven but everyone agreed that he had the talent to reach the very top. The next step would be moving from *futsal* to association football.

## CHAPTER 7

# SCOUTED BY SANTOS

Zito had been keeping an eye on Neymar Jr for a while. As a Santos FC legend with over fifty caps for Brazil, he was a well-informed man. If there was a great young player in São Paulo, he knew about him. He had first heard the name 'Neymar Jr' from Alemão, a massive Santos supporter who ran a bar near the Vila Belmiro Stadium.

'I think you'll really like him,' Alemão told him with a smile. 'He plays *futsal* for Gremetal and he's got unbelievable talent for an eleven-year-old!'

When Zito asked one of the other Santos youth coaches if he had heard of Neymar Jr, he laughed. 'Oh yes! Gremetal thrashed our Under-12s 9–0 two weeks ago. That kid scored a hat-trick and set up most of the other goals too. He's special, that's for sure!'

'Do you know if he's playing association football for a club?' Zito asked.

'He's at Portuguesa Santista, I think.'

As Zito waited for the Santista match to begin, he watched Neymar Jr warming up. He was laughing with his teammates, while doing keepy-uppies at the same time. He made it look as easy as walking. The kid's height wasn't a problem but he did look far too skinny.

'There can't be any muscle on his body at all,' the Santos youth coach thought to himself. 'A gust of wind might blow him over!'

But once the game kicked off, Zito saw that it didn't really matter. Neymar Jr's dribbling skills made it almost impossible for anyone to get near enough to push him around. Everything about him was so quick: his feet, his change of direction, and his football brain.

He was the best player on the pitch by miles. As soon as the ball came to him, space seemed to open up in front of him like magic. He sprinted forward, nutmegged one defender, played a one-two with a teammate and then hit a fierce shot into the bottom corner.

*Gooooooooooooooaaaaaaaaaaaaaaaaaaaalllllllllllllllll lllllllllll!!!!!!!!!!!!!!!!!!!!!!*

'We have to sign him!' Zito shouted out loud. He was on his own but he didn't care if he sounded crazy; he had never been so excited about a youngster before. He looked around to see if any other local scouts were watching. Surely Santos couldn't be the only club chasing this wonderkid?

That same day, Zito marched into the office of the club chairman, Marcelo Teixeira. 'I'm sorry to disturb you but I've just found a superstar and we have to act fast before another team gets him!'

Teixera was shocked. 'Wow, I've never seen you like this. The kid must be amazing – sure, go get him!'

Neymar Jr couldn't believe it when he heard the news. His dream was coming true. He would be following in his dad's footsteps: first Portuguesa Santista and now Santos.

'Are you absolutely certain that they've got the right player?' he asked his dad. His Gremetal strike partner, Léo Dentinho, was also very highly-rated. Maybe the club had mixed the two of them up.

'Son, they're desperate to sign you!' Neymar Sr told him proudly. 'They're offering a five-year contract with a salary.'

Neymar Jr smiled. 'Now I'll really be earning a wage for the family!'

Nadine laughed. 'Yes, but you know you won't just be playing football all day every day, don't you? You'll still be going to school – education is important too.'

As the family celebrated at dinner, a horrible thought crossed Neymar Jr's mind.

'Dad, what about Betinho? Is he coming too?'

He really didn't want to leave his coach behind. What would he do without him after so many years of success together?

'I'm not sure, Junior,' his dad replied, looking sad. 'I'll speak to Santos but I'm afraid he may have to stay with Santista.'

Fortunately, Neymar Sr was brilliant at negotiating and a few days later, he had great news for his son. 'Betinho is going with you! I told them that the deal was off unless they signed your coach too. And they agreed!'

Neymar Jr was delighted. With his dad and Betinho at his side, offering support and advice, he truly believed that he could fulfil his great potential. This was his big chance to develop into a top professional footballer and, hopefully, a Brazilian international. He was ready to make the most of the opportunity.

He went to Gremetal to say goodbye to his teammates. He would really miss them.

'Don't worry, we're going with you,' Dudu said, after listening to his friend's farewell speech. 'Apparently, you weren't enough; they wanted all of us!'

It was more good news for Neymar Jr. 'Santos, here we come!' they all cheered together.

As he arrived at the Meninos da Vila training centre, Neymar Jr was buzzing. There were skilful youngsters everywhere, playing on perfect green pitches in white and black shirts. He was one of them now – a Santos footballer, just like Brazil's greatest ever player, Pelé.

'I'm going to be very happy here!' Neymar Jr said to himself. He couldn't wait to get started.

## CHAPTER 8

# FINDING SPACE
# TO SHINE

'No way!' Zito said, shaking his head. 'Junior's not strong enough to play eleven-a-side football for you yet. He's only just arrived at the club. Maybe next year, when he's developed more muscle.'

But Lima, the Santos Under-15s coach, wasn't going to give up. He had seen Neymar Jr's talents on the *futsal* court. He was exactly the kind of exciting player that his team needed. 'He's far too good to be playing with your Under-13s!' he argued. 'He needs a bigger challenge. At least let him come and train with us. I promise he won't play a match until you think he's ready.'

In the end, Zito lost the fight and Neymar Jr joined

the Under-15s. He was the smallest and youngest player in the team but that never scared him. His dad and Betinho had taught him well. He understood that he had to keep testing himself if he wanted to become a Brazilian hero.

'I've played against older kids all my life!' Neymar Jr told Lima with a confident smile on his face.

That smile didn't last long, however. Under-15s football was much tougher than Neymar Jr had expected. The problem was that some of his opponents were far too old for the age group.

'That kid looks closer to thirty than fifteen!' Betinho shouted as a huge defender barged into the back of Neymar Jr. The skinny thirteen-year-old went flying to the floor. 'Referee, I'd like to see his date of birth please!'

'It's ridiculous,' Neymar Sr said angrily. 'They're fouling him every time. He's got no space to shine.'

Every week, Neymar Jr left the pitch covered in cuts and bruises but he never gave up. Instead, he just worked even harder in training.

'Come on, it's time to go home!' Lima shouted. It was dinner time and he was hungry.

'Just five more shots!' Neymar Jr replied.

His coach sighed; it was the same old story. 'Why are you hitting them all with your right foot?' he asked.

'My right foot is much more powerful than my left.'

'That's not a good reason!' Lima said. 'The best players can shoot with both feet and that makes it much more difficult for defenders to stop them. If you practise, you can make your left foot just as powerful. Not now, though. It's time to go home!'

Neymar Jr was improving every day in training but for the first time ever, he wasn't enjoying the weekend football matches.

'Are you okay, son?' Neymar Sr asked as they drove home from a game.

Neymar Jr nodded slowly. 'I can play so much better than that but I don't know what to do against those giants. They don't even care about the ball – they just want to hurt me!'

They needed to find a solution to the problem. A talent like Neymar Jr's could not be wasted.

'Do you think he should go back to the Under-13s?' Betinho asked. 'Perhaps he needs to play with kids his own age for a bit longer.'

Lima thought for a few minutes. Suddenly, he banged the desk with his fist. 'No, I've got a better idea!'

At the next training session, the coach spoke to his young attacker. 'How are your ankles after the last game?'

Neymar Jr looked down and shrugged. 'They're fine, thanks.'

'For next week's match, we're going to make a change,' Lima explained. 'This time, you won't be playing as the centre forward.'

Neymar Jr looked very upset. 'I know I haven't been scoring enough goals but please don't–'

His coach interrupted him. 'No, I'm not putting you on the bench! I want you to play as the playmaker instead, in between the midfield and the strikers. At the moment, you're too close to the defence to use your skills and speed. They're much stronger than you and so they push you around. Let's see what you can do with a bit more space to dribble!'

The youngster nodded. He was relieved to hear that he was still in the team and he liked the sound of his new role.

Neymar Jr got the ball just inside the opposition half. One of the defenders rushed out to tackle him but Neymar Jr had time to turn and flick the ball past him. He sprinted towards goal. The other centre-back tried to stop him but Neymar Jr did one step over and then another, and then another. Which way would he go? The defender tried to keep his eyes on the ball, rather than the magical, dancing feet, but it was impossible. Neymar Jr nutmegged him and ran into the penalty area.

'It's working!' Betinho shouted on the touchline.

As the goalkeeper slid out to block his shot, Neymar Jr faked to go right as he normally did, but then kicked the ball into the bottom corner with his left foot.

*Goooooooooooooooooooooooaaaaaaaaaaaaaaaallllllll lllllllllllllllllllllll!!!!!!!!!!!!!!!*

Neymar Jr's teammates had stopped to watch the wondergoal. They couldn't believe their eyes. Once the ball was in the net, they chased after him and jumped on top of him.

'I've never seen anything like it!'

'Those defenders are still looking for the ball now. That's magic!'

In his slightly deeper position, Neymar Jr was happy again. Even when there were four opponents surrounding him, he used the tricks and flicks that he had learnt in *futsal* and street football to escape and move his team forward. He loved the ball and he did everything he could to protect it.

'As long as you look after it too, I'll pass it to you!' Neymar Jr joked with his teammates, as they celebrated another goal. He had set it up with a killer through-ball and the smile was back on his face.

After the game, Neymar Jr hugged his coach. 'Thanks!' was all he said.

Lima was very pleased. With one small tactical switch, he had brought Neymar Jr back to life. Now there was no stopping him.

## CHAPTER 9

# THE BOY WHO TURNED DOWN REAL MADRID

'I know I should have told you earlier but I wanted to be 100 per cent certain before I mentioned it,' Wagner Ribeiro began. The agent looked nervous but slowly, a smile spread across his face. 'Real Madrid are interested in signing Junior!'

Neymar Sr was amazed; his son was still only thirteen years old and Real Madrid were one of the biggest clubs in the world. The boy's hero, Ronaldo, was playing there and so was Robinho, Betinho's other great discovery. Could Neymar Jr really be the latest member of their big Brazilian gang? The family truly believed in his footballing gift but this was beyond their wildest dreams.

'It's not a joke, I promise!' Wagner said when he saw Neymar Sr's shock. 'I sent them Junior's details and some videos of him in action, and they love him! They're willing to offer the kind of deal that Barcelona offered to Lionel Messi.'

If he accepted, Neymar Jr would move to Spain and begin training at the famous Madrid academy. He would learn from the best players in the world and he would earn lots of money for his family. It was an incredible deal but it had to be Neymar Jr's decision.

'Wow, that's amazing!' he shouted when he heard the news. He couldn't wait to tell all his friends at Santos. 'Where's the contract? I'll sign it right now!'

Neymar Sr laughed. 'Okay, calm down a minute! They want us to go to Madrid for a few weeks so that you can see if you like it. If you're happy, you can sign after that.'

Neymar Jr had never travelled on a plane before and neither had his dad. The trip was a big adventure for both of them. They didn't speak much Spanish and the big, busy European city was very different from the São Paulo that they were used to.

'Where's the nearest beach?' Neymar Jr asked. 'I can't imagine living this far away from the sea!'

At first, he seemed excited by all of the new experiences but after a couple of days he grew quiet. His dad noticed that something was up.

'Are you okay, son?' he asked.

Neymar Jr nodded but he didn't smile. 'It's just such a massive change for me. I'm so glad you're here, Dad; otherwise, I would probably have run away by now!'

'Junior, there's no pressure on you to stay here,' Neymar Sr said. 'I just want you to be happy playing football.'

Life was always good on the football pitch. Neymar Jr loved the modern training facilities at *La Fábrica* and he enjoyed the sessions. He was able to show off his amazing technique and he scored lots of great goals. The Real Madrid youth coaches were very impressed and the big contract was ready for Neymar Jr to sign.

But *off* the football pitch, he was finding life difficult. Everything was so scary and overwhelming.

He had met his Brazilian heroes, Ronaldo and Robinho, and watched a match in a VIP box at the huge Bernabéu Stadium. But where was the time and space to relax and have a laugh? And where were his old mates to play football with in the streets?

'Junior, you don't look happy,' his dad told him one evening as they watched a game on TV. 'You're only thirteen and there will be plenty more opportunities to come and play in Europe when you're older. The Madrid academy is excellent but if you don't feel comfortable here, you won't be able to play your best football.'

Neymar Jr felt very relieved to hear that. He had been worried about letting his dad down. 'We haven't even been here for a week yet and I already feel really homesick. I miss Mum and Rafaela, I miss my friends and I miss Santos.'

They went home to Brazil the next day. As the plane flew higher and higher above Spain, Neymar Sr looked at his son and said, 'I'm proud of you, Junior. And I'm sure you'll be back here one day.'

Neymar Jr smiled. It was really nice to know that

great clubs wanted to sign him but he wasn't quite ready to leave the familiar sights and sounds behind.

'Look, there's the beach,' he said, pointing out of the window as the plane prepared to land at São Paulo airport. 'It feels like we've been away for months!'

Once they were home, Neymar Sr phoned Wagner. 'I'm sorry but Junior wants to stay at Santos. Can you please speak to the club and ask for a better deal?'

The agent was disappointed but he spoke to the Santos President, Marcelo Teixeira.

'As you know, everyone loves Junior at this club,' Teixeira told him. 'If I said no, Zito would never leave me alone! He's the future of this club and so we'll make you a good offer.'

Some people thought Neymar Jr was crazy for rejecting such a brilliant offer from a top European team. But other people were very happy to see him again.

'He's back!' his Santos teammates cheered when he arrived at training. 'The boy who turned down Real Madrid!'

## CHAPTER 10

# WELCOME TO
# THE FIRST TEAM

'He's not even seventeen yet!' Márcio Fernándes, the
Santos first team coach, argued.

'I know but did you see his goals for the Under-20s
last week?' another coach asked. 'That free-kick was
amazing! I think he's ready to be in the squad.'

Fernándes shook his head. 'No, I don't want to
rush him. He's training with us and that's a great
learning experience for him. Hopefully next year
he'll be strong enough to play in the Brazilian league
but right now, he's too skinny. If he tries his tricks,
what do you think defenders will do? He'll be in
hospital in seconds!'

Everyone at Santos was talking about Neymar Jr.

There was no doubt that he was the future of the club but the big question was: when would he make his debut?

'Junior will play soon,' was all Fernándes would say to the media.

In the end, the fans ran out of patience and the coach was sacked. The new coach, Vágner Mancini, did not wait long to select the local wonderkid.

'I'm on the bench for the home game against Oeste!' Neymar Jr told his dad. It felt so good to finally see his name on the teamsheet.

'Congratulations, I'm so proud of you!' Neymar Sr replied. He had never quite achieved his dream of playing first-team football for Santos but his son was about to do it for him. It would be the happiest day of both of their lives.

And the most nerve-wracking. The other players tried to calm him down but Neymar Jr couldn't sit still in the dressing room, or on the substitutes' bench. He was just so excited about making his Santos debut. Would he come on for five minutes? Ten minutes?

As soon as the match kicked off, the supporters were cheering for him.

*Neymar! Neymar! Neymar!*

'I haven't even played a match yet, and they already know my name!' he thought to himself. The Santos fans had great expectations for 'the new Pelé'. He just hoped that he could live up to that name.

Early in the second half, the score was still 0–0 and so Mancini told Neymar Jr to start warming up. As he ran along the touchline, the crowd roared and his heart began to beat even faster. He couldn't wait to entertain them with his skills.

'Be fearless out there,' Mancini told him. 'Work hard and enjoy yourself – are you ready for this?'

Neymar Jr nodded. 'I've never been so ready for anything in my life!'

He ran onto the field wearing the black-and-white shirt with the Number 18 on his back. Every Santos supporter stood up and clapped for their new hero. It was a moment that Neymar Jr would never forget. As a seven-year-old boy playing in the streets, he had often imagined playing for his local team. But the reality was much, much better than that.

The first thing he did on the pitch was untuck his shirt; he needed to play with freedom. The next thing he did was attack. As Neymar Jr dribbled towards the defender, he moved his body to go left but then moved to the right instead. It was one of his classic tricks and the defender could only stand and watch him skip away.

*Neymar! Neymar! Neymar!*

Out on the right wing, Neymar Jr looked up for someone to cross to in the penalty area. He aimed for the back post but he hit the ball so hard that it smacked against the bar.

'Unlucky, that would have been an amazing start!' his teammate Paulo Henrique Ganso laughed.

Whenever the Oeste defenders got the ball, Neymar Jr sprinted over to try to win it back. He had forty minutes to impress Mancini and he wasn't going to waste any of them. Each time he got the ball, he used his quick feet and speed to play one-twos and create chances for his teammates. He never stopped moving, just like his dad had taught him on the beach many years before.

'Wow, can you play like that for the whole ninety minutes?' Ganso asked him at the final whistle. Santos had won 2–1 thanks to Neymar Jr's energy and flair.

'Of course!' he replied.

'But can you play like that for the whole ninety minutes *every week?*' Ganso asked.

Neymar Jr gave a cheeky smile. 'There's only one way to find out!'

Eight days later, he was in the starting line-up for the match against Mogi Mirim.

'If you play like you did last week, you'll be fine,' Mancini said, giving him the Number 7 shirt. 'Just don't tire yourself out in the first thirty minutes!'

The big, strong defenders kicked and fouled him all game long but nothing could stop Neymar Jr from dribbling, passing and shooting. He was enjoying himself and he was desperate to get his first Santos goal.

'Relax – you'll score soon!' Mancini told him at half-time.

In the second half, Triguinho crossed the ball into the box. Neymar Jr made sure that he was onside and then threw himself forward for the diving header.

*Goooooooooooooaaaaaaaaaaaaaaaaaaaaalllllllllllllllll llllllll!!!!!!!!!!!!*

Neymar Jr leapt into the air and punched his fist. He was so happy to score his first goal for the club. Then he pointed up at the sky to one of his biggest fans. Ilzemar had sadly died just before he could see his grandson in action for Santos, his favourite team since the days of Pelé. Neymar Jr hoped that his grandad was watching proudly from above.

As his teammates came to celebrate, Neymar Jr pointed to Triguinho and jumped into his arms. 'Thanks for the pass!' he shouted in his ear.

'No problem, welcome to the first team!' Triguinho replied.

## CHAPTER 11

# THE FUTURE OF BRAZIL

'Junior, wake up! Wake up!' André shouted.

'Why?' Neymar Jr mumbled. His teammate had interrupted an awesome dream about winning the World Cup for Brazil. He wasn't ready to get up yet.

'The King is here!'

Neymar Jr jumped out of bed in a flash, got dressed and ran down the corridor. At Santos, Pelé was known as 'The King'. He had scored an incredible 619 goals for the club and he still came to watch a lot of the matches. All of the Santos players were desperate to impress Pelé because the whole football world listened to him. Praise from 'The King' was a really big deal.

Neymar Jr was out of breath by the time he joined his teammates. Pelé was walking around, shaking their hands and chatting to each of them. He seemed very friendly but Neymar Jr was very nervous at meeting his hero. After all, the Santos fans were calling him 'the new Pelé'.

'The future of Brazil, it's nice to meet you!' Pelé said with a big smile on his face.

Neymar Jr smiled back but he didn't know what to say. 'The King' had just called him 'the future of Brazil'! He couldn't wait to tell his dad. 'Thanks, it's a real honour to meet you, Sir,' he managed eventually.

'I watched your debut last month – you've got skills, kid!' Pelé laughed.

Neymar Jr thanked him again. He had a question that he really wanted to ask his hero and, taking a deep breath, he plucked up the courage. 'D-do you have any advice for me, Sir?' he stuttered.

Pelé took a minute to think about his answer. 'Here in Brazil, we put so much pressure on our great footballers. They often have more responsibility than our president! My advice would be to ignore that pressure as much as you can, especially when you're so young. Enjoy your football and entertain the fans – that's all. The World Cups can wait for now!'

Neymar Jr was very grateful for Pelé's words of wisdom but 'The King' was wrong about one thing; the World Cups couldn't wait. Neymar Jr was selected in Brazil's squad for the 2009 Under-17 World Cup in Nigeria.

'It's so exciting that we get to go to Africa!' he told his teammates at the pre-tournament training camp. He already knew a few of the players from Santos but he had also made lots of new friends.

'Yes, but we're not going for a safari holiday, Junior!' joked Philippe Coutinho, a skilful midfielder who played for Vasco da Gama in Rio de Janeiro. 'We're going to Africa to win!'

Neymar Jr was full of confidence after his great start at Santos. The tournament was the perfect place to introduce himself to the world as 'the new Pelé'.

In the first match, Brazil were drawing 1–1 with Japan when Neymar Jr chased after a great pass from midfield. He was too quick for the defenders and soon he had just the goalkeeper to beat.

'Should I shoot?' Neymar Jr asked himself. No – he decided that he was too far from goal and the keeper had rushed out to block him. Instead, Neymar Jr did what street football had taught him to do: improvise. He kicked the ball around the goalkeeper and then ran through to tap it into the net.

*Gooooooooooooooooooooaaaaaaaaaaaaaaaaaallllllllllll llllllllllllllll!!!!!!!!!!!!!!!!!!!!!!*

'Great pass to yourself!' Philippe cheered as they celebrated. 'Why didn't you shoot first time?'

Neymar Jr laughed. 'Too easy!'

But after the victory against Japan, Brazil suffered a shock defeat to Mexico. Neymar Jr and Philippe were both substituted in the second half.

'That wasn't good enough,' Neymar Jr said, throwing his shinpads on the floor. He hated not playing the full ninety minutes but he accepted that he hadn't played well. 'We didn't score a single goal!'

'That Mexican defence was like a wall!' Philippe argued. 'There was just no way through.'

'No, we can't make excuses for ourselves,' Neymar Jr replied. 'With our talent, we should have found a way.'

Unfortunately, the same thing happened again in their next match, and so they were knocked out in the first round.

'I can't believe it!' Neymar Jr said on the flight back to Brazil. He was very disappointed to be leaving Nigeria so early. 'It's really embarrassing to fail like that. We were supposed to return home as heroes. That was our chance to shine!'

Philippe nodded glumly. 'Let's just hope we get another chance to make our country proud.'

The Under-17 World Cup was an important learning experience for Neymar Jr. It helped him to keep his feet on the ground as his career took off.

## CHAPTER 12

# FAME AND GLORY

'Junior, what have you done?!' Neymar Sr cried out. 'I told you that your hair was too long, but I didn't want you to do *that!*'

His son had just come home with a bold new 'Mohawk' haircut. The sides of his head were shaved but in the centre, there was still a strip of long hair.

'Don't you like it?' Neymar Jr asked with a smile on his face. He didn't expect his dad to like it. He liked it and his fans, the '*Neymarzetes*', would love it – that's what mattered.

In only six months, Neymar Jr's life had completely changed. He wasn't just a footballer anymore; he was a famous celebrity across the whole of Brazil. He travelled to events in Rio de Janeiro in helicopters. And every time he left his house, his fans were waiting for him. They queued for hours just to see his face and get his autograph or a photo with him. It was crazy to know that his new hairstyle would be copied by kids all over the country.

'You look like a punk,' his dad began, but he knew that it wasn't worth arguing with his son. 'Fine. As long as you play well on the pitch, I don't care about your fashion sense!'

Luckily, Neymar Jr was playing very well indeed. He had formed a great attacking trio with Ganso and André, and it got even better when Robinho made his big return to Santos.

'He's one of my heroes!' Neymar Jr told his dad happily. 'I used to watch him on TV and then pretend to be him when I played street football. Now, I'll be playing alongside him!'

Neymar Jr and Robinho became great friends straight away and together they made up cool celebrations for all the goals that the team scored.

'Remember, we're entertainers!' his hero told him.

'Now we'll be even more determined to score.'

When Neymar Jr scored from Robinho's pass against Naviraiense, his teammates rocked him like a baby and then Robinho pretended to polish his boot. And when Robinho scored from Neymar Jr's pass, the players joined hands and danced around in a circle.

'This is so much fun!' Neymar Jr shouted, with a big grin on his face. As he looked up at the crowd, the Santos fans were enjoying it just as much as the players.

In the second half, he dribbled into the penalty area with opponents all around him. He was feeling very confident. He brushed off the first defender, danced past the second, fooled the third with some fancy footwork and then dummied the goalkeeper too.

*Goooooooooooooooooooooaaaaaaaaaaaaaaaaaalllllllll lllllllllllllllllll!!!!!!!!!!!!!!!*

'I'm sorry, I've run out of celebrations!' Robinho joked as he hugged Neymar Jr. 'That deserved something very special – it was one of the best goals I've ever seen!'

The final score against Naviraiense was 10–0 to Santos. By April 2010, the victorious team were heading towards a league and cup double: the *Campeonato Paulista* and the Copa do Brasil – the Brazilian Cup.

'If we win both, we'll be the most successful Santos team since Pelé's side in the 1960s!' Neymar Jr told Ganso. It would be amazing to go down in club history.

Against Guarani in the Copa do Brasil, Neymar Jr scored a penalty after only two minutes. He ran to one of the stewards behind the goal and collected five baseball caps. Putting them on, they danced around and pretended to be rappers. Then they threw the caps up into the crowd.

'Don't worry, I've got twenty celebrations planned for this match!' Robinho told him with a big smile.

The goals kept coming. Neymar Jr scored, then Robinho scored, then Neymar Jr scored, then Robinho scored. There was a carnival atmosphere in the Vila Belmiro Stadium but they wanted the fans to make even more noise.

'Come on!' the Santos superstars shouted, raising their arms up into the air.

The match finished 8–1, with Neymar Jr scoring five goals. He was having the time of his life.

'The newspapers are calling us "The Santastic Four" – that's brilliant!' he told his dad at dinner one night.

Neymar Sr laughed. 'It's great to see you playing with such joy, but stay focused and win these trophies. Otherwise, all those goal celebrations will look pretty silly!'

Neymar Jr nodded. He loved to have fun but he also knew when it was time to get serious.

In the semi-finals of the *Campeonato Paulista*, Santos faced their local rivals, São Paulo. They had to win the big derby but at half-time it was still 0–0.

'I missed so many great chances,' Neymar Jr said as he replayed the first half in his head. He was very frustrated with himself.

'Don't worry – we'll score,' Robinho told him. He always stayed positive.

Neymar Jr wasn't giving up. He made another run towards the six-yard box to get on the end of a cross. A defender tripped him but as he fell, he headed the ball into the net.

*Gooooooooooooooooooaaaaaaaaaaaaaaaaaaaaalllllllll llllllllllllllllllll!!!!!!!!!!!!!!!*

Neymar Jr lifted the Santos badge on his shirt towards his lips and kissed it. He loved his home club very much and he was delighted to be their hero.

Robinho was waiting for him with a big grin on his face. 'You're always improvising, aren't you?' he said. Together, they performed the samba dance that they had practised in training.

In the final, they were up against Santo André. Santos won the away leg 3–2 but Neymar Jr knew that the tie wasn't over yet.

'We can't take it easy today,' he said in the dressing room before the home leg. 'Let's play our normal game, like the score is still 0–0.'

But his teammates didn't listen and Santos were losing 1–0 after only thirty seconds.

'Focus!' Neymar Jr shouted as the match kicked off again. They couldn't let their fans down.

Robinho flicked the ball to Neymar Jr and he dribbled into the penalty area. He glided past a few

sliding tackles and curled the ball calmly into the net.
One-all! Later in the match, he saved Santos again.
Robinho passed to Ganso, who flicked it straight to
Neymar Jr. With his weaker left foot, he slotted the
ball into the bottom corner, just like his old coach
Lima had taught him. Two-all!

*Gooooooooooooooaaaaaaaaaaaaallllllllllllllllllllllll
ll!!!!!!!!!!!!!!!!!*

Neymar Jr pointed at the name on the back of his
shirt but it wasn't really necessary. Everyone in Brazil
already knew it. He had the fame but he wanted the
glory too.

The match finished 3–2 to Santo André, making
it 5–5 on aggregate. But Santos were the league
champions because of the number of goals they had
scored earlier in the competition.

'See, I told you those goal celebrations were
important!' Robinho joked.

As Neymar Jr collected his winner's medal, there
were tears in his eyes. It was a very emotional day
for the eighteen-year-old, especially with his family
and Betinho watching proudly in the crowd. It was

a great feeling to know that all of the hard work had been worth it. But the season wasn't over yet.

'Now for the double!' Neymar Jr told his teammates once the first party had ended.

In the Copa do Brasil Santos beat Vitória 3–2 on aggregate. Neymar Jr was very relieved when the referee blew the final whistle. He had missed a penalty in the first leg but thankfully, it didn't matter.

'We did it!' Robinho cheered, lifting Neymar Jr high into the air.

With forty-two goals and lots of assists, he had been the star player in a historic season for Santos. But what next for Neymar Jr? Should he stay in Brazil or move to Europe? Was he ready for a bigger challenge?

Many clubs tried to sign him but Santos didn't want to sell. In England, West Ham's £15 million offer was rejected. They wanted a lot more money than that for the best young footballer in the world – £35 million. Meanwhile, Chelsea's starting offer of £20 million was also turned down – but when they returned with a £30-million bid, the Brazilian club couldn't say no.

'It's a great deal but it's still your decision,' Neymar Sr told his son. 'Let's see what Santos say first.'

To persuade them, the club chairman made a powerful presentation, called 'Project Neymar'. 'If you stay here, we'll make sure that you become Brazil's next national sporting hero.'

That was Neymar Jr's dream and they were offering him a big new five-year contract too. Other than his hero, Ronaldo, he would be the highest paid player in the country. The phone rang and the chairman passed it to Neymar Jr. The caller was Brazil's greatest sporting hero of all: 'The King'.

'You're still very young and you still have so much more to win at Santos,' Pelé told him. 'There's no need to rush to Europe – I didn't! Wouldn't you like to win the *Copa Sudamericana*, the *Copa Libertadores* and the FIFA Club World Cup before you leave?'

For the second time in his life, Neymar Jr chose to say no to Europe, and yes to Brazil.

'I don't want to leave until I've won everything I can here,' he told his dad. 'This country needs a new national hero and that's going to be me!'

## CHAPTER 13

# UPS AND DOWNS

As the 2010 league season ended, the Brazilian people looked ahead to the World Cup in South Africa. After losing in the quarter-finals in 2006, they wanted the national team to do better this time and Neymar Jr was the number one hot topic.

'He hasn't even made his international debut yet!'

'Yes, but no-one else has as much creative flair as him. He could be our secret weapon!'

'He only made his league debut a year ago. We need experience in our team.'

'Don't forget that Pelé was only seventeen when we won it in 1958!'

'The King' was one of the many Brazilian legends

who argued that Neymar Jr was worth the risk but in the end, the team manager, Dunga, decided that he wasn't quite ready.

'He's a great talent for the future,' Dunga told the media, 'but right now, I want strong players who have played more football.'

Neymar Jr was disappointed to miss out but he knew that he would have many more opportunities ahead of him. He was the future of Brazil, after all.

'It's okay – this time, it's not my turn,' he told his dad. '2014 will be my turn!'

Neymar Jr watched on TV as Brazil were knocked out by the Netherlands in the quarter-finals. The whole country was very upset and the fans called for big changes.

'Why aren't the youngsters playing?' they asked angrily. 'We need to go back to the old days of exciting, Brazilian football!'

Dunga was sacked after the tournament, and the new manager, Mano Menezes, called Neymar Jr up to the squad straight away for a friendly against the USA.

'Guess what – this time I'm coming with you!' he

told Robinho, who had been playing for Brazil for years.

'And me!' Ganso added.

'And me too!' André said.

Three of 'The Santastic Four' started the match and André came on in the second half. It was a day that Neymar Jr would never forget. As he waited for kick-off, he looked down at the famous yellow Brazil shirt that he was wearing and thought back to the days when he used to play FIFA with Luiz, Dudu and Michael. They had dreamed of playing for their country and now Neymar Jr was about to make that dream come true.

'I hope they're watching!' he thought to himself.

He was determined to make a big impact. He worked hard to find space and create goalscoring chances for him and his teammates. When Robinho passed to André Santos, the left-back looked up for the cross. The ball flew over Pato's head but Neymar Jr was there at the back post. Heading wasn't his best talent but one he had worked hard to improve. He guided the ball perfectly into the bottom corner.

*Goooooooooooooooooooooaaaaaaaaaaaaaaaaaaaallll llllllllllllllllll!!!!!!!!!!!!!*

Neymar Jr fell to his knees and pointed to the sky. He had scored on his Brazil debut – it didn't get any better than that.

'I hope you enjoyed that, grandad!' he said to himself.

As Neymar Jr kissed the Brazil badge on his shirt, the other players celebrated with him. Robinho was right in the middle of the big team hug.

'Welcome to the team, Junior!' he shouted. 'I wish you were there at the World Cup. We needed you!'

Neymar Jr was already on the path to greatness. But at the age of still only eighteen, he still had important lessons to learn. He was playing with so much confidence that he believed he could do anything. Sometimes, however, he made mistakes.

When Neymar Jr stepped up to take the penalty in the Copa do Brasil final against Vitória, he decided to go for a Panenka, a chip down the middle of the goal. It was a brave choice because if the goalkeeper didn't dive, he would save it easily and Neymar Jr would look like a fool. And that's exactly what happened.

'What an awful penalty!' Neymar Jr said to himself, putting his hand to his face.

He tried to move on and make up for his error but the supporters in the stadium wouldn't let him forget.

*Booooooooooooooooooooooooooooo!*

Even the Santos fans were angry with him. 'That kid thinks he's already the best player in the world. He's too cocky!'

Neymar Jr loved to do tricks in games but sometimes they got him into trouble. Opponents didn't like his showboating at all.

'We're losing badly and he's trying to do keepy-uppies and rainbow kicks over our heads!' they complained. 'He doesn't need to show off like that. He needs to grow up and be more respectful.'

Teams also accused Neymar Jr of diving to win free-kicks and penalties. 'I know he's skinny but he goes down far too easily,' they argued. 'He's like a gymnast, jumping up into the air and then rolling around on the floor. He's cheating!'

It was a difficult time for Neymar Jr. After so many years of love and praise, the criticism really hurt him.

'I'm just trying to enjoy my football and win games for Santos,' he told his dad. 'What's wrong with that?'

'People will always be jealous of your talent,' Neymar Sr told him. 'But you have to make sure that you stay humble and kind.'

Against Atlético Goianiense, Neymar Jr dribbled into the penalty area and as he dragged the ball back, the defender fouled him. Penalty! He got up, collected the ball and walked towards the spot but his teammate Marcel stopped him.

'Sorry Junior, Coach says that I'm the penalty taker today,' he said.

Neymar Jr was furious. 'I won the penalty and I always take the penalties!' he argued.

'Calm down, mate!' Marcel replied. 'I'm only telling you what Coach told me.'

'Whatever,' Neymar Jr muttered and he threw the ball down and stormed off.

His teammates tried to talk to him but he pushed

them away; Coach Dorival shouted to him but he ignored his instructions. Neymar Jr carried on playing but he wouldn't pass to anyone.

'Who does he think he is?' the Santos fans demanded. 'No player is bigger than the team. He's become so arrogant!'

Neymar Jr just dribbled and dribbled until a defender tackled him. When the other players moaned, he shouted at them. At the final whistle, he walked straight off the pitch and went home.

After giving him an hour to think about his behaviour, his mum went to speak to him. Neymar Jr's eyes were red from crying.

'Son, what happened to you today?' Nadine asked. 'I've never seen you like that before. That's not the Junior I know – you looked like a spoilt teenager!'

'I'm sorry,' he replied. 'I just got so frustrated. I know it was really bad but it won't happen again, I promise.'

'It's not me that you need to say sorry to,' she told him. 'It's your teammates, your coaches and your fans.'

Neymar Jr nodded. It was time to grow up and take responsibility. He needed to show them that he was still the same happy, friendly, football-loving team player that he had always been. He couldn't let his success and fame go to his head.

The next morning, he spoke to the media. 'I want to apologise to everyone for what I did yesterday. It was unacceptable to act like that. I've let myself down but please forgive me for my mistakes. I'm going to improve my attitude and become a Santos hero again.'

## CHAPTER 14

# FOLLOWING IN THE FOOTSTEPS OF 'THE KING'

Once again, Santos were in the final of the *Campeonato Paulista*, and this time their opponents were Corinthians. After a 0–0 draw in the away leg, Neymar Jr couldn't wait to help his team to victory back home at Vila Belmiro.

'They're a good team but we've got nothing to fear!' he told Ganso.

They were now the 'Santastic Two' because Robinho and André had both left the club. Neymar Jr had even more pressure on his young shoulders but that only seemed to improve his game.

With ten minutes to go, Santos were winning 1–0. As he got the ball on the left wing, Neymar Jr had two options in his head: 1) dribble towards the corner to waste time or 2) dribble towards goal to score a second and secure the victory. He chose the second option, of course.

As the defenders backed away, Neymar Jr aimed for the bottom corner. The shot wasn't very powerful but it was very accurate.

*Gooooooooooooooooooaaaaaaaaaaaaaaaaaaaalllllllll lllllllllllllllllll!!!!!!!!!!!!!*

By the time the ball trickled over the goal-line, Neymar Jr had already taken his shirt off. He had scored yet another important goal for his club. After a year of ups and downs, it was amazing to hear the fans cheering his name again at the top of their voices.

*Neymar! Neymar! Neymar!*

What a feeling! At the final whistle, Neymar Jr took his shirt off again. He hugged his coaches and his teammates. Together, they had won the league for the second year in a row. As Santos lifted the trophy, black and white confetti filled the air.

'We're the champions of São Paulo!' Ganso cheered.

But Neymar Jr had bigger targets in mind. 'Yes but next month, we could be the champions of the whole of South America!'

Santos had reached the quarter-finals of the *Copa Libertadores*. They hadn't won the big tournament since the 1960s, when Pelé was at his best. This was why Neymar Jr had stayed at the club – to bring the glory days back to Santos.

There was no stopping Neymar Jr. He scored a wondergoal against the Colombian team Once Caldas, and then another against Cerro Porteño from Paraguay. Santos were now only one win away from the trophy – they just had to beat Peñarol from Uruguay.

'That's the same team that Pelé beat in the final forty-eight years ago,' Neymar Sr told his son.

'Did you watch that game?' Neymar Jr asked with a big smile on his face.

'Don't be so cheeky – I wasn't even born!'

After a 0–0 draw in Uruguay, Neymar Jr felt confident that his team could win with the crowd's support back in Brazil. The match was moved to the Pacaembu Stadium so that more Santos fans could cheer them on. The players held hands as they ran on to the field and then waved to the supporters. The atmosphere was electric.

Neymar Jr's mohawk hair was even bigger than usual. He was ready to be the star but the opposition marked him very tightly. Santos had many chances to score but at half-time, it was still 0–0.

'There's no need to panic!' Neymar Jr told his teammates. He was trying to be positive like his good friend Robinho.

At the start of the second half, Arouca dribbled forward and passed to Neymar Jr on the left side of the penalty area. He shot straight away without even controlling the ball. It was a brilliant decision because the goalkeeper didn't have enough time to dive and stop it.

*Goooooooooooooooooooooaaaaaaaaaaaaaaaaaaaaalllllllll llllllllllllllll!!!!!!!!!!!!!!!*

Neymar Jr jumped up and punched the air. Thanks to him, Santos were now a goal ahead of Peñarol and just forty-five minutes away from winning another major trophy.

'Focus – no mistakes now!' their captain Edu Dracena shouted.

It was a tense finish but the Brazilians held on to win 2–1. The fans went wild and some even ran on to the pitch. Neymar Jr fell to the floor and pointed up to the sky. He tried to hold back his tears but he couldn't. It was the biggest moment of his life.

His family were watching in the crowd and so was Pelé. 'The King' came down on to the pitch afterwards to congratulate the players. A journalist asked him about Neymar Jr.

'He's a great player with a huge talent,' Pelé replied.

His words were ones that Neymar Jr would treasure all his life. After the trophy presentation, the celebrations moved to the dressing room. Everyone was singing and dancing and pouring champagne around. Neymar Jr loved every minute of it.

*Campeones, Campeones, Olé Olé Olé.*

Eventually, his dad found him at the centre of the crowd.

'Congratulations, son!' Neymar Sr said, giving him a big, emotional hug. 'I'm so proud of you.'

'Thanks!'

'You missed a couple of good chances in that second half, though,' his dad continued. 'You'll need to do some more shooting practice with your left foot.'

Neymar Jr laughed. 'Can't we talk about that tomorrow? Dad, we're the Champions of South America!'

## CHAPTER 15

# MEETING MESSI

'You know what this means, don't you?' Neymar
Jr said to Ganso once the celebrations were over.
'We're going to the Club World Cup in December!'

At the FIFA Club World Cup, one team
represented each football region. In 2011, it would
be Al-Sadd for Asia, Espérance for Africa, Auckland
City for Oceania, Monterrey for Central America,
Santos for South America and Barcelona for Europe.
Kashiwa Reysol from Japan were the hosts and the
sixth and last team in the tournament.

'So we might get to play against Lionel Messi?'
Ganso asked excitedly on seeing that Barcelona were
participating.

Neymar Jr nodded. 'Yes, but we'll have to get to the final first!'

In the semi-final, Santos were up against Kashiwa Reysol. Neymar Jr dyed the top of his mohawk blonde for the big day. He was ready to shine. After four minutes, his powerful shot hit the post and bounced into the goalkeeper's arms.

'Next time!' Neymar Jr said to himself. His game was brimming with confidence.

When Ganso passed to him just outside the penalty area, Neymar Jr could see a defender rushing in for the tackle. It was time to improvise. He pretended to shoot and as the defender dived in, he shifted the ball on to his left foot instead and curled a shot into the top corner. The goalkeeper didn't even have time to move.

*Goooooooooooaaaaaaaaaaalllllllllllllllllllll!!!!!!!!!!!!!*

Neymar Jr was delighted with his start to the tournament.

'I'm not sure even Messi could have done that!' Ganso cheered.

The match finished 3–1 and Santos were through to the final against Barcelona.

'I'm confused; are you just playing one-versus-one?' Edu Dracena joked in training. 'I thought the rest of us were playing too!'

The media were nicknaming the match 'Neymar versus Messi'. Neymar Jr knew it would be a team battle but it was also an international one: Brazil versus Argentina. In addition, he was really looking forward to testing himself against Messi. The best player in the world would face the future best player in the world. Who would be victorious?

'This is my big chance to prove myself,' Neymar Jr said to his dad. He felt far more nervous than he usually did before a match.

'It's an important game because it's a final but you don't need to put any extra pressure on yourself,' Neymar Sr reassured him. 'Junior, the biggest clubs in Europe are already desperate to sign you!'

In the summer, Neymar Jr had signed a new contract at Santos, despite interest from Real Madrid, Chelsea and Manchester City. He was the Brazilian League's Player of the Year but there were still things that he wanted to achieve before he moved away.

The first was winning the FIFA Club World Cup.

Unfortunately, in the final, Santos lost 4–0 to Barcelona. Messi, Xavi and Andrés Iniesta were simply too good for Neymar Jr and co. Their pass-and-move football was so fast and skilful that the Santos players could only chase and watch as the goals went in.

'How do we even get the ball off them?!' Edu Dracena complained at half-time. 'Those guys are incredible!'

Neymar Jr tried to create something special for his team but in the end it was Messi's night. The Argentinian wizard scored two goals and won the Player of the Tournament award.

At the final whistle, Neymar Jr wiped the sweat off his face with his shirt. He had done his best for his team but it wasn't enough. He had learnt a lot of lessons, though. He hugged each of the Barcelona players but Messi was the one that he really wanted to speak to.

'Wow, that was a football masterclass,' Neymar Jr told him. 'I felt like I was back at school today. I don't know how you guys do it!'

'Thanks, you played well too,' Messi replied as

they swapped shirts. 'So when are you moving to Europe? You should come and play with me at Barcelona – it would be fun!' Neymar Jr's frown turned into a smile. 'That would be amazing!'

He always hated losing but luckily there wasn't any time for a tantrum. He had other trophies to collect. First, he travelled to Uruguay to win the South American Footballer of the Year award.

'Congratulations, you're the second Santos player to win the prize!' his dad told him.

Neymar Jr laughed. 'Let me guess who the other player was – Pelé?'

'Of course!'

Next, at the start of 2012, Neymar Jr travelled to Switzerland for the famous Ballon d'Or ceremony. He was on the shortlist for The FIFA Puskás Award for best goal of the year.

Neymar Jr's wondergoal started on the left wing, just inside the Flamengo half. With three quick flicks of his boot, he escaped from two defenders and then played a great one-two. Running at full speed towards the penalty area, he rolled the ball from his right foot to his left foot and kicked it round the last defender. It was another magical piece of skill. In the penalty area, he lifted the ball over the diving goalkeeper and into the net.

*Goooooooooooooaaaaaaaaaalllllllllllllllllllll!!!!!!!!!!!!!!*

'And the winner of the FIFA Puskás Award is…' the presenter began, '…Neymar Jr!'

With his mohawk dyed red this time, Neymar Jr walked onto the stage. He couldn't believe what was happening. His goal had beaten brilliant strikes by Wayne Rooney and Lionel Messi.

'I'm so happy to win this award against two of my heroes,' he told the audience. 'Thank you!'

He was too nervous to say much more. He sat back down at his table and watched Messi win the Ballon d'Or for the third year in a row.

'That guy is simply amazing!' Neymar Jr said to himself. What would it be like to play with him? He was sure that Messi could teach him so much.

Later that night, the best player in the world came over to congratulate Neymar Jr. 'Remember: you, me and Barcelona. It's a match made in heaven!'

## CHAPTER 16

# THE HAT-TRICK

Ganso curled the free-kick into the penalty area with his brilliant left foot. His target was always the same. Neymar Jr stood between the two central defenders and waited. When the ball flew over the first defender, he was in the right place to head it powerfully past the goalkeeper.

*Goooooooooooooooooooaaaaaaaaaaaaallllllllllllllllllllllll llllll!!!!!!!!!!!!!!!!!*

Neymar Jr ran towards the fans and his teammates chased after him. Soon, he was in the middle of a big circle and everyone was patting him on the back and on the head. Even the substitutes joined in.

'Congratulations, Junior!' Ganso cheered. 'One hundred goals!'

Neymar Jr smiled. 'And on my twentieth birthday too – it's the best present ever!'

He was very proud of his achievement but it was still a team game, and he never forgot the defenders and midfielders who worked so hard to help him.

'I couldn't have done it without you,' Neymar Jr assured Ganso. 'We have such a great understanding – you know exactly where I'll run.'

'Yes, if you ever leave Santos, you'll have to take me with you!' Ganso joked.

Neymar Jr had prepared a special dance for the fans. He moved to the left and then moved to the right. The fans cheered loudly as the steps got faster and faster. They loved his *ginga* rhythm.

'That's enough,' the linesman told him eventually. 'We've still got thirty minutes of the match to go!'

During 2012, Neymar Jr was scoring more goals than ever. Free-kicks, penalties, headers, chips, long-range strikes, wondergoals – he scored them all.

'You're a proper striker now!' his dad told him.

'Before, every goal had to have a beautiful piece of skill but now you're happy even if you score a tap-in.'

Neymar Jr was growing up. He now had more responsibility, both on and off the pitch. After the birth of his first son, Davi Lucca, he needed to set a good example, so he saved his tricks for important moments when they could help to create goals. Otherwise, showing off didn't really help anyone. And when opponents fouled him, he tried to stay on his feet and if he couldn't, he got straight back up and carried on.

Against local rivals São Paulo in April 2012, he received the ball on the edge of the penalty area and took a shot straight away. The goalkeeper was surprised and he couldn't make a save. The strike was just too powerful.

*Goooooooooooooooooooooooaaaaaaaaaaaaaaaallllllllllll llllllllllll!!!!!!!!!!!!!!!!*

Santos were winning 3–1 and Neymar Jr had scored a hat-trick. He celebrated by doing his favourite thing: dancing in front of the fans.

'We're going to win three league titles in a row!' he told his dad. 'Did Pelé ever do that?'

Neymar Sr nodded. 'I'm afraid so – twice! 1960, 1961, 1962 and then 1967, 1968, 1969.'

'The King did everything – I'll never beat him.'

'No, but if you keep playing like this, you might well match him!'

There was no stopping Neymar Jr in the *Campeonato Paulista* final against Guarani. He glided past defenders as if they were just obstacles, like the mattress and the wardrobe in his childhood bedroom. He scored two goals in the first leg and Santos won 3–0. Victory was almost theirs but Neymar Jr wasn't ready to relax yet.

'I want to score another hat-trick!' he told Ganso.

When Neymar Jr had scored his first from the penalty spot after only eight minutes, the hat-trick looked likely. He took shot after shot but the goalkeeper made lots of great saves. After seventy minutes, he scored his second goal but as hard as he tried, he couldn't score a third.

'Never mind. There's always next year!' Ganso

told him at the final whistle, as the first fireworks filled the sky.

Neymar Jr wasn't too upset. How could he be when he had just got a different kind of hat-trick? Three league titles in a row! It was celebration time for Santos and Neymar Jr had planned everything carefully.

The players all wore black T-shirts saying '*Campeonato Paulista* 2010 2011 2012'. Neymar Jr also wore a white headband, just like the ones he had made for his Gremetal teammates many years before. After they lifted the trophy, there was lots of singing and dancing. By the time he got to the changing room, Neymar Jr didn't have his T-shirt or his shorts!

After a team dinner, the party really started at *Neymarzetes*, the nightclub named after his crazy fans. Neymar Jr arrived in style, driving a brand new white Porsche. He didn't leave until the early hours of the morning. He was always the life and soul of the party.

Once he had rested for a few days, Neymar Jr focused on his next goal: the 2012 London Olympics. Brazil had won silver twice and bronze twice, but never gold. It was the one trophy missing from their impressive collection. Ronaldo, Rivaldo and Ronaldinho had all tried and failed. Now it was Neymar Jr's turn.

'This is going to be our tournament!' he told Ganso confidently as they arrived in England.

There was a great team spirit in the Brazil camp and the squad was brilliant. They had the experience of Thiago Silva, Marcelo and Hulk, combined with the exciting young flair of Oscar, Pato and Neymar Jr.

The team got off to a great start with wins against Egypt, Belarus and New Zealand. Neymar Jr scored twice – his second goal was an amazing free-kick. He was playing well and the goal celebrations were excellent too.

'What are you going to do if we win gold?' Marcelo asked.

'*When* we win gold,' Neymar Jr corrected him. 'Don't worry – I've got big plans!'

He scored a penalty against Honduras in the quarter-finals and then created all three goals as Brazil beat South Korea in the semi-finals.

'Just Mexico to beat now!' Neymar Jr told Ganso.

But the Gold Medal match was a disaster for Brazil. Mexico scored in the first minute and then defended very well. Neymar Jr hardly touched the ball on the right and when he did, there was no space to work his magic.

'You need to pass it to me more quickly!' he shouted to Oscar.

Neymar Jr was becoming more and more frustrated. When he did get the chance to shoot, he kicked the ball too hard and it flew high over the bar. The match finished 2–1 to Mexico and Brazil went home with a third silver medal.

Neymar Jr sat on the pitch at Wembley, staring down at the grass. His teammates tried to help him up but he wasn't ready to move yet. He was very upset about letting his country down.

'We lost in the quarter-finals of the Copa América last year and now this,' Neymar Jr said, wiping away his tears. 'Brazil haven't won anything for years!'

'You'll have more chances to win gold,' Marcelo told him. 'The next Olympics are in Brazil and you'll need to be our star!'

## CHAPTER 17

# BARCELONA

In four years of first-team football, Neymar Jr had scored over 120 goals for Santos and won three league titles, one Brazilian Cup, one *Copa Libertadores* and reached the final of the Club World Cup. And he was still only twenty-one years old! By 2013, what was left for him to achieve in Brazil?

When his best friend Ganso signed for their rivals São Paulo, Neymar Jr thought long and hard about his future. Was it time to finally accept the challenge of playing in Europe? He and his dad thought so but Santos were desperate to keep him at least a little longer.

'Why don't you wait one more year?' his coach,

Muricy Ramalho, suggested. 'Stay here for the 2014 World Cup and then move to Spain.'

Brazil's legends all gave their opinion on Neymar Jr's big transfer dilemma. Pelé thought that he needed to be stronger before he played in Europe but Ronaldo thought that he was ready to test himself against the best. While everyone kept talking about him, Neymar Jr kept scoring goals but it was difficult to ignore all of the attention.

'One day, I dream of playing in Europe,' he told the Brazilian media. 'I'd like to play for a big club like Barcelona, Real Madrid or Chelsea. Who wouldn't want to play in the same team as Messi, Xavi and Iniesta? But for now, I play for Santos.'

Barcelona were very pleased to hear that they were leading the race to sign Neymar Jr. The club had been following his progress for years but it was now time to make an offer. Messi, their superstar, needed a partner in attack and the club believed that the Brazilian was the best man for the job.

However, Barcelona's big rivals Real Madrid hadn't given up on Neymar Jr, despite their disappointment seven years earlier when he had chosen to stay in Brazil. Barcelona were the Spanish League winners but Real were the Champions League winners. Cristiano Ronaldo, their superstar, also needed a partner in attack.

'How does it feel to have the two biggest clubs in the world fighting over you?' Neymar Sr asked his son with a smile.

'It's tiring!' he replied. 'I need to take some time to think about each offer and make my decision.'

In the end, Neymar Jr chose the style of Barcelona and the chance to play with Messi. He left the contract negotiations to his dad and his agent, Wagner Ribeiro, and began his long goodbye to Santos. Despite his best efforts, however, he couldn't win a fourth *Campeonato Paulista* for his club. That would have been the perfect leaving present.

'I am going but I'll be back!' he wrote on the wall at the training ground.

Next, he told his *Neymarzetes* around the world. 'On Monday I will sign for Barcelona,' he posted on Twitter, Facebook and Instagram. 'I want to thank all the Santos fans for these ten incredible years. I will always be Santos!'

Over 60,000 fans came to watch Neymar Jr's final match for Santos in May 2013 against Flamengo. It was a very emotional day and he was crying even before the game kicked off. He was desperate to be the matchwinner yet again. Neymar Jr's free-kick flew towards the top corner but the Flamengo goalkeeper made a great save.

'The keeper should have let that in on purpose!' Neymar Sr joked to Nadine. 'Junior deserves to say goodbye in style.'

In the end, it finished 0–0. As he left the pitch for the last time, Neymar Jr clapped and waved to the fans. He would never forget their love, energy and support. When he threw his shirt into the crowd, a fight nearly broke out.

Neymar Jr arrived in Barcelona on a private jet. He posed for photos next to the club badge with his baseball cap on backwards and a big smile on his face. It was still hard to believe that his dream was really coming true. After medical tests, Neymar Jr went to the Nou Camp to sign his five-year contract.

'Are you ready for this?' Sandro Rosell, the club chairman, asked him.

Neymar Jr nodded. He knew what happened next. Once he was dressed in the Barcelona kit, he walked out onto the blue carpet that covered the pitch. The 56,000 fans in the stadium roared. They had been queueing for hours to meet their new signing.

*Neymar! Neymar! Neymar!*

'Welcome, Neymar Jr!' was written on the big screen.

He had played football in front of very big crowds before but this was a completely different experience. There were no teammates by his side; it was just him: The Neymar Jr Show. He turned around in circles, waving to everyone.

Luckily, he had a football in his hands. Since he was very young, Neymar Jr had always felt safer with a football. It was his safety blanket. On the stage, he did some keepy-uppies to entertain the fans.

Now, Neymar Jr had to make his speech. It was the part that he had been dreading for weeks. As a

Brazilian, he spoke Portuguese and a bit of Spanish. But the people of Barcelona had a language of their own – Catalan. He had been learning one phrase all day.

'Hello, I'm very happy to be a Barcelona player. It is a dream come true. *Visca el Barca!*'

The supporters went wild. *Neymar! Neymar! Neymar!*

Neymar Jr's last task of the day was to speak to the Spanish journalists. He had a clear message for them.

'Barca is a great team and I want to help Messi to continue to be the greatest player in the world,' he told them.

Some people were worried that the two superstars wouldn't play well together in the same team but Neymar Jr was very happy to support Messi. He knew that he still had a lot to learn, especially in European football, and the Argentinian was his friend and hero.

'What a day!' Neymar Jr said to himself as he returned to his hotel.

He was exhausted but he didn't have long to rest. In a few days, Neymar Jr would be returning home to play in the Confederations Cup.

## CHAPTER 18

# CONFEDERATIONS CUP

Brazil were the hosts for the 2013 FIFA
Confederations Cup, a tournament featuring the best
teams from around the world: Uruguay also from
South America, Spain and Italy from Europe, Japan
from Asia, Nigeria from Africa, Mexico from Central
America, and Tahiti from Oceania.

'This is our warm-up for next year's World Cup,'
Brazil's coach Luiz Felipe Scolari told his players.
'Let's show what we can do!'

Brazil had won the tournament in 2005 and 2009
but could they make it three wins in a row? Most of
the players had played together at the 2012 Olympics
but Neymar Jr had one new teammate in attack: Fred.

'I'm here to score goals,' Fred told Hulk, Oscar and Neymar Jr happily. 'You guys do the skills and I'll just make sure that the ball goes in the net!'

Neymar Jr now wore the famous Number 10 shirt, passed down to him by legends like Zico, Rivaldo, Ronaldinho and, of course, Pelé. It put even more pressure on his skinny shoulders but Neymar Jr didn't mind at all. With a smart new shorter haircut, he was ready to show that he could lead his country to glory.

In the first match against Japan, Fred chested the ball down and Neymar Jr hit a beautiful shot into the top corner. 1–0 – what a start!

Brazil's second match was against Mexico, a repeat of the 2012 Olympic Final. It was time for revenge. When Dani Alves put an early cross into the box, the defender headed it away but straight to Neymar Jr. He watched the ball carefully as it fell and hit a sweet volley into the bottom corner.

*Gooooooooooooooooooaaaaaaaaaaaaaaaaalllllllllllllll llllllllllll!!!!!!!!!!!!!!!*

The Brazilian supporters went wild as Neymar Jr ran towards them and jumped into the air. This time, he wouldn't let his country down.

'What a strike!' Marcelo screamed as he jumped on the hero.

In the last minute, Neymar Jr set up a second goal to complete his 'man of the match' performance.

Brazil were already through to the semi-finals but Neymar Jr didn't want to miss the final group game against Italy.

'I'm ready to play!' he told Scolari.

'I know but we need you at your very best in the next match,' his manager replied. 'And what if you get hurt in this game?'

'Please let me start,' Neymar Jr begged. 'If we're winning, you can take me off for the last twenty minutes.'

In the end, Scolari agreed. After all, he needed to keep his star player happy.

Early in the second-half, Brazil won a free-kick just outside the penalty area. It would be difficult to beat a world-class keeper like Gianluigi Buffon but

Neymar Jr was fearless. His shot flew like an arrow into the corner of the net.

*Goooooooooooooooooooooaaaaaaaaaaaaaaaallllllllllllll lllllllll!!!!!!!!!!!!!!!!!*

He pointed to the number on his back – yes, he was more than good enough to wear the 10. He was a superstar. With twenty minutes left to go, Neymar Jr left the pitch to a standing ovation.

It was a South American semi-final – Brazil vs Uruguay.

'We've played so well so far,' Scolari told the team. 'We just need two more great performances – we can't lose to our local rivals!'

At the end of the first half, Neymar Jr chested the ball down as he ran into the penalty area and tried to lift it over the keeper. The keeper saved it but Fred was there to score the rebound. 1–0! Fred ran to the fans and Neymar Jr jumped up on his back.

'You're a goal-hunter, always waiting for your next chance to score!'

Uruguay equalised but Brazil never gave up. With

five minutes to go, Paulinho scored from Neymar Jr's corner to put them through to the final.

'Rio here we come!' Dani Alves shouted as the whole squad celebrated. The final would be played at the Maracanã Stadium in Rio de Janeiro, in front of more than 70,000 supporters.

'And at least 90 per cent of the crowd will be Brazilians!' Neymar Jr added. He couldn't wait for the big day.

Their opponents would be Spain, the 2010 World Cup and Euro 2012 winners. Neymar Jr and Dani Alves would be playing against their Barcelona club-mates Gerard Piqué, Sergio Busquets, Xavi and Andrés Iniesta. For one day only, they would be enemies.

'There's only one way to test how good we are,' Scolari said to his players. 'And that's by taking on the best team in the world.'

Neymar Jr had never been so excited about a match in his life. With just two minutes gone, Brazil scored after a goalmouth scramble.

'You kicked that in while lying on the floor!' Neymar Jr shouted.

Fred smiled. 'I was in the right place at the right time again!'

Just before half-time, Neymar Jr got the ball on the edge of the penalty area. He took one touch and then smashed his shot into the roof of the net with his left foot. The goalkeeper didn't have a chance.

*Goooooooooooooooooooooooaaaaaaaaaaaaaalllllllllllll llllllllllllll!!!!!!!!!!!!!!*

Neymar Jr ran straight into the waiting arms of the Brazilian fans. It was the best feeling in the world to make them so happy.

'Wow, how do you kick it that hard?' Oscar asked him as they ran back for the restart. 'You're as skinny as me!'

Neymar Jr had a good answer for that. 'Hard work and a gift from God.'

In the second half, Neymar Jr dribbled forward from his own half. They were winning 3–0 but he always wanted to score more. Piqué backed away, scared of Neymar Jr's skill and speed. As the Brazilian shifted the ball to the left, Piqué went for the tackle but he was too late to win the ball. Instead, he fouled Neymar Jr and got a red card.

At the final whistle, Iniesta hugged Neymar Jr. 'What a performance! There was nothing that we could do to stop you today. Just make sure that you play like that for Barcelona this season!'

Neymar Jr didn't stop smiling for days. The 2013 Confederations Cup was a time that he would never forget. He won the award for the tournament's best player but it was a brilliant team effort. Together, the Brazilians had made their nation proud again.

'We won every match and beat the World Champions,' Neymar Jr said to Dani Alves. 'Bring on the World Cup now!'

## CHAPTER 19

# NEW START
# IN SPAIN

In the 2013 Spanish Super Cup, league winners Barcelona faced cup winners Atlético Madrid. Neymar Jr was determined to get off to a great start but Barcelona's manager Gerardo Martino chose to play a front three of Lionel Messi, Pedro and Alexis Sánchez.

'Don't worry – you'll get your chance in the second half,' Martino told him. He didn't want to rush his new superstar.

Neymar Jr watched from the bench as Barcelona went 1–0 down. He was raring to get out there and help his team but when Lionel came off at half-time, it was Cesc Fàbregas who replaced him.

'There's still plenty of time,' Neymar Jr told himself. He needed to be patient.

After sixty minutes, Neymar Jr finally entered the game, wearing the Number 11 shirt. As Dani Alves attacked down the right, he ran from the left wing towards the penalty area. The Brazilian teammates knew each other well. The cross was perfect and Neymar Jr headed the ball into the bottom corner.

*Goooooooooooooooooooaaaaaaaaaaaaaaaaaalllllllllllll llllllllllll!!!!!!!!!!!!!!*

It was an amazing feeling to score his first official goal for Barcelona. Neymar Jr ran straight to Dani Alves and jumped into his arms. Xavi, Andrés and Alexis hugged him too.

'Welcome to Barca!' they all cheered.

It was exactly what Neymar Jr needed as he adapted to his new life in Spain. He missed Brazil and his old club. At Santos, they never worried about his size. They believed that being small and skinny helped him to skip past defenders but Barcelona wanted him to build lots of muscle.

'I hate the gym!' Neymar Jr told his dad.

'I know but you have to listen to your coaches,' Neymar Sr replied. 'They want to make you an even better player.'

That was why Neymar Jr had come to Barcelona – to improve. He wasn't scoring as many goals as he had at Santos but he was playing well for the team and creating lots of chances for Lionel.

'The fans love you!' Dani Alves reassured him. 'You're doing exactly what Martino has asked you to do.'

Soon it was time for Neymar Jr's biggest test – Barcelona vs Real Madrid, his first *El Clásico*. It was the battle of the superstars: Neymar Jr and Messi against Cristiano Ronaldo and Gareth Bale. Who would win?

'Are you ready to shine?' Lionel asked him as they waited in the tunnel.

Neymar Jr could already hear the incredible noise of the Nou Camp crowd. He had never heard anything like it. There were nearly 100,000 fans in the stadium. 'You bet I am!' he replied. He was buzzing.

Neymar Jr ran past one defender and then cut inside past another. He took a shot but he fell over as he kicked it and the goalkeeper made a comfortable save. Undeterred, Neymar Jr got back up and carried on.

'Take your time,' Lionel told him.

A few minutes later, Andrés dribbled through the middle and passed to Neymar Jr on the left side of the penalty area. He took Lionel's advice and placed his shot carefully through the defender's legs and into the far corner. The goalkeeper could only turn and watch the ball go in.

*Goooooooooooooooooaaaaaaaaaaaaaaaaaaalllllllllll llllllllllllll!!!!!!!!!!!!!!*

Lionel ran to celebrate with his strike partner. 'What a clever finish!' he screamed.

It was certainly one of the best moments of Neymar Jr's life. All of his teammates hugged him and the fans chanted his name.

*Neymar! Neymar! Neymar!*

Barcelona won 2–1 and Neymar Jr was the big game hero.

'I'm so glad we signed you!' Lionel told him as they walked around the pitch, thanking the supporters.

In December, Lionel was injured and so Neymar Jr

got his chance as Barcelona's central striker. He didn't let his team down. He scored his first Champions League hat-trick in a 6–1 victory over Celtic and then both goals in a 2–1 win over Villarreal.

'Five goals in four days – you're on fire!' Cesc shouted.

Neymar Jr was enjoying his new life in Spain enormously. But just when he was finding his best form, disaster struck. Against Getafe, he dribbled down the left wing and as he stretched to cross the ball, he twisted his right ankle.

*Owwwwwwwwwwwww!*

As he lay on the grass in agony, Cesc ran over. 'What happened?'

Neymar Jr was in too much pain to speak. All he could do was raise his arm in the air to ask for help. With the physios supporting his weight, he limped off. The supporters were very sad to see him go.

'How bad is it?' he asked as he sat on the treatment table. Each movement of the ankle hurt so much.

'The good news is that it's not broken,' the team

doctor told him. 'The bad news is that it's sprained. You'll need to rest it for at least a month.'

Neymar Jr was frustrated to miss so many matches but he focused on recovering as quickly as possible. His team needed him.

By the middle of February 2014, Neymar Jr was fit enough to be on the bench again. As Barcelona were beating Rayo Vallecano 4–0, Martino told him to warm up. When Neymar Jr ran on to the pitch, the fans chanted his name. It was great to be back in action and there was plenty of time to grab a goal.

Alexis passed to Andrés, who passed to Neymar Jr just inside the Rayo Vallecano half. The Brazilian had lots of space to run. He glided past one tackle and as the defenders backed away, he decided to shoot. He was at least thirty yards away from goal but Neymar Jr had nothing to lose. The ball flew into the top corner.

*Goooooooooooooooaaaaaaaaaaaaaaaaaalllllllllllllllllll llllllll!!!!!!!!!!!!!!!!!!!!*

What a return! Neymar Jr ran to the fans and jumped into the air. Then he looked for Dani Alves. They had prepared a special dance.

'Next time, you need to do more practice,' Neymar Jr joked with his teammate. 'Robinho is a much better dancer!'

Unfortunately, Neymar Jr's first season at Barcelona ended in disappointment. They were beaten by Atlético Madrid in the Champions League and the Spanish League, and also by Real Madrid in the Spanish Cup.

'I can't believe it – we didn't win any trophies this year!' Neymar Jr said to Lionel. Losing to their bitter rivals was hard to accept.

'I know, this can't happen again,' he replied. 'Next season, we'll have to win everything.'

Neymar Jr nodded and managed a smile. He was satisfied with his start in Spain but there was plenty of room for improvement.

'Right, we need to stop talking to each other now!' Lionel joked.

Neymar Jr laughed. 'Oh yeah! For the next six weeks, we're not friends – we're enemies!'

It was time for the massive tournament that they had both been waiting for: the 2014 World Cup.

## CHAPTER 20

# WORLD CUP 2014

'When I was young, I watched Romário and Ronaldo win World Cups,' Neymar Jr told the media. 'Now I want to do that too and this time, it will be right here in Brazil!'

As the first match got closer, the pressure only increased. There was no Kaká, no Pato, no Robinho and no Ronaldinho. So all hopes rested on Brazil's star Number 10, Neymar Jr. After some difficult years, the country was desperate for a reason to celebrate.

'We played so well together at the Confederations Cup last year and everyone's back here again,' Dani Alves reassured Neymar Jr. 'You won't be doing this alone!'

Neymar Jr believed in himself and his teammates but he knew that it would be very difficult to make his nation happy. Brazil were one of four favourites to win, alongside Germany, Iniesta and Xavi's Spain, and Lionel's Argentina. With his hair dyed blonde, Neymar Jr was determined to shine.

After ten minutes of Brazil's opening match against Croatia, Marcelo scored an own goal. The big crowd in the São Paulo Arena fell silent. It was the worst possible start for Brazil. They needed Neymar Jr's magic, and quickly.

When Oscar passed to him, Neymar Jr was still forty yards from goal. But the Croatian defence backed away and gave him the space to dribble forward. Suddenly, the Brazil fans were excited.

*Shoot! Shoot! Shoot!*

From just outside the penalty area, Neymar Jr hit the ball with his left foot through a crowd of legs. It wasn't his most powerful strike but it was deadly accurate. The goalkeeper dived across but he couldn't quite reach it as it rolled right into the corner.

*Goooooooooooooooooooooaaaaaaaaaaaaaaaaaaallllllllll llllllllllllllllllllll!!!!!!!!!!!!!!*

The sea of yellow shirts danced in the stands but down on the pitch, Neymar Jr hardly made time to celebrate. Instead, he ran straight back for the restart. He wanted to score again as soon as possible.

'Come on!' he shouted to his teammates.

With twenty minutes to go, Fred won a penalty and Neymar Jr had the chance to put Brazil ahead. He just had to stay calm. He ran up slowly and kicked it as hard as he could. The goalkeeper dived the right way but he managed to push the ball into the roof of the net.

*Goooooooooooooooooooooaaaaaaaaaaaaaaaaaaallllllllll llllllllllllllllllllll!!!!!!!!!!!!!!*

This time, Neymar Jr did celebrate. He ran towards the fans and his teammates joined him. It hadn't been their best performance but thanks to their superstar, Brazil had won the game. That was all that really mattered.

'We need to be much better next time,' Scolari warned his players.

But against Mexico, Brazil played even worse. Neymar Jr was marked closely and without his creativity, the team struggled. It finished 0–0.

'At least we didn't lose,' Dani Alves said afterwards, trying to stay positive.

'That's true but we're here to win!' Neymar Jr replied, kicking the air in frustration. 'If we play like that again, we might not make it to the second round.'

The Brazilian people were not impressed. They demanded more from their countrymen in their final group stage game against Cameroon. Luiz Gustavo dribbled down the left wing and put a perfect cross into the box. Neymar Jr ran between the centre-backs and sidefooted the ball into the net. He made it look so easy.

*Goooooooooooooooooooaaaaaaaaaaaaaaaaaaaalllllllllll llllllllllll!!!!!!!!!!!!!*

'That's more like it!' he cheered.

But ten minutes later, Cameroon had equalised. Neymar Jr needed to do it all over again. As he dribbled across the penalty area, the goalkeeper dived one way and he shot the other way, through the legs of the defender.

*Goooooooooooooooooaaaaaaaaaaaaaaaaaaaalllllllllll llllllllll!!!!!!!!!!!!!!!*

'I thought you said I wouldn't be doing this on my own!' Neymar Jr joked as Dani Alves ran over to hug him. He was very happy to be the hero.

In the second round, Brazil faced their South American rivals Chile. It was a very tense match. David Luiz's goal calmed Brazil down but when Neymar Jr's Barcelona teammate Alexis made it 1–1, the host team became very nervous. If they made one mistake, they could be knocked out and the nation would be furious. In the end, it went to penalties.

'I'll take the last one,' Neymar Jr told Scolari. That gave him a little time to rest. He was exhausted after 120 minutes of football.

Neymar Jr stood with his teammates on the halfway line and waited. After eight penalties, it was 2–2. It was his turn. The walk to the penalty area seemed to take forever. The referee handed him the ball and Neymar Jr put it down carefully on the spot. Despite all of the noise and pressure, he felt calm. He sent the goalkeeper the wrong way and scored.

'Come on, save this last penalty and we win!' Neymar Jr shouted to Júlio César as they high-fived.

Júlio didn't have to save it; the ball hit the post. The Brazil players ran to celebrate with their keeper.

'We did it!' Neymar Jr screamed with relief. He fell to his knees on the pitch and began to cry tears of joy and relief. Their World Cup dream was still alive.

Against Colombia in the quarter-finals, Brazil's captain Thiago Silva scored an early goal from Neymar Jr's corner and David Luiz made it 2–0 with an incredible free-kick. It was all looking good for Brazil, even when Colombia scored a penalty.

But in the last few minutes, as Neymar Jr went to chest the ball down, his opponent pushed his knee into his back.

*Owwwwwwwwwwwwww!*

Neymar Jr fell to the floor and screamed with pain. The crowd went quiet and Marcelo rushed over to him.

'What happened? Are you okay?'

'I don't know but I can't feel my legs!'

As Neymar Jr was carried off on a stretcher, he cried and cried. He feared that his World Cup was over.

'I'm afraid you've fractured one of the vertebrae in your back,' the team doctor told him.

Neymar Jr thought he knew the awful answer but he had to ask. 'Is there any chance that I can play in the semi-final against Germany?'

The team doctor shook his head sadly. 'I'm afraid you need to rest for at least a month.'

The whole of Brazil was devastated, from the players to the fans. How could they continue without their superstar and leader?

'You can do it without me,' he told his teammates. 'I'll be cheering you on!'

For the semi-final, however, he didn't cheer them on live at the Mineirão Stadium. He needed to rest and he knew it would be a nightmare to be so close to the pitch when he couldn't help his country. Instead, he watched the game at home with his friends and family. It turned out to be the worst TV that Neymar Jr had ever seen.

'That's it – I'm turning it off!' he shouted as Germany scored yet another goal, to make it 7–0.

It was too painful to watch any more. Without Neymar Jr, Brazil completely fell apart and suffered their most humiliating defeat of all time.

'We have to move on,' he told his teammates the next day. They were all still in shock. They didn't dare look at what the newspapers were saying about them. 'The preparations for World Cup 2020 start today!'

**CHAPTER 21**

# THE TREBLE

'Let's just forget about the World Cup and focus on the new season,' Lionel said to Neymar Jr. Lionel was upset too because his Argentina team had lost to Germany in the final.

The Brazilian smiled. 'Sounds good to me!'

As his back injury healed, Neymar Jr got ready to show the Barcelona fans just how good he could be. He now had a year's experience of Spanish football and a year's experience of playing with Lionel.

'This is going to be your season!' Dani Alves predicted.

There had been some major changes at Barcelona.

Cesc and Alexis had both moved to England, team captain Carles Puyol had retired and Martino had resigned as manager. Former player Luis Enrique was the new man in charge and Lionel and Neymar Jr had a new partner in attack: the Uruguayan striker Luis Suárez.

'Welcome to Barca!' they said to Luis on his first day in training. 'Let's score lots of goals and win lots of trophies together!'

Soon, the whole football world was talking about 'MSN' – Messi, Suárez, Neymar Jr.

Neymar Jr dribbled in from the left and passed to Luis. Luis flicked the ball through for the one-two and Lionel was already making his run to the back-post to tap in Neymar Jr's cross.

*Goooooooooooooooooooaaaaaaaaaaaaaaaaaallllllllllllll llllllllllllll!!!!!!!!!!!!!!!*

'It's like we've been playing together for years!' Lionel joked as the three superstars hugged.

'Don't forget about me!' Andrés shouted as he joined them.

And Neymar Jr wasn't just setting up goals for Luis

and Lionel; he was also scoring lots of goals of his own, like the good old days at Santos.

'I've already scored as many goals as I scored in the whole of last season and it's not even November yet!' he told Lionel.

Barcelona lost *El Clásico* against Real Madrid's 'BBC' – Gareth Bale, Karim Benzema and Cristiano Ronaldo – but they were still top of the Spanish League and had reached the knockout stages of the Champions League.

'We're still on for the Treble!' Dani Alves said confidently.

That was the team's big target. Against Paris Saint-Germain in the Champions League quarter-finals, Andrés dribbled forward and passed to Neymar Jr. He glided past his Brazilian teammate David Luiz, rounded the keeper and tapped the ball into the net.

*Gooooooooooooooooooooaaaaaaaaaaaaaaaallllllllllllllllllllllllllllll!!!!!!!!!!!!!!!!!*

'Great pass!' Neymar Jr shouted as he hugged Andrés.

'Great finish!' his teammate replied.

Twenty minutes later, Neymar Jr scored again to send Barcelona through to a semi-final against Bayern Munich. Everyone was excited about the battle of the two best teams in the world. Bayern's manager was Pep Guardiola, the man who had won everything with Barcelona a few years earlier.

'Pep was one of the reasons that I wanted to come to Barcelona,' Neymar Jr told his teammates.

'But I was the main reason, right?' Lionel said and everyone laughed.

In the first leg at the Nou Camp, the Argentinian was the hero. He scored two goals and then played a great through-ball for Neymar Jr. In the penalty area he faked to shoot one way, faked to shoot the other way and then shot through the keeper's legs.

*Goooooooooooooooooooooooaaaaaaaaaaaaaaaalllllllllllll llllllllllllll!!!!!!!!!!!!!!*

Neymar Jr and Lionel rolled around on the grass together, and Luis joined them. MSN were having so much fun.

In the second leg, Neymar Jr and Luis were the joint heroes. Neymar Jr scored both goals and in each case Luis set them up. Barcelona were through to another Champions League final.

'I know you're an old pro now but Luis and I are excited!' Neymar Jr joked with Lionel. 'This is our first time in the final!'

Before that, Barcelona had two other trophies to win. Lionel's goal secured the Spanish League title and then Lionel and Neymar Jr's goals secured the Spanish Cup. The team celebrated both achievements but they knew that their biggest test was still to come.

'It's time for the Treble!' Dani Alves reminded them.

With one game left in the season, Neymar had scored thirty-eight goals and MSN had scored 120 in total.

'We're officially the best front three ever!' Luis reported.

But to really go down in history, they had to win the Champions League final against Italian giants Juventus in Berlin. Neymar Jr wasn't nervous ahead of the biggest match of his life; he was focused on winning.

In the first few minutes, he played the ball into Andrés's path as he ran into the penalty area. He passed to Ivan Rakitić, who scored. 1–0!

'When we play flowing football like that, we're unstoppable!' Neymar Jr shouted as they celebrated.

But after sixty-five minutes, Juventus had equalised. Barcelona needed more goals. MSN to the rescue! Lionel ran through the middle, dribbled past one defender and then created a powerful shot. The ball swerved through the air and the keeper could only push it away. Luis was ready for the rebound. 2–1 to Barcelona!

Neymar Jr and Lionel chased after their strike partner as he ran around the pitch. Eventually, they caught up with Luis and they celebrated in style with the fans.

'We're nearly there!' they cheered.

Barcelona kept attacking. Jordi Alba made a great run down the left and crossed into the box. Neymar Jr was there to flick the ball into the bottom corner. He began to celebrate but his smile quickly changed to a frown. The referee had disallowed the goal for handball.

'No way!' Neymar Jr said, waggling his finger from

side to side and shaking his head. 'It hit my shoulder, not my arm.'

But the referee wouldn't listen.

'Keep going!' Andrés told Neymar Jr. 'There's still time to score again.'

With seconds to go, Lionel played a brilliant through-ball to Neymar Jr. As he ran towards goal, he passed to Luis, who then passed back to him. The tired Juventus defenders couldn't cope with their brilliant teamwork. As he entered the penalty area, Neymar Jr struck the ball with his left foot and it flew through the goalkeeper's legs.

*Goooooooooooooooooaaaaaaaaaaaaaaaallllllllllllllllll llllllllll!!!!!!!!!!!!!!!!*

This time, the goal counted. What a moment! Neymar Jr took his shirt off and ran towards the supporters, pumping his fists like crazy. It was the perfect way to finish an incredible year. He had scored in his first Champions League final and Barcelona had won the Treble.

'It doesn't get any better than this!' Dani Alves screamed as they hugged each other.

With a Brazil flag wrapped around his waist, Neymar Jr walked around the stadium, holding hands with Davi Lucca. Both father and young son had matching '11 Neymar Jr' shirts and matching white headbands too.

'Wave to the fans!' he said as he lifted Davi into the air like a trophy. His son was proudly wearing his winner's medal around his neck. 'They love you already.'

It was party time for Barcelona. Neymar Jr jumped up and down with his teammates. He was delighted to be one of the heroes. After a decent first season at Barcelona, he had come back so much more strongly for a super second season.

## CHAPTER 22

# MSN

'What do you think?' Neymar Jr asked as he arrived for a training session. His teammates were used to seeing his new hairstyles each week but this one was really radical.

Lionel and Luis look shocked. 'Where did all your hair go?'

'Dani Alves said it would look cool!' Neymar Jr said as he rubbed his shaved head.

Lionel laughed. 'You're very brave to let him touch your hair!'

'Yeah, if I wanted style advice, Dani Alves is the last person I would speak to!' Luis added.

The Nou Camp crowd was also surprised by

Neymar Jr's new look but as long as MSN kept scoring goals, they didn't mind.

Against Rayo Vallecano in October 2015, Neymar Jr dribbled forward and then slowed down to think about his options. Luis was calling for the ball in the middle but with a burst of pace, he kept dribbling. The defender couldn't keep up; all he could do was foul him. Penalty! Neymar Jr took it himself and scored.

*Goooooooooooooooooaaaaaaaaaaaaaaaaaaalllllllllllllllll lllllllll!!!!!!!!!!!!!!!!!!!!!!!!!*

Ten minutes later, he did it again. This time, Neymar Jr's skill was even more magical. He rolled the ball from one foot to the other and did a step over and then a nutmeg, all in one movement. The defender had no idea what was going on and stuck out his leg to trip him. Penalty! Neymar Jr scored again.

'Are you ever going to pass to me?' Luis joked.

'Not when I can beat them on my own!' Neymar Jr replied with a smile. 'This new haircut has given me super powers.'

With Lionel out injured, Neymar Jr was enjoying

his starring role. Just before half-time, he raced into the box once more and a defender kicked him again. But this time, the referee waved to play on. Neymar Jr was furious.

'How was that not a foul?' he complained to Luis.

'Don't be so greedy!' his strike partner teased him. 'The referee can't give you three penalties in twenty minutes.'

Neymar Jr's glory was not over. In the second half, he scored his third and fourth goals of the match. He celebrated like the old days at Santos with Robinho. Dani Alves pretended to polish his boots and then he danced for the fans.

'What a performance!' Luis said as they high-fived after the final whistle.

'It was my turn today,' Neymar Jr told him. 'It will be your turn next week!'

He would be right. Against Eibar, Barcelona won 3–1. Luis scored a hat-trick, although even then Neymar set up two of the goals.

'I'm not sure we need our "M",' Luis laughed. 'How does "SN" sound?'

'I prefer "NS"!' Neymar Jr replied cheekily.

The 'M' would soon make a comeback of sorts; Lionel was back for the first *El Clásico* of the season but he was only on the bench. Neymar Jr and Luis would have to take on Real Madrid's 'BBC' without him.

'Don't worry – you'll be able to take it easy when you come on!' they told Lionel.

They were both playing with joy and confidence. By half-time, Barcelona were winning 2–0 and Neymar Jr and Luis had scored one goal each. By full-time, they had thrashed their rivals 4–0 away at the Bernabéu.

'What a win!' Neymar Jr shouted as his team celebrated a memorable victory.

Barcelona were top of the Spanish League and it was soon time to travel to Japan to challenge for another trophy – the 2015 FIFA Club World Cup. It was a particularly important one for Neymar Jr.

'I was so upset when I lost in the final with Santos four years ago,' he told Lionel. 'Do you remember? I was crying on the pitch!'

How times had changed. Now Neymar Jr was a Barcelona star and he was determined to collect a winner's medal. He would be absent through injury for the semi-final against China's Guangzhou Evergrande but he returned for the final against Argentina's River Plate. Although he didn't score on that occasion, both Lionel and Luis did.

'Thanks, I feel much better now!' he told his teammates as they stood with the medals around their necks.

The good times continued in 2016. Neymar Jr was back at the Ballon d'Or ceremony and this time, he was on the shortlist for the Best Player in the World award.

'Congratulations, son! You deserve this after winning the Treble last season,' his dad told him as they arrived in Switzerland together.

Neymar Jr was sure that either Cristiano or Lionel would win the top prize but it was great to be one of the other players on the list, alongside amazing players like Luis and Andrés. He didn't worry about writing a winning speech.

'I'm going to enjoy myself tonight!' Neymar Jr told his Barcelona teammates.

He was wearing a very cool suit for the big day with a velvet waistcoat, a spotted bow-tie and a bowler hat. He stopped to take lots of photos on the red carpet outside.

'My fans will love these on Instagram!' he told his dad as they took a selfie together.

When Lionel won the Ballon d'Or, he turned to Neymar Jr and they kissed each other on the cheek. The Brazilian was delighted for his Barcelona strike partner and he was delighted for himself too – he had finished third, behind Cristiano but ahead of his other teammates.

'I'll beat you next year!' Luis said, displaying his competitive spirit.

Unfortunately, Barcelona were knocked out of the Champions League in the quarter-finals, but they still finished top of the Spanish League and faced Sevilla in the final of the Spanish Cup.

'I wanted to win another treble this season but the double will have to do,' Neymar Jr told his teammates before kick-off. He was desperate to end the season in style.

'Did Dani Alves cut your hair again?' Lionel joked, pointing at Neymar Jr's new slicked-back look.

'At least I try new things – you're just boring!' he replied with a smile.

As soon as the game against Sevilla started, MSN got serious. But when their defender Javier Mascherano was sent off in the first half, Barcelona's Spanish double was in danger. Luis went off injured early in the second half but Luis Enrique kept Neymar Jr on the pitch. His manager trusted him to be the matchwinner. He worked hard in defence and attacked at every opportunity.

In injury time, Neymar Jr raced on to Lionel's through-ball but just outside the penalty area, he was fouled, to his great disappointment.

'I was going to score the winner!' he moaned as he got back to his feet.

'There's still time for that,' Andrés reminded him.

In extra-time, Lionel set up goals for Jordi Alba and then Neymar Jr. After he slid the ball past the goalkeeper, Neymar Jr ran over to hug Lionel.

'Thanks mate!'

'No problem. I know how much you love scoring in finals!'

Neymar Jr had learnt so much from playing with amazing players like Lionel, Luis and Andrés, and he was still learning every game. He wasn't quite the best in the world yet, but he was getting closer and closer to Lionel and Cristiano's level.

## CHAPTER 23

# BRAZILIAN SUCCESS

'What do you mean you're not playing in the Copa América?' Dani Alves asked. He was the Brazilian captain for the 2016 tournament and he was relying on Neymar Jr to be their star.

'I'm sorry!' Neymar Jr explained. 'Barcelona won't let me play in the Copa América *and* the Olympics. They said I had to choose and I chose the Olympics. I want to win that gold medal in front of the nation!'

Without Neymar Jr, the national team were knocked out by Peru in the first round. It was like the 2014 World Cup all over again.

'What a disaster!' Dani Alves told him when

they met up afterwards. 'Junior, we can't even score goals without you, let alone win a tournament.'

But even with Neymar Jr in the team, Brazil were struggling to score goals. In their first two Olympic matches, they drew 0–0 against both South Africa and Iraq. Their fans had been dreaming of a glorious home victory and they weren't happy at all. Neither was Neymar Jr.

'What's happened to my shooting?' he complained to his teammates. 'I've got to do better. I'm the captain now and I've been scoring goals for Barcelona all season!'

'Relax!' his young strike partners Gabriel Jesus and Gabriel Barbosa told him. 'We're a team and we're going to help you.'

In the third game, against Denmark, Douglas Santos crossed from the left. Neymar Jr stretched out his foot but he couldn't quite reach it. Luckily, Gabriel Barbosa was there to score instead.

'Well done!' Neymar Jr cheered. Brazil were finally off the mark at the Olympics and it was a great relief. 'Now that we've got one goal, they're going to flood in!'

He was right. Gabriel Jesus, Luan and Gabriel Barbosa all scored to make it 4–0.

'That's more like it!' the coach Rogério Micale told his players in the dressing room after the match. But Neymar Jr still wasn't happy.

'The others are playing well but I'm not doing my job properly,' he told Micale.

'Your job is more than just scoring goals, Junior,' his coach told him. 'You're the team leader and you were involved in creating all of those goals. Don't be so hard on yourself.'

Neymar Jr nodded. There were plenty of matches left in the tournament for him to be a national hero. Against Colombia in the quarter-finals, Brazil won an early free-kick. It was a long way from goal but Neymar Jr stepped up and curled the ball right into the corner of the net.

*Goooooooooooooooooaaaaaaaaaaaaaaaaaaaalllllllllllll llllllllll!!!!!!!!!!!!!!!!*

Neymar Jr was so pleased to be on the scoresheet at last. He pointed to the sky and jumped for joy.

'What a strike!' Luan shouted as the whole team celebrated together.

In the semi-finals, Neymar Jr tackled the Honduras centre back and lifted the ball over the goalkeeper. In the first minute of the match, he had made it 1–0 to Brazil. In the last minute of the match, he scored a penalty to make it 6–0.

'One goal in the quarter-final and then two goals in the semi-final. That means you should score a hat-trick in the final!' his teammate Marquinhos joked.

'No pressure, then!' Neymar Jr replied. The smile was back on his face.

In the final, Brazil faced Germany. It was the perfect opportunity to get revenge for that embarrassing 7–1 defeat at the 2014 World Cup. And this time, they had Neymar Jr in their team.

'I won't accept another silver medal,' he told Gabriel Jesus before the big match. 'Especially not when it would mean losing to Germany again!'

No, with nearly 60,000 Brazilians in the Maracanã Stadium, they had to win the gold. In the twenty-seventh minute, Neymar Jr scored another free-kick.

*Goooooooooooooooooooooaaaaaaaaaaaaaaaaalllllllllllll lllllllllllll!!!!!!!!!!!!!!!!*

It was one of the best moments of his life as the stadium went wild and his teammates hugged him. But the match wasn't over yet. Germany equalised and it was still 1–1 after extra-time. The final would be decided on penalties.

'I'll take the last one,' Neymar Jr told Micale, just as he had told Scolari in the shoot-out against Chile at the World Cup two years earlier. He had been a hero that day – could he be a hero again?

As Neymar Jr made the long walk to the penalty spot, he knew this was his chance, the one that he had dreamed of since the age of three. It was the opportunity that Neymar Sr had dreamed of long before his son was even born.

'Come on, Junior!' he shouted from the stands. His crossed his fingers firmly and so did his grandson Davi next to him.

If Neymar Jr scored, Brazil would be Olympic Champions for the first time ever. He would be the hero, the captain and the star. He would

win something that not even Pelé had
achieved.

Neymar Jr kissed the ball, placed it down and
took the perfect spot-kick. The goalkeeper dived to
the right and his strike went high to the left. Brazil
had won the Olympic Gold! By the time the ball
hit the net, he was already in tears. It was the most
emotional moment of his life.

Once his tears had dried, it was carnival time.
Neymar Jr put on his favourite white headband for the
medal ceremony and pretended to bite into the precious
metal. His celebrations didn't end there. By the time he
returned to Spain, the Olympic rings had been tattooed
on his wrist and his hair was dyed blonde.

At the age of twenty-four, Neymar Jr had lived up
to his huge reputation as his country's next great
superstar. After his big move to Barcelona, many
Brazilians feared that he would forget about his
home. But they didn't need to worry. The smiles, the
skills, the dancing, the *ginga* rhythm, the incredible
natural footballing talent – Neymar Jr was 100 per
cent made in Brazil.

Turn the page for a sneak preview of
another brilliant football story by
Matt and Tom Oldfield. . .

## LIONEL MESSI

**Available now!**

**CHAPTER 1**

# TREBLE TIME

'Hey, how's it going?' Lionel said, giving his fellow Argentinian Carlos Tevez a big hug as they waited in the tunnel.

Lionel was about to play in the 2014–15 Champions League final but he wasn't nervous at all. It was the third time he had played in the final with Barcelona and he had won both times before. He was a born winner and he was the best player in the world. So he felt very confident as he walked out on to the pitch at the Olympiastadion in Berlin to face Italian giants Juventus.

Lionel looked up into the stands and saw the huge wall of red and blue, or '*azulgrana*' as they called it

in Spanish – the colours representing Barcelona, one
of the world's biggest clubs and Lionel's home since
the age of thirteen. He had played in some amazing
Barcelona teams but this was perhaps the best team
of all. They had already won the Spanish League
and the Spanish Cup – now could they win the
Champions League to make it an incredible Treble?

'Yes we can!' they cheered together.

Lionel's old friends Gerard Piqué and Javier
Mascherano were the rocks in defence, Andrés
Iniesta and Xavi controlled the midfield, while 'MSN'
scored the goals up front. That's what the media
were calling the world's best ever strikeforce – Lionel
Messi, the Uruguayan Luis Suárez, and the Brazilian
Neymar. Together, they had scored 120 goals already,
with one big game left to play.

'Come on!' Lionel shouted as they waited for kick-
off. When he was younger, he was too shy to speak
to his teammates but he was twenty-seven now and
one of their leaders.

Within four minutes, Neymar passed to Andrés,
who passed to Ivan Rakitić, who scored. Barcelona

were 1–0 up. They made everything look so easy with their quick, passing football, and Lionel hadn't even been involved – but he knew how important teamwork was.

'Great work!' he shouted to Ivan. Even he couldn't do everything on his own.

Playing just behind Neymar and Luis, Lionel kept searching for the space to work his magic. He was known as The Flea, buzzing around everywhere and terrorising his opponents. With his close control, quick feet and footballing brain, he only ever needed one second. Especially in his favourite area: just outside the penalty area on the right side, he could dribble with his amazing left foot. Lionel loved scoring goals but he loved creating goals too – there was nothing he couldn't do.

Barcelona were playing well but in the second half, Juventus equalised. Just when his team needed him most, Lionel came alive. He passed to Neymar, who flicked it back to Lionel, who passed to Luis, who passed back to Lionel. His shot went wide but 'MSN' were looking dangerous.

'If we keep this up, we'll score again!' Lionel told the others.

Minutes later, he dribbled forward again. The defender tried to tackle him but Lionel was too quick and too skilful. When he grabbed his shirt, Lionel shrugged him off. He wasn't the biggest footballer but he had worked hard to build up his strength.

As Lionel flew towards goal, Neymar made a run to make space for him. On the edge of the penalty area, Lionel decided to shoot. The ball flew straight at the goalkeeper but it swerved and dipped and he couldn't hold on to it. Luis sprinted towards the ball and smashed it into the net. 2–1!

As Luis jumped the advertising board, Lionel and Neymar were right behind him. It was yet another 'MSN' goal and Barcelona were one step closer to another Champions League trophy.

'There's plenty of time to score another!' Neymar said with a big smile on his face. Their favourite form of defence was attack.

In injury time, a clearance fell to Lionel. He looked up and saw his Brazilian teammate sprinting forward.

Stretching out his leg, he played a perfect through-ball. Neymar and Luis had a two-on-one against the Juventus centre-back. Neymar passed to Luis and as the defender moved across, Luis passed it back to Neymar. His shot rocketed into the bottom corner. 3–1! Barcelona were the Champions of Europe.

At the final whistle, Lionel hugged Andrés and Xavi. Together, they had conquered the football world again. He was so grateful to his amazing teammates. Their clever passes always arrived at his feet, no matter where he was on the pitch.

'After my injuries last year, some people thought that my best days were over,' Lionel said. 'They were so wrong!'

In the 2014/15 season he had helped Barcelona win the Treble with fifty-eight goals and twenty-five assists in only fifty-seven games. He was very proud of his return to form.

As Xavi lifted the trophy into the air, Lionel was right at the centre of the celebrations. He hadn't scored a goal in the final this time round, but he had still played a very important role.

'Thiago!' Lionel called to his three-year-old son, who was wearing a Barcelona shirt with '10 MESSI' on the back. He kissed his girlfriend Antonella and carried Thiago around the pitch to wave to the fans. His little family meant the world to him.

'Look, there's your Grandpa and Grandma!' Lionel said to Thiago, pointing to Jorge and Celia in the crowd.

Without the love and support of his parents, Lionel wouldn't have made the brave move from Argentina to Spain to chase his dream of playing professional football. He had arrived at Barcelona as a tiny teenager with amazing natural talent but some of his coaches had their doubts. Did he really have the strength and desire to make it to the very top?

Nearly fifteen years later, the answer was there in Lionel's trophy cabinet: seven La Liga titles, four Champions League trophies, four FIFA Ballon d'Or trophies and one Olympic Gold Medal. He was the best player in the world but The Flea had plenty more magic up his sleeve.

**NEYMAR DA SILVA SANTOS HONOURS**

## Santos

🏆 Campeonato Paulista: 2010, 2011, 2012

🏆 Copa do Brasil: 2010

🏆 Copa Libertadores: 2011

🏆 Recopa Sudamericana: 2012

## Barcelona

🏆 La Liga: 2014–15, 2015–16

🏆 Copa del Rey: 2014–15, 2015–16, 2016–17

🏆 UEFA Champions League: 2014–15

🏆 FIFA Club World Cup: 2015

## Paris Saint-Germain

🏆 Ligue 1: 2017–18, 2018–19, 2019–20

🏆 French Cup: 2017–18, 2019–20, 2020–21

🏆 League Cup: 2017–18, 2019–20

## Brazil
🏆 South American Youth Championship: 2011

🏆 Olympic Silver Medal: 2012

🏆 FIFA Confederations Cup: 2013

🏆 Olympic Gold Medal: 2016

## Individual
🏆 Brazilian Golden Ball: 2011

🏆 FIFA Puskás Award: 2011

🏆 South American Footballer of the Year: 2011, 2012

🏆 FIFA Confederations Cup Golden Ball: 2013

🏆 FIFA World Cup Bronze Boot: 2014

🏆 UEFA Champions League Team of the Season: 2014–15

🏆 FIFA FIFPro World XI: 2015

# NEYMAR

**10 THE FACTS**

**NAME:** Neymar
Da Silva Santos Júnior
**DATE OF BIRTH:**
5 February 1992
**PLACE OF BIRTH:**
Mogi das Cruzes,
São Paulo
**NATIONALITY:** Brazilian
**BEST FRIEND:** His dad,
Neymar Sr.
**CURRENT CLUB:** Paris Saint-Germain
**POSITION:** LW

## THE STATS

| | |
|---|---|
| Height (cm): | 175 |
| Club appearances: | 452 |
| Club goals: | 265 |
| Club assists: | 205 |
| Club trophies: | 24 |
| International appearances: | 116 |
| International goals: | 70 |
| International trophies: | 2 |
| Ballon d'Ors: | 0 |

★ ★ ★ **HERO RATING: 91** ★ ★ ★

# GREATEST MOMENTS

## 27 JULY 2011,
## ANTOS 4-5 FLAMENGO

Neymar scored lots of amazing goals for his Brazilian club Santos but this is the best of them all. He was only nineteen when he tricked his way past two defenders, played a great one-two and then dribbled past another defender before lifting the ball over the diving goalkeeper. This wonder goal won The FIFA Puskás Award for best goal of the year.

## 30 JUNE 2013,
## BRAZIL 3-0 SPAIN

In the Confederations Cup Final, Brazil faced the European and World Champions, Spain. It was the biggest game of his career so far and so Neymar put on a match-winning display. He scored a brilliant goal and played so well that Gerard Piqué got sent off trying to tackle him. This was a very proud moment for Neymar and a sign of things to come.

## 26 OCTOBER 2013,
## BARCELONA 2-1 REAL MADRID

This was Neymar's first ever *El Clásico* match but he didn't show it. With nearly 100,000 supporters watching him in the Nou Camp, he scored the first goal and then set up Alexis Sánchez's winner with a brilliant pass. If the Barcelona fans didn't already love their big new signing, they certainly did after this.

## 6 JUNE 2015, BARCELONA 3-1 JUVENTUS

Neymar took his first ever Champions League final in his stride. He helped Ivan Rakitić to score Barcelona's first goal and then combined with Lionel Messi and Luis Suárez to score the third himself. It was a special way to end a special night. 'MSN', Barcelona's superstar strikeforce, was on fire.

## 20 AUGUST 2016, BRAZIL 1-1 GERMANY (5-4 ON PENALTIES)

After the embarrassing defeat at the 2014 World Cup, this was the perfect chance for Brazil to get their revenge on Germany and win another major trophy. With the pressure of the nation on him, Neymar captained his country to glory. Not only did he score an amazing free-kick but he also scored the winning penalty in the shoot-out.

# PLAY LIKE YOUR HEROES

## THE NEYMAR FLICK

**STEP 1:** Wait for a defender to charge towards you.

**STEP 2:** Get the front of your foot under the ball and at the perfect moment, flick it up in the air.

**STEP 3:** Don't put too much power or height on the flick. You want it to go just over the defender's head and then land the other side.

**STEP 4:** Dodge the defender, who may well try to foul you for trying such outrageous skills.

**STEP 5:** Run onto the ball and bring it down with perfect control.

**STEP 6:** If you're a real entertainer, flick the ball back over the defender's head.

**STEP 7:** Once you're bored of that trick, move on to some step-overs or even a rainbow flick.

# TEST YOUR KNOWLEDGE

## QUESTIONS

**1.** How did Neymar have a lucky escape when he was a baby?

**2.** What did Neymar give to his teammates at Gremetal?

**3.** How old was Neymar when he joined Santos?

**4.** Which Spanish club tried to sign Neymar first and how old was he?

**5.** What are Neymar's fans called in Brazil?

**6.** Who was Neymar's childhood hero, who he then played with at Santos?

**7.** Neymar scored on his Brazil debut – true or false?

**8.** When and where did Neymar first meet Lionel Messi?

**9.** Which Barcelona manager signed Neymar and how much did they pay for him?

**10.** Who joined Barcelona first – Neymar or Luis Suárez?

**11.** What number does Neymar wear for Brazil and who else famously wore that shirt?

**Answers below. . . No cheating!**

1. *'He survived a serious car crash.* 2. *White headbands* 3. *11* 4. *Real Madrid tried to sign him when he was 13* 5. *Neymarzetes* 6. *Robinho* 7. *True* 8. *At the 2011 FIFA World Club Cup in Japan.* 9. *Gerardo Martino was the manager and Neymar cost Barcelona about £72million* 10. *Neymar. Neymar joined in 2013 and Suárez joined in 2014.* 11. *He wears Number 10, just like Pelé.*

## CAN'T GET ENOUGH OF
# ULTIMATE FOOTBALL HEROES?

**Check out heroesfootball.com
for quizzes, games, and competitions!**

**Plus join the Ultimate Football Heroes
Fan Club to score exclusive content
and be the first to hear about new
books and events.
heroesfootball.com/subscribe/**

# Climate Change
# Begins at Home

## Life on the two-way street of global warming

Dave Reay

## Macmillan

London　New York　Melbourne　Hong Kong

First published in hardback 2005
First published in paperback 2006 by
Macmillan
Houndmills, Basingstoke, Hampshire RG21 6XS and
175 Fifth Avenue, New York, N. Y. 10010
Companies and representatives throughout the world

ISBN-13: 978–1–4039–4578–5 (hardback)
ISBN-10: 1–4039–4578–0 (hardback)
ISBN-13: 978–0–230–00754–3 (paperback)
ISBN-10: 0–230–00754–6 (paperback)

This book is printed on paper suitable for recycling and made from fully managed
and sustained forest sources. Logging, pulping and manufacturing processes are
expected to conform to the environmental regulations of the country of origin.

A catalogue record for this book is available from the British Library.

A catalog record for this book is available from the Library of Congress.

10   9   8   7   6   5   4
15   14   13   12   11   10   09   08   07

Printed and bound in China

*To Sarah*

# contents

*acknowledgements* **vi**
*permissions* **viii**
*note on units* **x**
*foreword* **xi**
*preface* **xv**

1. the power of one  **1**
2. going places  **28**
3. home start  **55**
4. flying strawberries  **81**
5. in my backyard  **99**
6. money matters  **121**
7. a green inheritance  **139**
8. lights out  **157**

*references and resources* **181**
*bibliography* **195**
*index* **197**

# acknowledgements

First among all, thank you Sarah and Maddy for the year's worth of weekends during which you put up with me shut in the bedroom, emerging only rarely for rocket-fuel coffee. Also, thank you Sarah for reading the draft chapters, for liking them and for laughing.

Thanks Flo for the head-clearing yomps over the fields. Thanks to my parents John and Joan for always being so interested, not to mention providing a great childhood with Mike, Paul and Elisabeth. Thanks to Glyn and Allan for all your support, good meals and great company. Thanks to Mahmoud Ibrahim, John McCrystal, Elspeth, Irene, Brian, Angie, Richard, Jenny, and all my good friends and neighbours in Threemiletown for making our little corner of West Lothian a Scottish Bedford Falls.

Thank you Keith Smith at Edinburgh University for being a friend as well as a boss, and for giving me the freedom to follow new ideas. Likewise, thank you to my other hugely supportive bosses at Edinburgh, John Moncrieff and John Grace.

Thank you to Scott, Mel, Ceri and Maud McEwan for all the afternoon walks and talks. Thanks also for, variously, help, advice and inspiration to: Simon Singh, Rachel Carson, Mark Lynas, George Monbiot, Richard Starkey, Paul Jacobson, Bernard Hutchinson, Douglas Adams, Gerald Durrell, the Intergovernmental Panel on Climate Change, the Natural Environment Research Council, and ABBA.

Finally, thank you to Sara Abdulla, my editor at Macmillan, for liking more than half of my jokes and for scraping the academic barnacles off my writing.

# permissions

The author and publisher are grateful for permission to reproduce pictures from the following sources:

Intergovernmental Panel on Climate Change (IPCC). *Impacts of or risks from climate change, by reason for concern.* TS-12. Climate Change 2001: Impacts, Adaptation and Vulnerability. Published by Cambridge University Press, Cambridge, 2001. Reproduced with permission.

Paul (Jake) Jacobson. *Jacob Marley and Ebenezer Scrooge.* http://bcpub.com/jake/. Reproduced with permission.

Patrick Minnis, NASA. *Flight frequencies over the US on 3rd and 11th September 2001.* NASA Langley Cloud and Radiation Group, US. http://www-pm.larc.nasa.gov/sass/airtraffic_shutdown.html. Reproduced with permission.

Imperial War Museum. *Daddy, What did you do in the Great War?* (Saville Lumley). Poster held by Imperial War Museum, London. Reproduced with permission.

# note on units

Throughout the book I refer to grams, kilograms or tonnes of greenhouse gas, by this I mean the amount of greenhouse gas as measured in so-called carbon dioxide equivalents. For this, emissions of powerful greenhouse gases like methane and nitrous oxide are multiplied by their global warming potential (GWP) which takes into account how much better they are than carbon dioxide at trapping heat on a molecule to molecule basis. So carbon dioxide has a GWP of 1, methane a GWP of 20 and nitrous oxide a GWP of 310.

A keen eye will also spot that while greenhouse emissions are given in metric, I have kept engine efficiencies in imperial units as, despite the best efforts of our governments, most people better understand fuel efficiency in terms of miles per gallon. Some other units are treated similarly.

# foreword

Perhaps the most shocking images from 2004's Asian tsunami were those taken by Canadian holidaymakers John and Jackie Knill on the beach at the Thai resort of Khao Lak. It's not the photos themselves that are shocking, but how they were taken. Each of the six images shows the unfolding catastrophe of the tsunami, from the receding tide in the first shot, to the wall of oncoming water in the last. John and Jackie were killed by the wave; the photos they took were recovered from their digital camera's memory card by rescuers searching the rubble.

The discovery raised searching questions – not just for the Knill family, but for all of us. Why had the two tourists just stood on the beach taking pictures as a gigantic wave rushed towards them? Why did they not run? I believe that John and Jackie's behaviour was all too understandable – a tsunami was outside their experience; they simply couldn't make sense of it. They were frequent visitors to Khao Lak, and had no doubt watched big waves break on the beach many times before. How were they to know that this wave was so different from all the others?

This sad story illustrates the difficulty we all have in adjusting to the reality of climate change, a looming catastrophe which is just as far outside our experience and understanding as the tsunami was for the Knills. Of course, humanity has experienced climate changes in the past. During the Mediaeval Warm Period – in a story much beloved of climate sceptics – the north of England was famed for its wines. Still longer ago, during the last Ice Age, humans were displaced far to the south as ice sheets advanced across the European landmass.

But this climate change is different. It could get as warm this century as it was cold during the last Ice Age – about 5 °C of difference from the present. That hints at the magnitude of what we are facing. Except that the world is already in a warm period, and human-induced global warming will make it warmer still, catapulting the globe into a super-hot greenhouse episode without precedent for tens of millions of years. That could put paid to much of what we call human civilisation; it is also likely to extinguish much of the world's biodiversity in what will be the planet's sixth great mass extinction.

Look around you, and remember the couple watching the approaching tsunami. Isn't that an aeroplane cruising overhead? Is that familiar distant roar not the sound of many thousands of engines, all pumping carbon dioxide through a thousand exhaust pipes to get a thousand busy commuters to work on time? Sometimes this peculiar disconnect is starkly highlighted in the media. The UK's *Independent* newspaper recently ran a scary front page splash about the likelihood that global warming tipping points were being crossed. Meanwhile in its editorial pages, it celebrated the late Freddie Laker for bringing cheap aviation to the masses.

The looming wave is already visible on the horizon. We're past the stage where the water simply retreats; it is now coming in again, and fast. 2005 was either the hottest year ever or the second hottest, depending on whether you believe NASA or the UK Met Office. The northern polar sea ice was at its lowest-ever recorded extent since the satellite era began, and across every mountain range in the world glaciers continued their headlong retreat. It was also a record-breaking year in the North Atlantic for hurricanes, in every conceivable sense: storms were so numerous that forecasters ran out of names and had to resort to the Greek alphabet; the season lasted longer than ever before, with a tropical storm keeping meteorologists busy until January 2006; and the record was also broken for the most intense storm ever recorded. Hurricane Wilma morphed from a minor tropical storm to a Category 5 monster in just 24 hours; its pinhole eye, a mere two nautical miles across, saw barometric pressures plunge to an incredible 882 millibars.

Yet this was the same year that politicians celebrated as a 'success' international negotiations in Montreal which turned out to be nothing more than an agreement to hold another meeting. And, thanks to the strenuous efforts of the US delegation, these future talks will be prohibited even from straying into the forbidden territory of what to do about emissions of greenhouse gases. So what will they talk about? Hotel breakfasts? Football scores? With every moment of delay the wave gets closer.

All is not quite lost. The first steps of the Kyoto agreement are putting a price on carbon for the first time in Europe. The atmosphere is no longer a free dumping ground for any corporation that wants to use it. Public concern and media coverage are increasing nearly exponentially: in just a few months climate change has gone from the preoccupation of sandal-wearing greenies to the top level of policy posturing of presidents and prime ministers. Even in the Bush-benighted United States, the north-east region is holding its own mini-Kyoto. At the local level too things are changing: a Cheshire village called

Ashton Hayes has decided to go carbon neutral, and nearly 400 people turned up to launch the project with home-made apple pie and English champagne. Sweden is the first country aiming to go fossil-fuel free – on an impressive timetable of 15 years.

At the same time, technologies for solar, wind and wave power are advancing in leaps and bounds – spurred, ironically, by high oil prices making them more competitive on the open market. Just as people in Hawaii and Chile know perfectly well to head off the beach if the water retreats, wiser heads across the world are waking up to the climate change threat and beginning to act on it.

Dave Reay is one of these wiser heads, offering a succinct and accessible analysis of how the global warming issue might appear to one typical developed world family, and the steps they – and all of us – must take to avoid contributing to it further. Dave illustrates how climate change is no longer a distant concern of people far away but must become the central governing principle of our lives if the worst impacts of global warming are to be avoided. The challenge we now face is that, like it or not, climate change is coming home – and we have to act before the house gets washed away by the oncoming tsunami.

Mark Lynas

# preface

Climate change isn't new. Since the first microbes, drifting in a bubbling prehistoric ocean, noticed it was getting a bit chilly, life on Earth has had to either adapt to changes in the climate or die. What *is* new is a rapidly changing climate driven by an enhanced greenhouse effect – humankind's uncontrolled experiment on the planet whereby we pump enough greenhouse gas into the atmosphere to double or triple its concentration and then see what happens.

The reason I've written this book is simple: I don't want to see what happens. I don't want my family and friends to see it, I don't want you or your loved ones to see it. Most of all I don't want our children and grandchildren to see it. I'm frightened by what climate change has in store, really frightened.

I haven't always been this worried. For years my interest in global warming was more professional than personal. As a fresh-faced graduate my research centred on the descendants of those chilly microbes in the frigid waters of the Southern Ocean, asking: how will they respond to a warming world?

(Some liked it, some died.) For the next seven years, I carried on counting the climate change beans in the belief that politicians would see the need for action, and act. When the Kyoto Protocol emerged in 1997 I knew that, by itself, the treaty wouldn't be enough. Nevertheless, I felt reassured that with so many nations on board something would finally get done. Then, in 2001, US president George W. Bush withdrew his nation – the world's single biggest greenhouse gas emitter – from Kyoto. For a while I just wandered about at work muttering "What the hell happened?". At the time it looked as though Kyoto was dead in the water, that there was to be no concerted action on cutting global greenhouse emissions, and all the scientific research (my own algae boiling included) counted for nothing.

It would have been easy to continue feeding George W dolls to my Labrador and moaning about politicians, but there was a way to fight back. Alongside the research I was being paid to do, I started to look into the greenhouse gas that I was directly responsible for, the emissions which were mine to increase or decrease as I saw fit. I found that I was a big emitter, but also that I could do something about it. The politicians may have been dithering, but I was going to cut my own emissions – to do my bit.

And so were sown the seeds of this book. First came a short paper in the journal *Nature* called "Kyoto Begins at Home" about a family of four in the USA who met their own equivalent of the USA's Kyoto commitment through a few simple lifestyle changes. During the subsequent years I researched everything from green burials to the global warming contribution of Labradors. Along the way our big car was swapped for a Smart car, low-energy bulbs spread through the house, and the mail-order composting worms arrived (a fun evening in, I can tell you).

During this time I was also running a website covering climate change research. Each month the workload increased as the column inches that global warming was attracting shot up. These stories were no longer only about its impacts in the developing world. There were now headlines about Alaskan communities sinking into the ground, heatwaves killing tens of thousands across Europe, flash flooding in the USA, drought in Australia, and even bankrupt ski resorts here in Scotland. Climate change, it seemed, was coming home.

All this, along with some severe sleep deprivation, led to this book. *Climate Change Begins at Home* takes a long hard look at life on the two-way street of global warming and brings our impact on the climate face to face with the shifting climate's impact on us, our neighbours, and generations of first-time buyers to come.

# 1

## the power of one

Meet the Carbones, a middle class family living in a typical street. A street, just like thousands of others in the Western world, with picket fences and trimmed lawns, with coffee mornings and a neighbourhood watch. The Carbones have worked hard to buy the house and cars they want, and to provide for their two young sons, George and Henry.

It's Saturday morning and the Carbones have just got back from the supermarket. They are unloading the week's shopping from their gleaming people carrier. The weather in Alabama is wiltingly hot again and it's a race to get the ice cream into the freezer before it melts completely. Once in the house, George racks up the air-conditioning and slides in front of the TV. Henry slopes off to his room, puts on some music and rejoins his online game. With shopping safely put away, and all the carrier bags stored for reuse, Mr and Mrs Carbone sit down with the newspapers and a fresh cup of fairly-traded coffee. Life is good.

Soon though, their chirpy conversation trails off and their buoyant mood is punctured by the doom-laden headlines. The *Greenville Herald* warns of the heatwave intensifying and prints an appeal from the local Senator for restraint in electricity use at peak times to avert a power blackout. Health officials estimate that 2,000 people across the county have already been hospitalised with heat stroke and 30 have died. They urge the public to keep an eye on elderly neighbours and not to leave dogs or young children unattended in cars. Two boys have drowned trying to cool off by swimming in a local lake. The national news isn't much better. Across the Mid-West there is strict water rationing, many farmers are watching their top-soil blowing away in the wind, and up in Alaska thousands of homes have been lost to thawing permafrost.

This haywire climate, not that of some distant African state, but here, at home, has the Carbones worried. Just five years ago both would have dismissed any suggestion of taking action on climate change, citing the economic arguments of politicians and hinting at the vested interests of climate scientists. Then, the warnings were dire but the evidence appeared scant – and both could still remember 1970s predictions of our falling into a new ice age.

Now, although the Carbones still feel that the threat has been exaggerated, they cannot deny the ever-earlier start to spring in Greenville, the disappointingly snow-free winters, and the scorching summer, which at that very moment is finishing off the last few living patches of Mr Carbone's formerly immaculate lawn.

As their worry about global warming has grown, the Carbones have become increasingly keen to 'do their bit' to prevent it. For a while now, Mrs Carbone has separated the bottles, tins and newspapers from the rest of their household trash and, each Thursday, filled the special crates for kerbside collection. Mr Carbone has replaced a couple of their traditional tungsten light bulbs with low-energy bulbs, and is always on at the boys for leaving lights, TVs and computers on. They may not wear knitted trousers and eat muesli for every meal, but the Carbones feel they do what they can for the environment and would describe their lifestyle as 'really quite green'.

So what help are the Carbones' various actions in mitigating climate change? The blunt answer is: not much. Their weekly car trips to the supermarket produce more greenhouse gas than all that saved by their efforts to recycle and cut energy wastage. The Carbones have fooled themselves into thinking that they can help tackle climate change without making real changes to their lifestyles. In fact, the only purpose their 'environmental' efforts currently serve is to massage their uneasiness about global warming while allowing them to carry on living just as they've always done.

Why don't they do more? Well, apart from finding some lifestyle changes hard to swallow, like getting rid of Mr Carbone's gas-guzzling SUV, they've tended to see climate change as a developing-world problem. Sure, they felt bad about the increase in hurricanes, droughts and floods in Africa, Asia and South America, but until global warming came knocking on their own door it was all too easy to ignore.

For the Carbones and millions like them, it takes a home visit to really stir up some action. Warn them that their greenhouse gas emissions may harm people thousands of kilometres away and they might try to do a bit – some recycling for instance – but then they can always avoid TV when the news gets too bad. Make them aware that climate change is likely to threaten their own friends, family and way of life though, and they'll be the first in line for low-energy light bulbs at the local hardware store.

This is the challenge faced by all those calling for action on greenhouse gas emissions. They can appeal to our humanity, listing the devastating consequences climate change will have, or is already having, in the developing world – try to tap that guilty streak that runs through all of us living in the luxury of the West. They can, and do, warn of the famine, plagues and migrations of biblical proportions that could occur as climate change takes hold in countries with scant or no resources to adapt. But as long as the apocalypses are remote many people will drag their heels.

Only when climate change starts to squeeze us directly will we really begin to take notice – when it's not only drought-stricken Sudan or flood-ravaged Bangladesh in the news, but our own neighbourhoods and economies taking a hammering. The most severe effects are still some years away and we have kidded ourselves into thinking we have ample time to head off any big problems. We haven't.

Like most families, the Carbones assume that unlobbied governments will deal with such global issues, or that scientists will come up with a technological fix – a silver bullet to solve climate change. Neither of these head-in-the-sand solutions is realistic. In the end the buck stops with you, me, and the Carbones: our lifestyles and our emissions. So how much greenhouse gas does the Carbone family emit and how?

## Mrs Carbone

Kate Carbone's life is, to say the least, hectic. Now in her late 30s, she successfully combines bringing up two sons, the bulk of the housework, at least two-thirds of the dog walking and a job as team leader in a local travel firm. Most mornings, it's non-stop demands from the moment she wakes up, from the dog whining for its walk, through the muttering husband unable to find matching socks, to George and Henry arguing about who opens the cereal packet. At the centre of this whirlwind Kate directs proceedings and somehow everyone ends up where they should be with the minimum of forgotten lunches and inside-out sweaters. Running George to and from school is invariably the most stressful part of her day. He always waits until the last possible minute before dashing out to her eight-seater people carrier, despite any amount of horn honking, threats of being left behind, pocket money restrictions and bedroom incarceration. Once the family are all safely off, Kate makes her way through the rush-hour traffic to her office and, with a cup of strong coffee, sits down for another day of placating disgruntled customers whose shower had been too hot/cold, whose hotel was too far from the beach, or who had found it inconvenient that not all Germans are fluent in English. Evenings for Kate Carbone are only slightly less hectic, with after-school clubs meaning more ferrying about of children, dinners to be prepared and eaten, and battles to be fought over when homework should be done and how much TV can be watched.

At the weekend Kate spends as much time as she can in the garden – her pride and joy. Over the years she has transformed it from a featureless waste of brown grass and bramble-ridden borders into a riot of colour and buzzing insects. She has turned a section over to herbs and vegetables, providing the family with fresh salads for much of the summer. There are always a hundred and one jobs to get done, with progress never helped by bored sons, husbands and Labradors. But Kate, aided by regular visits from her mother-in-law, Grandma Carbone, somehow keeps the weeds under control and the flowers dead-headed.

Kate Carbone's climate impact is dominated by her car-driving. All those school runs, the slow drag into work and back, and the numerous food-shopping trips add up to over six tonnes of greenhouse gas each year. She does, though, cut her emissions by growing some of the family's food and so avoiding all the transport normally associated with it.

## Mr Carbone

John Carbone is hugely proud of his family, his house and the life he has helped make for them all. It has been hard work, particularly in the early days when he and Kate had a young baby, only one insecure job between them and an income which could only just about cover the mortgage repayments. John still puts in long hours at the office and has his sights set on moving higher up the career ladder, but the money is now pretty good and he can take more time off without worrying that his job will be given to someone else. His day starts with a hasty shower and coffee to go, then it's into his brand new SUV and off to join the slowly moving queue of cars on the main road into the centre of town. John works for a large insurance firm and has recently been made acting manager of his branch. He reckons that in a year or so he should make full branch manager. Every year he flies to Seattle for the company's Annual General Meeting and, through some blatant networking, has earned himself the reputation as a rising star in the company.

At the weekends John usually has some paperwork to get out of the way. Once that's done its down to the usual weekend chores of watering the lawn, child ferrying, food shopping and DIY. He usually manages to squeeze in an hour or two of TV sport and, in the summer, a few beers with the neighbours and the odd barbecue.

Again, it's transport which dominates John's climate burden. His large-engined car clocks up a massive 12 tonnes of greenhouse gas emissions a year. His annual Seattle flight adds another tonne. At home he and his wife must take the blame for the bulk of greenhouse gas emissions, being responsible for how the house is heated or cooled, and for the efficiency of the many electrical appliances.

We all face the same problem as our families and/or our salaries grow. With greater affluence, the opportunity to increase greenhouse gas emissions through energy-rich activities also rises and the financial incentive for keeping down energy use fades. The climate impact of the two-kid, double-income Carbones has rocketed from those early days as newly-weds who always caught the bus to work and wouldn't dream of leaving a light on. Their household energy expenditure is now in the 'high-user' category, the resulting emissions adding up to 13 tonnes a year. With growing boys to feed; bought-in food alone totals over 30 kg of goods each week; the greenhouse gas arising from the transport of all this food adds up to about four and half tonnes a year. The household and garden waste that doesn't get recycled leads to yet another tonne of emissions as it slowly rots in the dark recesses of the local landfill.

## George Carbone

George is nearly eight. What he lacks in age he more than makes up for in energy. He is the main reason the Carbones' front and back lawns are bedecked year-round with trampolines, slides, and all manner of other plastic tat. Play in the back garden can sometimes lead to clashes with his mother, particularly when a plant mysteriously loses its flowers heads or develops snapped stem disease. Being so young, George's climate contribution is mainly determined by his parents. His daily drive to and from school in Mom's people carrier clocks up over 600 kg of greenhouse a year. But this youngest member of the family is already damaging the planet through his waste of energy around the house. He frequently leaves on lights, TVs and countless battery-powered toys, despite the threats and pleas from his Dad. This squandered energy equates to an extra 120 kg of greenhouse gas emission each year.

## Henry Carbone

Henry is 12 and becomes obsessed with any craze that passes through his high school. One week it is collecting game cards, the next skateboarding. A month later the oh-so-desperately-needed skateboard will be gathering dust in the Carbone shed while Henry clocks up his fourth straight hour playing an online fantasy game. His room looks like mission control; TV, stereo, PC, mobile phone and modem flash and hum away to themselves day and night.

Like his little brother, Henry routinely leaves his gadgets on, whether in use or not, resulting in 160 kg of greenhouse emissions each year. He's also got into the habit of turning on the electric radiator in his room at the first hint of chill through his Black Beelzebub T-shirt. This additional two hours of heating each day pumps out 700 kg of greenhouse gas every year.

Fortunately, Henry's decision to travel to school by bus (it gives him more time to swap Orc Ascension cards) saves more than half a tonne of greenhouse gas compared to going in his mother's car. The bus emits only 53 kg to get each card-sharp to and from school for a year.

## Molly

Molly is the Carbone Labrador. At nine years old her penchant for socks means no one in the family can claim to have more than a couple of matching pairs (and these all have holes in). Molly's climate impact is wholly the responsibility of John and Kate Carbone. It centres around whether or not they choose to drive to her favourite walking spots. They usually do, as most of the best are either too far or too dangerous to walk to.

An average walk entails a 6 km drive in the people carrier (the SUV is too new for muddy Labradors), which belches 300 g of greenhouse gas for every kilometre it travels – about 4 kg on each round trip. With two such walks every day of the year, rain or shine, Molly's annual emissions soar to nearly three tonnes.

## Grandma Carbone

Grandma Carbone lives about half an hour's drive south from Kate, John and the boys. She has dwelt in the same large, rambling house for over forty years and every corner is home to a happy memory. Grandpa Carbone built a good deal of it with his own hands, back when most of the land about was still fields and the traffic-clogged road at the front was just a dirt track. As a young couple, Grandma and Grandpa Carbone worked like Trojans to keep up the loan repayments. They spent all of their weekends painting, decorating and planning more improvements. Their son, John, was born and raised in the house, and he and Kate had their wedding reception in its garden. Since Grandpa Carbone's sudden death eight years ago, Grandma Carbone has lived alone in the house – not that she spends much time there, being out almost every day at some fundraiser, playing golf, or helping out with the grandchildren.

When Grandpa Carbone died, Grandma swapped his pride and joy – a 1968 gas-guzzling classic car – for a bright yellow hatchback in which she clocks up around 9,000 kilometres a year. This new car emits two tonnes of greenhouse gas a year, a great improvement on the old one which drank twice as much fuel and was a pig to park in town.

Grandma Carbone flies each Easter to visit her sister in Beaverton, Oregon, adding about a tonne to her own annual greenhouse gas budget in the process. Since the death of Grandpa Carbone, energy use at home has dropped into the 'low' household bracket with the related emissions adding up to five tonnes a year. The old place is feeling too big and Grandma Carbone has plans to move into a more up-to-date and compact retirement flat.

Though her son and daughter in-law have mentioned things like recycling and 'the environment' on numerous occasions, Grandma Carbone has no truck with such lefty concepts. She does hanker for the cooler summer days of her youth, but not the enforced thriftiness of the war years. As such, her green-house gas emissions add up to ten tonnes each year and the recycling boxes in her backyard collect only dead leaves and rain water.

Over at Kate and John's house where, unlike Grandma, they are 'doing their bit' for the environment, how do they compare climate-wise? Let's take the good things first. They recycle most of their newspapers and cardboard, saving about 400 kg of greenhouse gas per year. The recycling of their glass bottles and jars each year, along with all the tin cans, cuts another 300 kg off their annual greenhouse budget. Kate Carbone grows enough salad and root vegetables in her garden to prevent 300 kg of greenhouse gas that would have been emitted from production and transport of this food. John has fitted three energy-efficient bulbs and intends to get around to replacing them all, so far cutting 225 kg of greenhouse gas off the yearly family budget and bringing their total reductions to just over 1,200 kg.

On the down side, the family's emissions are dominated by transport: between them their two large-engined cars pump out a total of 18 tonnes of greenhouse gas per year. And then there is the summer holiday. For the past six years, the entire Carbone clan, (apart from Molly who goes into kennels), has jetted off to Cancun in Mexico for two weeks' swimming and sunbathing at the same self-catered house. For every kilometre flown, each family member racks up a further 150 g of greenhouse emissions. So the round trip to Cancun adds 400 kg to each of their annual budgets. Throw in John's AGM jaunt to Seattle and family air travel produces more than two and a half tonnes of greenhouse gas a year.

Totting things up, we have 20.5 tonnes of greenhouse gas from transport, 13 tonnes from home energy use, four and a half tonnes of food-related emissions, and the tonne produced due to household waste. In other words the 'we're doing our bit' Carbone household puts 39 tonnes of greenhouse gas into the atmosphere each year – enough to fill their house 40 times over.

The Carbones have managed to cut their greenhouse gas emissions by an embarrassingly small 3%. This doesn't even get them to the 5.2% target that politicians have set with the Kyoto Protocol, let alone the 60% cut scientists urge. It's a shock to a family who felt that they were doing well in mitigating their damage to the environment. The lifestyle changes they actually need to make go a tad beyond leaving the newspapers out for collection once a fortnight.

↔

The south-eastern USA, home to the Carbones, has been a boom area in the past few decades. It produces about a quarter of all US-grown food and half of the timber. The population has shot up by around a third since the 1970s, with most people moving into new homes along the coast. Climate change poses a real threat to hundreds of thousands, maybe millions, of people in this region, endangering their homes, their jobs, and even their lives.

Summertime temperatures across the south-eastern states are projected to soar by more than 10 °C by 2100, the most dramatic rises predicted anywhere in the USA. Such big hikes threaten people right across the region, especially the young, old and poor. As temperatures soar, so does the danger to those without expensive air-conditioning systems and those physically more vulnerable to heat stress. In Atlanta, Georgia, for example, temperatures on a sunny July day could top 54 °C during this century, unbearable for the most sturdy lumber-jack, let alone a new-born baby or its bedridden grandpa.

The huge energy demand from those who are lucky enough to have air-conditioning will mean more air pollution from power stations, and therefore more respiratory health problems due to low-level ozone and particulates. All in all, not the ideal recipe for a carefree summer in the south-eastern USA.

Another big concern is flooding. It is already a leading cause of deaths due to natural disasters in the south-eastern USA, and in the USA as a whole, causing about 100 fatalities each year. Sea level has risen almost 30 cm since the mid-19th century and models suggest it could rise a further 90 cm or more by 2100. Around 400,000 hectares of wetland have disappeared in the past century. Many hundreds of hectares of coastal forest have been destroyed, the saltwater slowly intruding inland, killing off the trees as it goes.

In recent decades, a combination of rising tides and land development has already led to the loss of 13,000 hectares of coastal salt marsh – the natural buffer that protects the land from flooding and erosion by the sea. As sea levels go up, yet more of these natural barriers will be lost, increasing the flooding threat to communities further inland. Rainfall is also expected to increase by about 25% by the end of this century, further adding to flooding risks.

Water quality right across the region is imperilled by climate change. Salt water is increasingly likely to contaminate drinking water supplies near coasts, while higher temperatures reduce the amount of oxygen in the water, damaging fish and other aquatic life. Flash flooding can lead to pollution of drinking water supplies by sewage, rotting carcasses, chemicals and fuel. North Carolina suffered exactly this fate in 1999.

The economic costs of such climate change sequelae are set to grow and grow. The bill for weather-related disasters in the south-eastern USA has topped $85 billion over the last 20 years – the heatwave and drought of 1998 alone cost $6 billion and 200 lives.

Crop yields are expected to rise in some areas but fall in others, particularly the Gulf coast, during this century. Some soybean farmers have already seen harvests drop 80%, while those growing irrigated wheat may see rises of 20% by 2090. Higher concentrations of carbon dioxide in the atmosphere are likely to boost tree growth in the south-east; models predict increases of up to 10% in pine production and up to 25% in hardwood production in the next 100 years. But there's bad news too for our sweaty lumberjack. On top of the destruction of forests by salt water, drier soils and more fires (brought about by those soaring summertime temperatures) will probably see large areas of forest replaced by grasslands by 2100.

The Carbone house is 160 kilometres from the coast and, at about 130 m, well above sea level. But, with heavier rainstorms predicted, the local river poses a serious flooding risk. Through his work in insurance John Carbone is all too aware of the danger. Since the last scientific assessment of the flooding risk in Alabama was published, his own insurance premiums have rocketed and almost every day he has to tell a potential customer that, as their house is within 30 kilometres of the coast, it is effectively uninsurable.

Grandma Carbone has suffered water contamination half a dozen times in the past 10 years, each time having to rely on rapidly diminishing supplies of bottled water from the local supermarket. John had to upgrade the air-conditioning system throughout his house last summer; the existing system couldn't cope with being run at full blast for such long periods and eventually gave up the fight completely – leading to a very sticky couple of days trying to persuade the air-conditioning company to fit a new one when they had hundreds of similar requests from across the county.

Soaring summer temperatures will also affect the Carbones' holiday. Though models of the effects of climate change are best for developed-world countries, it is clear that Mexico will be hit hard. Summer heatwaves are expected to intensify and cause many more deaths, mainly through heart and respiratory illnesses. The problem is exacerbated in Mexico by the general lack of air-conditioning, high population density and a fragile health-care system. Things will likely be worst in Mexico City and other large, overcrowded, polluted urban areas. Cities experience the 'heat island' effect: roads and buildings absorb and trap warmth, keeping temperatures several degrees higher than in the surrounding countryside, even at night. This, combined with overall temperature increases, is likely to push up average temperatures in Mexico City by 5 °C during this century. Add in the very real threat to water supplies across Mexico, as increasing demand clashes with falling availability, and you have the recipe for a human health disaster.

Around 18 million US citizens currently holiday in Mexico every year. Like the Carbones, these tourists will start staying away in droves if the summer temperatures rise too high. This is the last thing Mexico's fragile economy can afford, given the huge costs it faces in coping with climate change.

The threats facing the Carbones and their neighbours in the south-eastern USA will be echoed around the world. For some, things will be much worse, for others, not as bad. The precise impacts of global warming are often hard to predict because the world's climate system is so complicated. One effect may cause another, resulting in a cascade of problems. Some effects may cancel out others. The global evapo-transpiration cycle is expected to speed up. This means that generally it will rain more, but water will evaporate faster – leaving soils drier during critical parts of the growing season and potentially causing widespread crop loss and famine.

Maximum wind speeds will increase and extreme weather events, such as hurricanes, may occur more frequently. Rising sea levels, from thermal expansion and/or ice-shelf disintegration, may result in mass migrations and the loss of huge tracts of farm-land. Some islands and low-lying coastal regions may disappear altogether: Tuvalu in the South Pacific and the Sundarbans delta in Bangladesh, for instance. Global average sea level has already risen by around 15 cm over the past 100 years, with another 18 cm rise predicted due to global warming in the next 30 years. If this trend continues, we could see a rise of up to 88 cm by 2100.

It's the poorest countries of the world – those least responsible for human-made climate change – that are likely to feel the most severe effects. Many areas will lose huge swathes of agricultural land to flooding, freak weather and pests, leading to starvation on an unprecedented scale. Clean water will become ever more scarce, which, in combination with poor sanitation, over-stretched medical services and bad nutrition, will provide a perfect environment for disease epidemics.

Expanding deserts, extreme storms, floods and starvation could displace many millions of people, causing civil unrest and a rising pressure on immigration systems. Tropical diseases are expected to spread to new areas. The geographical zone of potential malaria transmission, for example, today covers around 45% of the world population; by 2050 that figure may be 60%. Finally, climate change will have a massive impact on ecosystems and wildlife right around the world, with the climate-warming scenarios for 2050 indicating that up to a third of all land species will by then be committed to extinction.

Long before the earliest hairy-backed hominids started lighting fires, our atmosphere already had greenhouse gases and a fully functioning 'greenhouse effect'. Just as the glass of a greenhouse lets the sunlight through but keeps a good deal of the reflected heat from escaping back outside, so our atmosphere lets the light of the Sun through but catches some of the thermal radiation (heat) emitted back towards space from the Earth's surface.

Look out of the window. If you're lucky the Sun is shining down and the birds are singing. Everything you can see, from your driveway and your patchy lawn, to the neighbours' car and their novelty garden toadstools, is throwing energy back towards space. The amount of energy bounced back to the atmosphere in this way has to balance the amount coming in from the Sun; if less is able to leave than comes in, as happens when greenhouse gases trap some of it, the Earth starts to heat up – global warming.

Without this warming the average temperature on Earth would be a frigid –18 °C rather than our more balmy average of 15 °C. The big problem though is that the greenhouse gas blanket that has been keeping the Earth warm for millennia is

**Figure 1** The Monkey Puzzle Tree (*Araucaria araucaria*). Busy doing its bit to lock up carbon dioxide.

being added to on a massive scale by humans. Take a look at the historical records of the amounts of the various greenhouse gases in our atmosphere and all the graphs have the same shape. They bumble along for thousands of years and then, around the end of the 18th and beginning of the 19th centuries, they start to rise, slowly at first and then faster, like a stock price in a world of boom and no bust. With the Industrial Revolution came a huge growth in the burning of fossil fuels. The amounts of carbon dioxide have risen by almost 30%, while methane – a greenhouse gas produced by rice-growing, landfills and burping cows – has leapt to more than double pre-1800 concentrations. The quantities of these greenhouse gases in our atmosphere are set to carry on increasing long after you and I have shuffled off this mortal coil. Carbon dioxide concentrations, for instance, are expected to more than double by 2100. As a result, global temperatures will rise by between 2 and 5 °C, having already gone up by about half a degree during the 20th century. It's this warming, and the catastrophic impact it may have on our global climate, that threatens us all.

Let's take a closer look at the key players in this – the greenhouse gases themselves. Carbon dioxide and methane are both big hitters, but there are another four that are also of real concern globally, and which politicians have specified as in need of control. First is nitrous oxide, commonly known as laughing gas. Much of it comes from fertilisers and cattle feeds. Then come the catchily named hydrofluorocarbons (HFCs), perfluorocarbons (PFCs) and something called sulphur hexafluoride ($SF_6$). These last three are entirely artificial and come from things like fridge coolants and propellants. Ironically the HFCs were introduced to replace the ozone-damaging CFCs that once chilled fridges and fired out our hairspray. Together these gases make up the so-called 'basket of six', each of them threatening our climate and all of them produced in part or wholly by us. (Water vapour is another powerful greenhouse gas, but, as our effect on it is largely via emissions of the other gases, it is left out of the greenhouse gas 'basket'.)

Some greenhouse gases are much better at trapping the heat radiated from the Earth than others. The most famous, carbon dioxide, is not actually the best heat-catcher but is present at higher concentrations than the others and so plays a bigger role in global warming. The HFCs on the other hand occur in vanishingly small amounts, but each molecule can be thousands of times more effective at trapping the heat radiated by the Earth than a molecule of carbon dioxide.

Take a look into the sky. Imagine all that radiated energy streaming back towards space, invisible to our eyes but on its way nonetheless. Up it goes through our atmosphere, much of it back into the cold vacuum of space, but some – that encountering a greenhouse gas – has a different journey. Think of what happens as like energy trawling, where the energy emitted from the Earth is like a shoal of fish making a dash for the cool of space. All those greenhouse gases in the atmosphere are like giant nets spread across the sky. The carbon dioxide net, though one of the biggest, has a rather coarse mesh and so lets most fish through. Methane, nitrous oxide and the others, despite having much smaller nets, also have a much finer mesh and so are much better at trapping our, by now, rather altitude-sick fish. Methane's net for instance is effectively 20 times finer than that of carbon dioxide, while the silk-stocking-esque nitrous oxide net is 300 times finer. To stay with our fishy example, humankind's emissions of carbon dioxide and the other greenhouse gases over the last century or so have given those atmospheric trawlers the equivalent of bigger nets, finer meshes and a catch which is growing by the day.

As emissions and global temperatures increased, and the predictions worsened, the international community, under the umbrella of the United Nations, began to wake up. In 1988 the Intergovernmental Panel on Climate Change (IPCC) was established to assess the risk of human-induced climate change. The UN Framework Convention on Climate Change (UNFCCC) was developed to provide the overall policy for addressing climate change and so forms the foundation of global efforts to combat global warming, such as those set out in the Kyoto Protocol.

The Kyoto Protocol was drawn up in 1997 by more than 160 nations to set targets for global reductions in greenhouse gas emissions.

Targets in the Kyoto Protocol ranged from a 7% cut for the USA to a 10% increase for Iceland. The developed-world target was for a 5.2% emissions cut, but the scientific consensus is that a worldwide reduction of 60% is required by 2050 to stabilise our climate and head off catastrophic impacts. Achieving such a cut could, for example, reduce the amount of flooding along the Bangladesh coastline of 2100 by 90%, compared to taking no action. The 60% cut is undeniably big. If we're going to achieve it we need meaningful action on emissions right now.

The Kyoto Protocol cuts are a start, but even they are being undermined. Two of the world's biggest emitters, the USA and Australia, have refused to sign up even to the small targets of Kyoto, while loophole exploitation by countries who have signed threatens to reduce the value of cuts set out in the Protocol even further.

To recap: thousands of top-notch scientists from all over the world are warning that if we don't reduce greenhouse gas emissions, we, our children, and our children's children, will almost certainly suffer dire consequences. Getting a wide array of science's big guns to agree on anything is like herding cats, yet on climate change they have reached this sobering consensus:

> most of the warming observed over the last 50 years is likely to be attributable to human activities.

This strong statement from an inherently conservative group was made back in 2001. And still emissions increase.

In the interests of even-handedness, I should mention that there are still some scientists who believe we shouldn't worry about global warming. There are about six of them. This small yet vociferous clique argues that our climate has always been changing and that the warming we see is simply a result of the natural fluctuations in global temperature. This sounds plausible, but their argument collapses though when you look closely at just how fast the Earth is warming. Include all the 'natural' things that control the planet's temperature – things like solar activity, volcanoes, and how close we are to the Sun – and you're still left with a big missing source of heating. The culprit? Artificially generated greenhouse emissions.

The climate change nay-sayers can babble on about natural variations all they want, but here are the bare facts:

- Greenhouse gases warm the planet.
- Global temperatures have risen 0.6 °C in the last 100 years.
- Concentrations of greenhouse gas in our atmosphere are now higher than at any time in the last 420,000 years.
- Since the Industrial Revolution greenhouse gas concentrations have risen by around 50%.

'Natural' variations? They've got to be kidding.

There may only be a dwindling handful of researchers who continue to deny the existence of human-induced climate change, but they have some powerful political allies. The US administration has often cited the 'scientific uncertainty' in defending its anti-Kyoto Protocol stance. For them the 420,000 year record is too short, still too uncertain. As I write, colleagues across Europe are working on an ice core from Antarctica that contains an even longer record of greenhouse gas concentrations in our atmosphere – almost a million years of climate history. The sceptics want more proof? They're going to get it.

Developed-world nations (essentially the industrialised West) are home to only about 20% of the world's population, but use about 80% of the world's resources. Ominously, the oil-powered standard of living we enjoy is what many in developing countries strive for. If the billions of people in the developing world progress to the same level of consumption and emissions as an average US citizen, we will be looking at climate meltdown. China, a nation of over 1 billion souls and possessor of huge coal reserves, is already the world's second largest emitter of greenhouse gas and is gaining fast on the USA.

That the warnings from the scientific community have not yet elicited a meaningful global response to climate change is astonishing. The Kyoto Protocol lives on, but still without the world's largest emitter on board. All is not lost though. A large, and growing, number of people around the world are starting to take their own steps to tackle global warming. The actions of individuals on a global scale could have a profound effect. Domestic and private transport emissions are huge, so individual action can have a big impact. Add to this the bottom-up effect that such lifestyle changes can have on community, business, and eventually government climate policy, and the huge importance of individual action on climate change is clear.

Throughout much of the past three centuries, we in the developed world have been emitting ever-increasing amounts of carbon dioxide, methane and nitrous oxide into the atmosphere, with no comprehension of the potentially disastrous consequences. We no longer have the defence of ignorance. The pressure is now on to turn off that light, get out that bike, and really 'do our bit'.

Why should you take action? Because it's you who will suffer the consequences if you don't – your family, your friends and most definitely your descendants. Our parents' and grandparents' generations will be remembered for huge technological changes, for great leaps forward in agriculture and medicine, and for fighting two world wars that allowed many millions of us to grow up in freedom. We, on the other hand, will be remembered as the 'selfish generations'. The ones who knew the damage their fossil fuel-driven lifestyles would do to the future but who carried on regardless. Our children will be angry with us, our grandchildren more so. And they will have fair reason. It brings to mind the War Office poster (Figure 2), shaming men into enlisting in the First World War. When your granddaughter asks "Grandad, did YOU drive a big car?" your face could well look like his.

Some time soon – maybe it's already happened somewhere – as a horde of children slope into their classroom and take their seats for another indigestible helping of double history and the Industrial Revolution, a teacher is going to surprise them. Instead of launching into a lesson on the significance of Jethro Tull and Thomas Edison to the food we eat and the lights we read by, the teacher will talk about another, very modern consequence of our ancestors' enlightenment – climate change. That class would go something like this:

Early in the 18th century night held sway over working practices and lifestyles. The setting of the Sun was usually the signal to cease work, with most jobs becoming impossible due to the lack of good-quality light. By 1721 the first 'factory' was in operation, signalling the start of the industrial era. By the late 18th century technological innovations, including the steam engine and the Spinning Jenny, were transforming production methods and working practices. Later, in 1831, Michael Faraday made generation of electricity practical and defying the darkness of night became possible on a large scale. Allied to changes in working practices and lifestyles during the 18th century

**Figure 2** Daddy, what did **YOU** do in the Great War?

was a large increase in both national and individual greenhouse gas emissions. With the spread of industrialisation across Europe and North America, rapid human-made global warming was born.

Along with rapid population increase in the 18th century came a big rise in consumerism. Indeed, the most important driver of the late 18th century iron-smelting boom was not industrial demand for machine parts, ship hulls and the like; rather, it was consumer demand for domestic hardware – pots, pans and fireplaces. More iron meant burning more coal and so rising carbon dioxide emissions.

The new generation of steam engines in the 18th century were coal-powered themselves and pumped mineshafts dry to allow yet more coal extraction. In many ways, coal both fuelled the Industrial Revolution and paved the way for the global warming we are now experiencing.

Per capita greenhouse gas emissions rose rapidly during the 18th century. In England, for example, individual emissions rose from around 1 tonne per person per year in 1700, to around 3 tonnes per year by 1800. In the 19th and 20th centuries our rate of development and emissions grew hand in hand. The advent of electric lighting, motor cars, refrigerators and the rest marked new highs on this inexorable climb. From the base camp of 18th century steam engines to the gadget-littered summit of today, it's a climb that's become steeper by the year. In the UK, per capita greenhouse gas emissions now stand at around 11 tonnes each year; in the USA they top 20 tonnes.

So, what makes up an individual's climate impact? As we saw with the Carbones, for most of us it centres on our behaviour at home and our burning of fossil fuels to get around (Figure 3).

Topping the lifestyle chart at close to half of all our greenhouse gas emissions is transport. The chief culprit here is the car: all those gas-guzzling saloons, people carriers and four-wheel drives make up a major part of the climate burden for the average developed-world family. Indeed, for those of us with big cars our love of driving can constitute well over half of all our contribution to global warming. Our deepening affair with flying, for work and pleasure, has also become a significant part of most people's emission budgets.

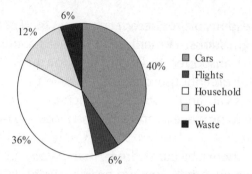

**Figure 3** What makes up your own climate impact?

Energy use at home is the next big hitter, accounting for over a third of emissions. Nearly half of this is due to the heating and cooling of our homes. Refrigerators, freezers and all the other appliances and gadgets come a close second. These appliance-related emissions are increasing, as we fill our kitchens with ice-cream makers and giant refrigerators, our living rooms with huge plasma TV screens and our shelves with music centres and computers.

Next comes water heating at about 15% of household emissions, depending on the fuel used. Gas, for instance leads to far less carbon dioxide than does electricity from a coal-fired power station. Lighting comes in at 5–10% – more for those with a penchant for floodlighting their property. Cooking and clothes washing complete the picture.

Food makes up another large slice of our total greenhouse gas pie. The expectation of year-round availability of everything from kumquats to lemon grass, via salmon, tiger prawns and wild boar, means that the items of food in an average shopping basket can collectively have travelled 240,000 km, giving them a huge climate change tag. Add to this the methane emissions from belching cows and the miasma of nitrous oxide rising from fertiliser-soaked farmland, and food is responsible for 10–20% of our impact on the climate.

Waste is responsible for between 5% and 10% of our greenhouse gas emissions. Primarily this is because old food and newspapers transported to landfill sites rot down to produce the powerful greenhouse gas methane. But every shampoo bottle, drinks can and toothpick that goes into our bins also took energy to produce it, and so represents even more greenhouse gas.

So, that's where it all comes from. Between 10 and 20 tonnes of carbon dioxide, methane and nitrous oxide a year for most of us, and a good deal more for jet-setting, SUV-driving types. Can we really make big cuts in these emissions? Sixty per cent cuts? Is it expensive? Are electric cars the answer? Is recycling a con? Let's find out....

# 2

## going places

Car and air travel, as with the Carbones, top most people's greenhouse gas budgets and so represent a huge opportunity for individuals to make a real difference. Unfortunately our way of life now so revolves around cars and planes that changing habits really does mean a break from the norm – taking the path less travelled. Look at the roads leading to your local mall: there are no pavements. Even if you wanted to walk to the shops you couldn't – not without risking being mown down by an SUV. The same is true of cycling. It's positively suicidal to ride a bike on many roads (Figure 4). Unless you are very lucky (or Swedish) there will be just a few kilometres of cycle path in your local town, probably scattered with broken glass, parked cars or potholes, or all three. Towns, cities, shops and offices, and even homes, are increasingly designed to fit the needs of that four-wheeled wonder that is the car, at the expense of less climate-damaging ways of getting around.

We've heard the pleas from politicians to use public transport, reduce speed, and drive a smaller car so many times we've become almost deaf to them. To date the effects of climate change on transport have tended to take the form of having the in-car air-conditioning on non-stop in the summer. Those of us who rely on an open window as opposed to a

**Figure 4** The joys of cycling.

whirring piece of cooling technology under the bonnet have certainly been feeling the heat in recent summers. Higher temperatures, though, are just the start of a series of impacts on our car driving.

Those journeys through torrential rain, gripping the steering wheel for all you are worth as another wall of water from the truck in front obliterates your view – expect more of them. Likewise, there will be more weather-related accidents and 'road flooded' notices. And climate change will attack the very road surface itself. If you don't find yourself in a jam waiting for a fallen tree to be cleared you're likely to end up in one caused by repairs as the surface melts in summer, cracks in winter, or sags and disintegrates due to both. Bad news then if you think of driving as an efficient, safe and rapid way to get around. It's also going to get very expensive. As oil runs out its price will go up; road tax will climb to pay for all those repairs, insurance premiums will rise to cover increased accidents and, if governments are brave enough, drivers will face escalating taxes on their greenhouse gas.

Relying on top-down government action to cut our emissions from transport, though, could mean a very long wait. Yes, private road transport, being mainly cars, is a major source of greenhouse gas globally, but curbing our driving addiction has proved a political hot potato. There are more cars in the USA than people to drive them: the average household has 1.8 drivers and 1.9 personal vehicles. That's over 200 million private vehicles in the USA alone. Lined up end to end these would stretch around the Earth more than 20 times. Over a fifth of them are SUVs, and another fifth are trucks, meaning big engines and bigger emissions. The average US car does about 20 miles per gallon – the worst 4×4s do only 4 miles to the gallon – and, altogether, transportation in the USA creates nearly 2 billion tonnes of greenhouse gas each year. This is more than the total emissions of any other country, except

China (a nation with four times as many people). Each day, on average, an American will make four car trips totalling about 65 kilometres. Together the nation's drivers clock up about 17.5 billion kilometres each day.

The trend is repeated around the world. England's leafy lanes are now more likely host to four-wheel drives and people carriers than nippy Minis driven by Michael Caine lookalikes. The bustling streets of Paris, once the honking-ground of compact Renaults and Citroëns, are now patrolled by the same hulking four-wheel drives you'll find on a Texan highway. The sleeping greenhouse gas giant of Asia is waking up to aspirations of mass car ownership and US lifestyles. This is very bad: with more than 1 billion people in India and another 1.3 billion in China, if they all drove cars too....

Talk about how bad cars are for the planet and most drivers will respond that their public transport services are either poor or non-existent and that government first needs to provide viable alternatives. But, just as the matter is too urgent to sit and wait for politicians to take decisive action on climate change as a whole, it's also too pressing to wait until they've put a shiny new bus stop outside our house and provided a reliable service to the office every half an hour. So, what to do? I could launch into berating car users for their damaging and wasteful ways, demanding we change to a fossil-fuel-free society, where our children would be healthier and safer, and one could cycle to work without needing full body armour. When you look at the figures – the amounts of greenhouse gas we are emitting and the predicted consequences – it's hard not to take this kind of radical line. Let's face it though: if all I did here was tell you that you shouldn't drive, you shouldn't fly and that foreign holidays were out of the question, you'd fleetingly think about what this would mean to your own life, shove the book down the side of your bed, and get out the 'Learn Esperanto While You Sleep' tapes.

Cutting emissions, as with all addictive habits, takes awareness and willpower. You're a smoker and you like smoking, but you also know that if you carry on smoking it will probably kill you, so you'd like to give up. Going overnight from a twenty-a-day user to a gibbering cold turkey doesn't appeal to most people, and often doesn't work in the long run. Instead, you cut down more gradually, you chew gum, put on patches, avoid the pub, whatever makes the transition easier. Then one day you get to a stage where the first thing you think of when you wake up isn't a cigarette, and you know you can do it.

Some lifestyle changes may seem so small as to be irrelevant, and on their own they are, but they represent that first nicotine patch – a start. Right now we live in a car-dominated culture with very limited public transport. It's very difficult for most of us to simply forgo cars altogether and a fantasy to believe that, like the cold turkey smoker, we can all just kick our car habit overnight. Try telling a harassed mother of three, lugging her shopping bags and children a mile home from the nearest bus stop through driving rain, that it's OK because she's doing her bit for the planet.

Reliable, affordable and accessible public transport is vital in tackling climate change and reducing traffic congestion. But in the USA, for example, public transport accounts for only 1% of the billions of kilometres travelled each day. In Canada, the UK and Australia the picture is similar, with public transport faltering and car use growing.

Each time a bus or train route is abandoned, it makes it harder for those without a car to get to work, the shops and school. We live busy lives, and it is hard to relinquish the sheer convenience of being able to get in the car, rather than trudging down to the bus stop to stand in the wind-blasted and ill-named shelter for twenty minutes looking at a poster advertising the latest BMW and trying to avoid the gaze of the rather worrying man with a ferret on a lead. Eventually, benighted public transport users give in and get themselves a car, so the bus or train company loses yet more customers and their ticket money, leaving them less cash to run services; so they make further cutbacks. This ever-diminishing circle culminates in sparse networks of deserted (apart from the ferret man) or crammed-full buses and trains, and roads jammed with honking cars.

To break this cycle takes top-down (government) and bottom-up (you and me) action. The government must subsidise public transport, ensuring a good network that gets us where we want when we want; and you and I must use it. George Carbone's decision to take the school bus, rather than demand a lift in his mother's car, slashed his contribution to global warming. The same applies to us all. If you are lucky enough to still have a usable bus, train or even tram route to work then you can cut tonnes off your annual emissions. The exact savings vary depending on the service. But if you can use public transport, do.

Take a standard daily commute into work, say a 30 kilometre round trip. Your shiny saloon is in the drive, *ABBA's Greatest Hits* is teed-up in the CD player and it looks like rain. Driving is tempting, but the roads are awful, parking a nightmare and the train station is just five minutes' walk. By grabbing your umbrella and strolling down to catch the train rather than using the car you're cutting over 7 kg from your greenhouse emissions each day. Keep this up, and over a working year you've stopped a massive tonne and a half of greenhouse gas from getting into the atmosphere, helped keep a good train service running and may even have broken that worrying ABBA habit.

The effects of such changes add up fast. In 2003 London introduced congestion charging to discourage people from driving into the capital and encourage use of public transport. This pushed around 29,000 extra people out of their cars and onto the capital's public transport, mainly the beefed-up bus network. Transport-related greenhouse gas emissions in the charging zone fell by around 20%, the city became a nicer place to live and work and scores of other cities realised that you could actually take on the seemingly omnipotent car and win.

Along with congestion charging there are a host of ways in which the authorities can help, rather than hinder, our efforts to cut greenhouse gas emissions. For their part, the planning offices around the world could make sure that there are footpaths when new buildings go up and that cycle lanes become standard in towns and cities. Instead of architects spending so much time showing how the 10 acre car park of every new gleaming office block could be 'softened' with a few plants they could be made to provide details on how public transport will be used to get there.

As long as trains are expensive and late, and buses infrequent, uncomfortable and inconvenient, we will keep picking up those keys, starting up our self-contained transport bubbles and bursting into another rendition of 'Dancing Queen'. The day when the hard-line environmentalists can be justifiably appalled at any use of cars is around the corner, but at the moment many of us have at least a passable defence in the shocking provision of alternatives.

So, for now at least, you plan to go on using your four-wheeled cocoon. In it you want your chosen music, your perfect temperature and to breathe your own recycled air. OK, but you can have all this without an engine big enough to power a tank and that spews out enough greenhouse gas each year to

fill the office block you're driving to. Increasing the efficiency of ·
the average car from around 20 miles per gallon to a not
unreasonable 40 mpg would cut US emissions by 500 million
tonnes. This is without altering the number of cars, or the comfort of their drivers – assuming they can bear not having to take
up two parking spaces wherever they go and put up with
climbing into their cars without the use of ladders.

John Carbone is facing up to this. His four-wheel drive is, or
rather was, his pride and joy. The car cost nearly a year's salary
and came with all the added extras. But in recent weeks the
pleasure of washing it each Sunday, polishing its chrome-work
and cruising to work and back has begun to diminish as his
worry about climate change has grown. Now, each time he
reaches down to flick on the 'Climate Control' button he shifts
uncomfortably in his seat and turns up the radio. For John, the
car is turning from a badge of status and power to one of ignorance and selfishness. For years he had been the first around the
water cooler to bring up the subject of cars and moan about the
price of gasoline. In the months leading up to buying his SUV he
became an expert on different engine sizes, top speeds and
even colours available, and imagined a thousand times the feeling of sitting high up in the new car, the engine roaring at the
turn of the key and Eric Clapton on the radio. On every drive he
had kept a special eye out for other models, admiring their relative merits. Now these same cars look ever more ridiculous to
him. This morning John was listening to another radio report of
the flooding and damage along the south coast and caught
himself angrily blaming the huge four-wheel drive in front. The
only time he feels smug about driving now is when he sees one
of the ever-growing number of ex-military personnel carriers
belching exhaust fumes around town.

John Carbone used to like going to the gas station. Though
the bill for filling the tank stung a bit, it was always a joy to walk
back to his big car after paying. Now he hates filling up the car

– he gets embarrassed at the shear volume of fuel it swallows. Watching the dials click round takes so long that smaller cars pull up, fill up, pay and leave while he stands there pumping in more fuel.

The erosion of John Carbone's enjoyment in his SUV reached a new low when Henry, spurred on by a classroom discussion, asked his dad why he drove such a big car to work when there was only him in it? John had no real answer. Some months ago he considered joining a local car pool and at least filling some of the acres of spare seat space. Several people in the street have the same route to work, but sharing really didn't appeal much. They might not like Eric Clapton, or they might be late, not pay their fair-share of the fuel bill, or just be irritating. In the end he had abandoned the idea. Now, with his conscience gnawing at him more every day, the time for some real action has come. Either he'll get involved with a car pool and divide the emissions of his car between more people, or the gas-guzzler will have to go. The latter appeals more: it entails more car research and shopping.

Persuading Kate is easier than expected. She had always felt the four-wheel drive was too ugly, too costly to run, and a risk to pedestrians, quite aside from its emissions. When John explains that his priority is fuel efficiency she actually gets quite interested. Together they go online to look for information. They are shocked to discover just how bad their SUV is for the climate. Compared to a standard five-door hatchback it emits twice the amount of greenhouse gas per kilometre. The hatchbacks they look at seem to have all the same comfort features as the SUV and, by getting a dual-fuel version, John Carbone can cut his fuel bill by three-quarters. Bye-bye SUV.

The Monday morning drive to work following delivery of the new car is one of the most enjoyable ranting sessions John Carbone has ever had. All around him are gas-wasting monsters driven by ignorant buffoons, each sitting by themselves in their climate-controlled boxes. He even signs up for the car-share scheme that coffee-time at work, the glowing feeling of superiority making him grin all day. The fuel station is a revelation. Rolling up to the liquefied gas pump, John notes the enquiring looks from the others on the forecourt and saunters up to pay his small fuel bill.

Each year, this move to a smaller-engined car will slash 6 tonnes from John's total greenhouse gas emissions, equivalent to a more than 50% cut in his total transport-related climate burden.

Despite this great potential for change without any big lifestyle compromises, US transport emissions are expected to increase 50% by the year 2020, to represent a third of total emissions in the USA (they already represent a quarter). If you do nothing else to fight climate change, if it all seems too much effort or just too inconvenient, then at least get a

**Figure 5** Jacob Marley and Ebenezer Scrooge discuss engine sizes (many thanks to Paul (Jake) Jacobson).

smaller-engined car. In the next life Dickens' Jacob Marley had money boxes hanging around his neck: how would you like a 4 litre engine?

There are lots of other ways to cut car-related greenhouse emissions. For a start there are a growing number of petrol alternatives – there's big money to be made, oil won't last forever and getting at what is left is proving fraught, to say the least. At my local petrol station there are three standard pumps at each bay, a green one (lead-free petrol), a red one (bad old leaded petrol), and a black one (smelly, sooty diesel). You'd assume that diesel would be the last choice for a climate-aware driver: a litre of diesel produces about half a kilo more greenhouse gas than a litre of petrol (about 2.7 kg compared to 2.3 kg). But modern diesel engines are roughly a third more efficient than petrol engines of equal size and diesel contains about 12% more energy per litre than petrol, so you get almost half as much distance again. Overall then, modern diesel vehicles tend to have between 5 and 10% lower greenhouse gas emissions than their petrol-powered cousins. New particulate filters, low-sulphur fuel and catalytic convertors are really starting to make diesel a viable option for the climate-aware driver.

Back at the petrol station, aside from the air and water pumps, the news stand, and the instant barbecues, you'll probably spot the odd-looking dual-fuel pump. Dual-fuel gas usually comes as CNG (Compressed Natural Gas) or LPG (Liquified Petroleum Gas), with the petrol relegated to a supporting role. It costs much less than regular unleaded petrol – commonly half the price – and produces up to 20% less greenhouse gas per kilometre. Most cars can be converted easily to run on dual fuel. The extra tank takes up about the space of a spare tyre and the cost is recouped in cheaper fuel bills within a few years.

I drive a Smart car – much less engine to lug around in the afterlife. Initially I hankered after one of the new hybrid cars that combine standard petrol power with backup from an electric motor, charged by the brakes. The petrol engine powers the car on the open road, when its efficiency is greatest; the electric motor helps when you're accelerating and takes over completely when you're braking or standing at the traffic lights waiting for green. These cars emit 30–40% less greenhouse gas than similar-sized petrol models. But they remain pricey and on my jobbing scientist's salary there is no way I can afford one. All these can reduce our greenhouse emissions, but all rely to some extent on burning fossil fuels and so will never be entirely climate-neutral.

Electric vehicles have been around for a long time and appear to provide potentially bigger cuts in emissions than hybrid vehicles and the rest. Yet the electricity used to power them is where they can come unstuck climate-wise. If it can be provided by renewable sources, such as wind or hydroelectric, then emissions are indeed vastly smaller than fossil-fuel based alternatives. But most people's electricity is generated using fossil fuels and so by plugging a car into the socket each night they are simply shifting the emissions away from their exhaust pipe and over to the coal-fired power station.

All-electric vehicles also tend to perform somewhat sluggishly. I have no interest in being able to accelerate like a jet fighter, or for my car to break the sound barrier, but when I'm running late and my daughter has tired of drawing snot pictures on the window and opted for all-out screaming, a top speed of 40 mph could get frustrating. Range too is currently rather restricted, being only about 40 miles between recharges in most models. With oil reserves plummeting and fuel prices rising, a switch to electric vehicles is increasingly likely. Their performance will improve and, for around town at least, they should become a very useful option. Still, the origin of the charge in their batteries is key to their success.

Biofuel is another growing, oft mistrusted, option that has the potential to provide climate-friendly driving. Occasionally newspapers run stories like 'Rooster Booster: man in New South Wales converts truck to run on methane from chicken manure', 'Chip Charged: Burnley chip shop owner tops up tank with old oil from pans', and 'Green and Drunk: cross-eyed Texan corn farmer swears home-made moonshine fuels truck and improves driving'.

Biofuels are either crops, like corn, made into alcohol (ethanol), or are byproducts of some other process, like manure methane or chip-shop oil. In theory, the carbon dioxide released when such fuels burn is offset by that taken up by growing more fuel crops, making the fuel effectively carbon-neutral.

In reality, the benefits are not quite so straightforward. Growing biofuels can itself lead to substantial emissions – nitrogen fertilisers for instance can produce large amounts of the powerful greenhouse gas nitrous oxide when soil bacteria use the nitrogen instead of the plants it's intended for.

After accounting for all the production-related emissions of growing, transporting and processing, most biofuel crops end up giving a cut of 20–30% compared to petrol – not climate-neutral, but still very worthwhile. The savings really shoot up when biofuel is made from the byproducts of other processes. Ethanol made by fermenting waste pulp – cellulosic biomass – from paper mills have zero greenhouse emissions.

Forecourt pumps offering biofuel, usually a mix of ethanol (known as E85) or methanol (M85) and petrol, are on the rise. In the USA there are already over two million flexible fuel cars on the roads, able to run on these fuel mixes. In Brazil, a country rich in cane sugar-derived ethanol, sales of alcohol-fuelled cars now top a quarter of a million a year. With more research, in laboratories and people's backyards, biofuels will get better. Fried fish fat may not be the final answer, but alcohol, so long a lethal mix with driving, could see climate-friendly car use take off on a large scale.

Hydrogen has been touted as the solution to car-driven climate change. As hydrogen is used up it produces nothing more harmful than water. Unfortunately, producing hydrogen in the first place tends to burn more fossil fuel than that saved by using it instead of petrol – not exactly the climate change panacea.

In the USA, over a billion dollars is being spent on improving this technology, where it is seen as a way of insuring motoring lifestyles against the uncertainty of oil supplies. The focus of this research is improving hydrogen fuel cells – batteries that sit in your car and convert hydrogen to electricity. The vision is one of US roads filled by these so-called Freedom Cars. The reality is that even with another 15 years of aggressive research and development their climate benefits will be no better than the hybrid cars already available.

Finally, solar power may still have its day, either as a booster to more conventional engines or, where the climate permits, a wholly emissions-free way to power a car. The potential of solar power is clear when you look at something like the World Solar Challenge, where teams from across the globe compete to see whose solar vehicle can cross Australia from Darwin to Adelaide in the shortest time (about four days is the aim). Doing this baking 3,000 km journey in four days powered only by the Sun is certainly impressive, but then Australia is not short on sunshine and the race rather grinds to a halt at night.

Solar energy's role may actually be more indirect. It has great potential to provide all that raw hydrogen needed by the fleets of whirring Freedom Cars and to make this and similar fuel cell technologies a realistic way to cut greenhouse emissions.

It's quite exciting to imagine what might actually make it onto our service station forecourts in the next few years. Will more biofuel ethanol pumps pop up beside the standard red, green and black fossil-fuel ones? Maybe manure-methane pumps will become standard, with a bright yellow chicken logo and a free egg with every cubic metre sold.

Meanwhile, by using dual fuel or, where possible, switching to biofuels, we can make anything from 20% to 100% cuts in our transport greenhouse emissions and encourage the spread and development of these new fuels.

Changing one's driving habits is probably the easiest of climate-friendly actions in theory. By driving habits I don't mean whether you like to wear shades and a baseball cap or have chemical toilet-scented air fresheners dangling from your rear view mirror, but when you use your car and how you then drive it. My bookcase holds several books on individual action, each containing top tips by which to cut your emissions through changing your driving habits. On paper these make absolute sense and every time I read them I nod and think "Great, that's easy – drive smoothly, save fuel and save the planet – no problem". But, such good intentions tend to evaporate when the first car accelerates to within a gnat's tongue of your rear bumper and flashes its lights. It takes real strength of character to cast off driving habits established over decades, but the benefits to the climate, your fuel bills and the safety of yourself and others on the road are undeniable.

The number one tip is to avoid short and unnecessary car journeys in the first place. As with the Carbones' dog, Molly, lots of short car trips can add up to a lot of emissions in a year.

In the UK cars are used for over 60% of journeys of between just 1.5 and 3 kilometres; and for nearly 20% of trips under 1.5 kilometres – a distance most of us could walk in less than 15 minutes. Popping down to the local shops twice a week for that oh-so-crucial extra packet of snacks or vital goat's milk for the dinner recipe can release a third of a tonne of greenhouse gas over the year. While it may be hard for the shopping bag-laden mother to see the attraction of public transport, we are all in real trouble if we can't avoid using our cars by using normal butter rather than popping out to find the last pat of organic hand-made slightly-salted butter in the county.

Out on the open road, speed really is king if you want to cut your greenhouse emissions – assuming for once you aren't too late and can drive pretty much at the speed you want. Instead of racing up to your normal 5 mph over the speed limit (if you usually drive faster then the benefits, both to climate and your life-span, of cutting your speed are even greater), get the car into top gear, put on some classical music and try gliding along at 5 mph under the limit. It feels odd at first, and all the cars whizzing by in the outside lane make you feel like you're going much more slowly. Try this as often as possible over the next week – you will annoy some of the still-speeding drivers, but you can always employ the universally recognised signal of conservative driving by wearing a hat for these trips. For some-one commuting 20 km into work and back 5 times a week the more efficient driving speed will make the tank last about a week longer. In a year of commuting this saving is equivalent to two full tanks of petrol and cuts over a quarter of a tonne off greenhouse gas emissions.

There are a whole range of other fairly common-sense things that help cut emissions. Car air-conditioning can soak up 10% of fuel, so use the vents or windows instead. Keeping tyres well inflated, the car properly serviced and its air filters clean, and not over-filling the tank are all rather dull but worth doing,

together saving up to 50% on fuel use. Avoiding sharp acceler-
ation or braking can also save a lot of fuel and so greenhouse
gas emissions. Those bunny-hopping tail-gaters that infest our
towns and cities are burning their way through an extra 40%
of fuel in their quest to shave two milliseconds off their journey.
Next time that white van screeches up behind you, adjust your
hat, turn up the Bach and pity their ignorance.

The average number of people per car is currently about 1.2
in the USA, adding up to about 10 trillion 'empty seat miles'
each year. Increasing car-sharing even a bit could take many
thousands of cars off the road. Joining the car pool now cuts
John Carbone's car use by two days a week and takes around
half a tonne off his annual greenhouse gas emissions. That's
another 15% off John's original car-based emissions.

Sadly, several valiant efforts by politicians to encourage car
sharing have had rather disappointing results. In Southern
California the introduction of high-occupancy vehicle lanes
(HOVs), where cars using these fast lanes had to have at least
one passenger, pushed up average occupancy from 1.22 to
just 1.25. Government schemes, both the carrot kind, like
giving cars with passengers their own lanes, or the stick kind,
like charging those without passengers, tend to fail because of
cheating by drivers. In the case of the HOV lanes, one woman
conned police for nearly a year by using a dummy passenger.
An undertaker prosecuted for his use of the HOV defended his
actions saying that the body he was carrying counted as a passenger, while a pregnant mother claimed a similar defence, her
unborn child this time being the 'passenger'. The undertaker
lost, but the mother-to-be won her appeal.

To achieve real change each of us needs to see the true incentive behind changing our driving habits – that of climate
change mitigation – before it is too late and floods carry off our
cars, passenger dummies and all. See Table 1 for a quick comparison of the ways to cut emissions from car use.

**Table 1** At-a-glance ways to cut greenhouse gas emissions from cars (savings in comparison to a 4 litre petrol-driven car).

| | Smaller engine | Dual-fuel car | Hybrid car | Biofuel car | Driving habits |
|---|---|---|---|---|---|
| Greenhouse gas savings | Up to 75% | 20–30% | 20–40% | Up to 100% | Up to 50% |

What about not travelling in the first place? It's something most of us have hankered after at one time or another. The idea of working from home seems an absolute winner when you're running late for work and a day in the stuffy office beckons, interspersed with long meetings about how to increase productivity, or when the traffic jam apparently starts at your front gate and that extra glass of Rioja from the night before is giving you supersensitive hearing and a tongue like a pub carpet. There are very few jobs these days which don't comprise a fair amount of paperwork and email. Some could probably spend only one day a fortnight going through administrative work at home, while others could swap full-time desk-jockey jobs for a decent computer and home Internet connection – as long as they have the willpower to resist reruns of *Cagney and Lacey*.

The climate benefits of home working are potentially great. The trend in recent decades has been for more and more of those living in rural areas to commute into the town or city for work. It's now common for office workers to make a 300 km round trip each day, so allowing them to live in a large house with a garden they never see in daylight. In the USA the average commute has gone up by a third since 1987.

A day without the office run can clearly make substantial reductions in our greenhouse gas emissions. Yet there are real dangers of pollution swapping here. Let's say you convince your boss that working 600 km away in an Internet-ready log cabin will increase your productivity and be a veritable gold-mine for blue-skies thinking. You make the big move to the sticks and, apart from the problem with your electricity supply going off whenever the wind gets above a strong breeze, all works well. No more of the daily 160 km drive/crawl to work and back. So far, so good. However, you still need to go into the office occasionally for special meetings – mainly because the best thing about working from a desk in a log cabin, with a view of a limpid lake and forested mountain, is being able to tell your colleagues how great it is.

So, you keep on a flat in the city for those trips back to the office, which average about one a week. The flight down and back clocks up just over 1300 km, almost 500 km more than you used to cover each week driving to work and back, and using a more climate-warming mode of transport to boot. The city crash-pad itself means an extra set of appliances and fur-nishings, all of which use up yet more energy in their manufac-ture. Through your 'climate-friendly' home-working, therefore, your related greenhouse gas emissions leap from 112 kg per week to about 180 kg.

Other pitfalls lie in the extra energy we use at home. Instead of the daytime being a period of low home energy use, we are now in the home, requiring air conditioning, illicitly watching TV and, usually at about 2 p.m. craving some human interac-tion and driving to the local garage for a newspaper and half a gallon of petrol. With two offices, one at work and one at home, we have all that energy used to make two desks and two PCs, two printers and two pen holders. At the same time, the energy for heating, cooling and lighting your office at work is still burning away, whether you are there to appreciate it or not. Home-working can potentially end up producing more greenhouse gas than sticking to the grind of the office run. The solution then, is to use the technology available in a way that makes a tangible difference to your climate impact: virtual conferencing for example, instead of swapping five short commutes in the car for one big one in a jet plane. Which neatly brings us to flying.

Flying these days plays a big part in nearly everyone's greenhouse gas budget. Air travel is already a huge climate problem and it's growing fast as flights get cheaper and more frequent and go to more destinations. A return flight from London to Sydney spews as much greenhouse gas into the atmosphere for every passenger as that given out by a good-sized car over an entire year (over 4 tonnes). The United Nations predicts that, by 2050, annual aircraft emissions will have reached well over a billion tonnes of greenhouse gas.

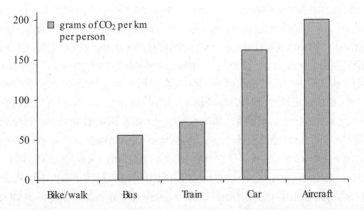

**Figure 6** Average carbon dioxide emissions for various modes of transport.

The climate-warming effect of air travel is magnified even further by the fact that most of the emissions occur high in the sky, at the very place where they can do most harm. As well as pouring out tonnes of carbon dioxide planes produce large amounts of so-called NOx gases (oxides of nitrogen). Up there in the troposphere, these NOx gases lead to the formation of yet another powerful greenhouse gas, ozone, effectively doubling the climate warming effect of our flights. Had we deliberately set out to cook our planet we couldn't have done much better.

Given its big role in global emissions you'd expect air travel to be feeling the pinch of efforts to tackle climate change. Not a bit of it. Because planes trickily fly backwards and forwards across international boundaries their emissions aren't included in national budgets under the Kyoto protocol. At the same time, aviation fuel goes untaxed and the industry benefits from large government subsidies. So we get a burgeoning budget airline industry, with seat prices less than the taxi fare to the airport and the true environmental costs of jet travel hidden away under the dirty aisle carpets.

Our love of air travel is going to turn into a rocky affair as global warming intensifies. Baking summer temperatures will attack runways, just as they attack our roads; and more frequent and intense storms will ground increasing numbers of planes. When it's not too windy and the runway is OK, planes may still struggle to get airborne with soaring summertime temperatures meaning less lift. Weather is already the cause of 70% of flight delays in the USA, causing a quarter of all air accidents and, through flooding, storm and hail damage, closing whole airports at a stroke. Just one diverted flight, due to a storm say, can delay 50 other flights and clock up $150,000 in costs. Cancelling a flight costs around $40,000 a time. Such diversions and cancellations already cost over $250 million dollars each year.

Where we actually want to fly to will also change. Many traditional summer sun destinations are facing failing water supplies, scorching summer temperatures and a host of disease outbreaks. Winter resorts in some countries are suffering from a decided lack of winter. In Scotland the ski industry is tottering on its last tartan pole, with the number of ski days having dropped by a quarter in the past 20 years.

With huge, climate change-fuelled increases in emigration, illegal immigration could soar. The political instability expected to arise from global warming may rule out some currently very popular destinations altogether, while increasing safety fears will lead to longer security checks.

All of which makes jetting off for that traditional getaway look less appealing. The benefits can be big to the climate of foregoing the dubious pleasures of sticky-carpeted departure lounges, intimate strip searches, and sitting on an overcrowded plane next to a time-share salesman with questionable personal hygiene. For an average long-haul flight, every kilometre you fly clocks up about 150 g of greenhouse gas. A flight from New York to London emits three-quarters of a tonne of greenhouse gas into the atmosphere for every person on board. Short-haul flights belch even more per passenger per kilometre because of the extra fuel used to haul those tonnes of plane, sweaty salesmen and limp egg sandwich into the air.

Rail or coach travel can radically cut emissions on journeys under 800 km. An average short-haul return flight from Amsterdam to Munich emits over 100 kg of greenhouse gas for each passenger; the same journey by train or coach results in emissions of just 30 kg.

As holiday travel makes up over 60% of air travel, rediscovering the delights of vacations in your home country can pay big dividends. Let's return to the Carbones.

It's going to be an odd summer. Seemingly forever now the family has flown *en masse* to Mexico for two weeks of blissful sun and relaxation. With Kate Carbone working for a travel agent they have always got fantastic deals on their flights and stayed in a wonderfully rustic farmhouse about a kilometre from the sea. Now though, for the first time in six years, the Carbones are looking elsewhere. Over the past couple of years the temperature has been unbearable. Even at night it was so warm that just sleeping was a challenge. Last year they had to go without showers for most of the holiday as water supplies hit an all-time low – the final straw for John and Kate.

Kate noticed from the holidays she had been selling over the past few years that Mexico was becoming much less popular during the summer. There were complaints and the temperature guidelines in the tour brochures had been amended upwards three times in as many years to cover the record-breaking summer heat. At first the company policy had been to say that the hot weather had been 'exceptional', but it was becoming obvious that ragingly hot summers were now the norm. So, no Mexican holiday this year. Instead, the family are consulted on an alternative destination. This is a great excuse for lots of arguing, re-reading of travel brochures and the making of unreasonable demands. Once the idea of trips to Antarctica (Henry), Afghanistan (George) or China (John) are all dismissed on the basis of price/danger/distance the family agree that what they all would really like to do is to go somewhere cool, with good food, swimming, and no flying. After a few phone calls to the office Kate confirms that their new holiday is booked. They're going down south to Tickfaw, Louisiana, to a lakeside cabin just north of New Orleans, for a winning mix of swimming, walking and, if John has anything to do with it, jazz.

When holiday time finally arrives, the Carbones are feeling ready for a break. The weather has been dry and hot and everywhere seems to be covered in a fine layer of dust. There is concern on the news that it could turn into a real 'dust-dreaming of slipping into the cool waters of Lake Pont-chartrain. The packing is the usual frenzied affair, with the added complication of a new holiday destination and so a barrage of questions about what might and might not be needed. After Kate has drawn the line at taking a TV 'just in case' and made clear to John that, no, there isn't room for him to take his entire Miles Davis collection to get himself in the mood for New Orleans, they are ready to go. After three false starts (for, respectively, a forgotten pair of sunglasses, another toilet stop for Henry, and retrieval of an errant Labrador), the Carbones are off.

This switch of holiday, from Mexico to Louisiana, swaps the two tonnes of greenhouse gas produced from the family's return flights to Cancun for less than a third of a tonne – Kate Carbone's barn-like people carrier is for once full of people.

In the USA there are 405 million long-distance (more than 80 km) business trips made each year, accounting for 16% of all long-distance travel in America. For business meetings less than 400 km away most people opt to drive, but as soon as the travelling distance gets up past the 800 km mark air travel is the usual choice.

For most international journeys air travel remains the only practical option, so what then? Several schemes have sprung up to massage our emissions guilt. These generally involve paying for trees to be planted or making contributions towards new renewable energy schemes to offset the emissions from your flight. During their 2003 tour, the Rolling Stones took their responsibility for greenhouse gas emissions to a new level. They paid for enough trees to be planted to offset the emissions of each one of the estimated 160,000 fans attending their UK gigs. At 13 kg of greenhouse gas per fan this meant a lot of trees – 2,800 to be exact. Great, but imagine the number of trees it would take to offset every tour these long-lived rock legends have ever made. Between 1997 and 1999 alone, over 5 million people went to see the Stones at 147 different gigs across Europe, That's another 100,000 trees.

It's unrealistic to think that all our air travel emissions can simply be offset by planting trees. The primary worth of such schemes is to get people thinking about their climate impact, rather than to solve it. Some schemes – 'ClimateCare' for example – now allow you to offset your emissions not with trees but through funding renewable energy schemes in the developing world. The climate benefits of doing this may be more transparent, but there's no easy way around this. To minimise your contribution to global warming fly less, or not at all.

As a scientist, one of the 'perks' of the job is going to international conferences. These are usually dominated by people with a penchant for wearing socks with sandals and for jokes about the time in '78 when Barnaby Lorimer-Smyth put up a slide of an anterior section of *Biterson vulgaris* upside down and didn't notice. They are part of every academic's working year. The premise is that they allow us to present our latest research and spark off new ideas in an atmosphere of convivial academic review. The reality is that the research presented is usually several years old and has already been published, and that most people go to network (young, dynamic and, most of all, desperate-for-funding researchers), or to meet up with old friends (socks and sandals). Occasionally, these conferences do work well and can get some useful discussions going. However, there is a tendency for them to be seen as jollies – free holidays paid for by the taxpayer to make up for a researcher's poor pay and working conditions. I'm sure it applies to business too. Barnaby Lorimer-Smyth may instead be Harris Baines, socks and sandals may be replaced by a novelty Simpsons tie, and the upside-down slide joke may instead be about Baines eating the boss's bread roll, but it all boils down to an awful lot of air travel.

Cutting greenhouse emissions due to conferences and meetings can be as simple as having them in the right place. For a meeting of 10,000 scientists in San Francisco (many of them climate change researchers) a couple of years ago it was estimated that associated emissions for the meeting topped 12,000 tonnes, with the average delegate travelling about 8,000 kilometres. Had the conference instead been held in the more central location of Denver, Colorado, the emissions would have been cut by 900 tonnes.

As well as getting the place right, you can slash emissions by attending meetings virtually. By avoiding just two medium-distance flights of, say, 1,600 km each way, you'll cut nearly a tonne of your annual greenhouse gas budget.

Several international conferences have already been run virtually. A recent genetics conference in the USA cut greenhouse gas emissions by about 900 tonnes through delegates swapping red-eye flights, soulless hotel rooms and complimentary soaps for their own office and the ability to go home for dinner each evening. For small island states there is now the 'Virtual World Forum on Small Island Developing States', an obvious use for this technology given all the water separating the interested parties. (The theme for Session 1 of the next meeting? Climate Change.)

The standard format of these virtual meetings is for the delegates from each place to get together in their own conferencing room and then, using a large screen, cameras, microphones and the power of the Internet, talk to groups in other cities, countries or continents.

On the large screen is the main speaker doing his or her thing, while windowed at the side are the other groups waiting their turn to speak. This high-tech conferencing allows you to download whole presentations – all the facts and figures – to peruse at your leisure. It also means that if anyone asks a particularly difficult question you can frown, point at your ears, and mutter something about Microsoft.

Real conferences will always have a place, but, given the many millions of air kilometres clocked up by delegates each year, even limited use of virtual conferencing has the potential to reduce greenhouse gas emissions by many thousands of tonnes.

Transport, then, plays a leading role in our individual contribution to global warming. But before you doze off to dreams of being run over by an SUV driven by a sandal-wearing chicken it's time to turn off the car-choked road and into the drive. It's time we took a look at the impact of our homes and, most worryingly, how climate change is planning to visit.

# 3

## home start

If you live close to a river, near the coast, or in a low-lying area, you may want to look away now. Each year, floods affect more than half a billion people and claim around 25,000 lives. Currently the United Nations designates about 1 billion people 'at risk' from severe flooding worldwide. Predictions are for this number to double during the 21st century as global warming intensifies storms and torrential rains. What's in store are not Hollywood-friendly new types of weather, but more of the existing devastating ones.

To get a good idea of how big the threats that our homes face are we only need look at house insurance. Insurers are essentially gamblers – well dressed, polite gamblers. Their livelihoods depend on correctly estimating the risk, say, of your house falling into a mineshaft or your chinchilla needing dental surgery. To refine their risk assessments they use the best information they can find, from detailed mining maps and surveys to in-depth studies of chinchilla eating habits and longevity.

So how have these cautious folk responded to climate change predictions? By offering soaring house insurance premiums to many and, to those in flood-risk areas, no insurance at all. Companies around the world are hiring climate experts, frantically drawing up new 'At Risk' tables, and upping their premiums. The most pessimistic are moving their head offices away from swanky docklands areas to locations well above sea level.

In the USA, 10 million homes are already at risk of flooding and the flood damage bill tops $7 billion a year. With sea levels set to rise somewhere between half a metre and a metre by the end of the century, 36,000 square kilometres of the USA – almost twice the area of New Jersey – may be lost. According to the US Environmental Protection Agency such flooding would cost between $270 and 450 billion. Insurance claims are likely to double or triple, and thousands of families could be displaced.

In Eastern Canada sea level rise could be even more devastating because the land itself has been steadily subsiding since the last ice age (about 2 cm a decade in some areas). In Australia the potential for displacement of communities is huge: 80% of the population live within just 50 km of the coast. In the UK, more than 3.5 million homes could flood this century – three times the number currently under threat. Globally, coastal flooding due to sea level rise will be threatening an extra 23 million people by 2050.

When the flood waters finally subside and that special post-flood smell – from a dilute mix of petrol and sewage – begins to disperse, at least it will be good drying weather. The predictions of temperature rise this century are big. Here in Scotland I've got my grapevine planted in anticipation of a Chateau Reay Rioja. Imagine a hot summer now, a real belter, say the hottest in ten years. In the Europe of 2080 nearly every summer will be just like that. Add to this a 30% drop in rainfall and the fact that summers are getting warmer and drier in the north, and it's bye-bye to the great wines of Bordeaux and hello to the cheeky reds of Brittany, Bognor or even Bute.

Summertime in New York by 2050 will be more like that currently experienced in Atlanta. In Atlanta, summers will be like those today in Houston. And in already-hot Houston? Think Panama (temperatures in the high 30s and close to 100% humidity). Heat stress already kills around 400 people in the USA each year. Europe had a taste of what is in store when, in 2003, over 20,000 people died as a result of an intense heatwave.

A table in the weighty volume *Climate Change 2001: Impacts, Adaptation and Vulnerability* – produced by the Intergovernmental Panel on Climate Change – sets out what climate extremes are coming our way. Below the heatwave section ('increased incidence of death and serious illness in older age groups and urban poor'), are similarly stark predictions for 'intense precipitation events' (heavy rainstorms), 'increases in peak wind and storm intensities', and 'intensified droughts and floods'. These worsening extremes will mean more damage to buildings, infectious disease epidemics, property losses and greater risk to human life.

Climate change will also have some less obvious impacts on homes. Already, extreme summertime temperatures and droughts have led to a big increase in subsidence as soil shrinks and trees suck the last drops of water from the soil. In Alaska thawing perma-frost has seen houses literally disappearing into the ground.

All in all, the outlook for our homes is pretty worrying. If you live 2 m or less above sea level, as millions around the world do, then buying that new carpet for the living room might not be such a good idea. If you're on a hill you might want to secure those loose tiles before the next storm, and if you're nestled in a city high-rise make sure you've got a good stock of bottled water and that the air-conditioning is regularly ser-viced. And order a Panama hat.

Alternatively we could work to keep the greenhouse gas con-centrations in our atmosphere below those we're currently speeding towards. In 2004 an otherwise grim report on the threat of flooding in the UK this century pointed out that by reining back global greenhouse emissions by 25% the costs of damage due to flooding could be cut by a quarter (from £21 billion to £15 billion a year in the 2080s).

Homes are massive energy users and so tend to be massive emitters of greenhouse gas. Happily, home is also where some of the most straightforward changes can be made. Take some-thing as simple as swapping an old-fashioned tungsten light

**Figure 7** Greenhouse emissions of an average home in the USA (% of 11 tonnes of greenhouse gas per year).

bulb for a low-energy one. Easy to buy, no extra effort to put in, and a money saver to boot. Just one bulb can stop up to 100 kg of greenhouse gas getting into the atmosphere each year. Indeed, almost all the climate-friendly strategies for the home – those listed on government websites, in books, even on the back of your electricity bill – reduce energy wastage and so save money as well as the environment. Making our homes more climate-friendly really can hit that 25% flood-stopping target, and go beyond it, even to the scientists' recommended 60%.

It's the control of our home climate that most threatens the global one. Like some loyal dog with a pair of chewed socks, the heating or air-conditioning system welcomes us with exactly the temperature we asked of it. We've come a long way from the spitting fires in damp caves that first constituted home heating. Gone are the winter nights which would freeze slippers to the carpet, or the summer days when even house-flies were too hot to bother buzzing. Now we can slop around our houses in Bermuda shorts and a Che Guevara t-shirt as the snow piles up against the windows. After some vigorous air guitar to Dire Straits, we can complain that it is too hot, pad barefoot across the shagpile and open the window.

Regarding transport I said that some environmentalists' criticism of car driving was a bit much, given the alternatives available. But with home heating and cooling they can literally pull on their woolly jumpers and get on their high, organically fed horses. I can hear my mother's words ringing in my head as I write: "If you're cold, put a jumper on, David. Nana knitted you that nice one for Christmas and you've not worn it once". Simply putting on more clothes when it's cold, or taking more off when it's hot, can slash household energy use, and so greenhouse emissions. Heating the average single family home in the USA emits about 4 tonnes of greenhouse gas each year; cooling it emits a further tonne. Here in Scotland, heating-related emissions also tend to be big, although air-conditioning isn't widely used – yet. For an average developed-world household, knocking the heating thermostat down just 1 °C, or the air-conditioning up by 1 °C, will cut a third of a tonne off annual emissions.

It takes a real shift of mindset to go from blithely cranking up the air-conditioning in our homes as the sun beats down outside, to turning it down in order to take some of the heat out of the summers to come. That whirring air-conditioning system is like a climate change loan shark: it gives you a cool house today but means a hotter world tomorrow, with interest.

Demand for housing is predicted to increase across the developed world, as more and more people aspire to home ownership, single living and bigger houses. Across Europe the demand for new houses will stay at well over 2 million a year for the next 20 years. In Japan, the number of single-resident households is expected to overtake the number of homes with two or more occupants by 2007, rising by a third in the next 25 years. Already, in Vienna almost half of households are one person only. Over the last 30 years the average number of people in Canadian and US households has dropped from 3.2

to 2.6 – like every two houses in the 70s sprouting into three houses today. At the same time the average house size in the USA has increased from 1,500 square feet (140 m$^2$) to more than 2,200 square feet (205 m$^2$).

Building design has become more energy-aware, but the trend is still one of increasing energy use in, and so greenhouse emissions from, housing. Over the next 20 years the combined energy burn in US homes is set to increase by another 20%. A person living alone gets through twice the amount of energy as someone in a three-person household, and nearly five times more than someone shacked up with five others. With more than one person in a house you share heating, lighting, and even that kettle of water for the coffee. Live alone and, though you'll always have the final say on what to watch on TV, you'll get through a lot more energy as an individual. The trend towards bigger houses has the same effect – bigger houses mean more materials, more heating and cooling and so more emissions.

In front of me is a pile of glossy government-sponsored brochures from the USA, the UK and Australia promoting energy-efficient strategies in the home. They each contain pictures of people drawing curtains, putting in loft insulation and closing double-glazed windows, all with rather off-putting self-satisfied grins playing on their faces. Grins aside, the energy savings, and so benefits to the climate, are impossible to ignore. Without exception, the brochures extol the virtues of improved insulation. This can take the form of thicker padding in the roof space, installation of double glazing, or simple draught-proofing of existing doors and windows. Getting cavity wall insulation, improving pipe and boiler cladding, and adding internal doors to provide enclosed hallways, can also prevent heat loss and energy wastage. The numbers are impressive: by better insulating your home you can almost halve the amount of energy used to heat or cool it – a cut of more than 2 tonnes of greenhouse gas emission a year for an average house.

As with transport, governments have recognised household energy use as a key battleground in the fight against global warming. As climate change intensifies we can all expect to see a lot more of those self-satisfied grins in government booklets and on our TV screens. The reach of governments in cutting household energy use can go way beyond posting booklets through our letter boxes and broadcasting 'Is your home behaving badly?' adverts. In some countries, Australia for instance, you may be able to claim back part or all of the expense of better insulating your home. Government-funded housing developments, with energy-efficient building designs, are also becoming more common. The Guguletu Eco-Homes project in South Africa is a good example of this, involving the construction of 6,000 energy-efficient homes over the next 50 years. By reducing energy use in space heating, primarily through solar heating, this project is set to cut emissions by a massive 40–50,000 tonnes of greenhouse gas over its lifetime.

Few, if any of us, bought our current home with climate change in mind. If we had, then all those flood-plain developments would be in serious financial trouble. When we do next choose a house, there are some key climate-related questions worth asking:

- Is the new house closer to work, the station and/or the cycle path?

- Is the house such a rambling, draughty, energy-guzzler that just keeping the thing warm in winter will eat up more power than your current house uses in a year?

- Is there a garden, no matter how small, to grow you own food in?

- Can you get renewable energy in the area?

And so back to the Carbones to see how housing decisions can radically affect our contribution to global warming. There's big news for the whole family and some major decisions to be made which could drastically affect all their climate impacts.

The Carbone family is going to get bigger. John and Kate Carbone have kept the news to themselves for the first few months just to play it safe, but now, 6 months in, Kate is showing clear signs of a bump and they've had to break the happy news to Henry and George. After initial apathy from both, George posed the tricky question of where this new addition was going to sleep. The Carbone house, seemingly so big when they first bought it, has since filled up with the detritus of modern life, not to mention a Labrador and two sons. Having assured both Henry and George that "No, they wouldn't be made to share bedrooms with the new baby", John and Kate have to admit that they will need more room. They aren't quite decided on whether to build an extension or start looking for another house. This decision is one of the biggest they will ever make climate-wise. The extension has a great advantage in that the Carbones could ensure that building design and materials were as energy-efficient as possible, while a new house has the potential to be much more, or less, energy-efficient throughout, depending on its design.

They're in a good position for a move as the housing market is fast-moving and there are several new building developments going up on the outskirts of town. With Grandma Carbone having made a present to them of several thousand dollars, they could stretch to quite a big place, or to a substantial extension. The building option, though, is limited to going upwards into the current roof-space, as anything going outwards would shrink the garden, something that the whole family, Kate and Molly in particular, would find unacceptable. After a long chat the Carbones decide that they'll have a look at a few places while the plans for the extension are drawn up and then decide for certain.

That same weekend the whole Carbone family set out to view the show houses on the new estate. It's certainly a very grand development. At regular intervals on the approach road there are huge billboards extolling the virtues of Hawthorn Hamlet: 'An exclusive development of 3-, 4- and 5-bedroom executive properties set in an unspoilt, secure setting'. Long before they get to the estate they can see its row of shining white flagpoles, each carrying the fluttering emblem of the development company. Drawing closer, the huge new entrance road comes into view bordered by a high brick wall and curving round to where two imposing black gates stand open to reveal the estate within. Once parked, the Carbones pick up the various brochures from the estate office and set off in the general direction of the nearest show house – a four-bedroomed example of the 'Manse' category, 'ideal for the growing family' according to the blurb. The house is certainly immaculate, with the dining table set for a sophisticated dinner, towels neatly folded on the bath rail and flowers on the reproduction mantlepiece. An hour later, the Carbones have had enough of looking at show homes to last them a lifetime. The sameness of all the houses, not to mention the enclave-like setting, doesn't appeal. For a comparable price they can get an older house with the same number of bedrooms, but with substantially more garden and at least some feeling of community.

So the search begins for an existing home in their area, with at least four bedrooms and a good-sized garden as must-haves. After a few false starts the Carbones find a property that seems to fit the bill, only a few streets from their own house. The house is quite old, 54 years old to be exact, and is 'in need of modernisation' according to the seller's details. However, it does have four good-sized bedrooms and a really big back garden which, though overgrown, sets Kate Carbone's eyes alight with its potential and gets the wholehearted approval of George, Henry and Molly. It's only when the survey comes back that the true import of 'in need of modernisation' hits home. The cost of this modernisation is likely to be as much as that of the house itself, and would make living there uncomfortable for a long time. With a new baby to think of, not to mention the bank manager, the Carbones finally plump for an extension.

Climate-wise, the flagpole-heavy new development houses are much more energy-efficient than the 'in need of development' old house. A new house will use about a third less energy for heating than an equivalent house built in the 1950s, mainly due to better insulation. But there's a catch to these hermetically sealed executive retreats: embodied energy. This is the energy that has gone into each brick, tile and faux Georgian fireplace. Indeed, every manufactured thing in our homes, everything that has taken energy to produce and transport, carries with it an invisible climate price tag. The PC I'm writing on now has one. It's using energy to power the monitor, to spin the discs and fans, power the processor, and to play *Californication*, but even before it arrived at my house it had used a great deal of energy. Even before I had torn open its box, unravelled its endless cables and sworn roundly at the author of the installation manual, the manufacture of the PC and its various components had used up the equivalent of 240 kg of fossil fuels.

The same goes for the bricks used to build a new house, the slates, the concrete and even the Welcome Home mat – all carry an embodied energy tag. Take just one brick in your wall: to get that brick where it is today required energy to mine the clay, transport it to the brick factory, cut it to shape, fire it in the kilns, ship it to the building site and then lay it in your wall. For a whole house, therefore, the embodied energy can be huge. On average, a brand new house has already used the same amount of energy as will be used by its owners over the next decade of home-living. As such, it has been responsible for around 70 tonnes of greenhouse gas, even before the occupants make their first coffee.

The case, then, for new houses being more climate-friendly than old ones is not so clear cut. Yes, old houses may be draughtier and waste more energy on heating, but as a house gets older its embodied burden on the climate is stretched thinner, and the energy used by those living in the house comes to the fore. Of the three options for the Carbones – old house, new house or extension – the of an extension wins hands down climate-wise.

As the extension is effectively a new build they are able to make it well insulated and energy-efficient, while keeping the amounts of energy-rich materials to a minimum. Aluminium and steel carry big tags due to the large amounts of energy used in their mining and processing. Timber, on the other hand, tends to be a far less energy-intensive building material. By choosing wood construction the embodied emissions of a house can be cut by 80% compared with those of a steel-framed one, and by more than 85% compared to those for a concrete dwelling. Where reclaimed building materials are used the embodied energies can be reduced still further.

The substitution of timber, or straw bales if you're feeling adventurous, for materials like concrete and steel can therefore make great savings in a building's contribution to global warming. Forests already have a big role to play in sucking up and trapping carbon dioxide, and by making the best use of the wood that comes out of them we can deliver a double blow to the enhanced greenhouse effect.

With the luxury of designing a house comes a wide range of climate-aware options. Long before the building starts, there's something called 'passive design' to consider. This is where the orientation of the house, specific roof pitches, window placements and aspects, can all be used to make the most of solar heating or to minimise the need for space cooling. Simple things, like putting the main living areas on the side of the house that gets the most sun, can mean substantial savings in the energy used for heating and lighting. Then there's the opportunity to use high-specification insulation throughout and to fit doors and windows that minimise draughts and heat loss.

There are also some big energy pitfalls to skirt around with any new build. Most of us, given the chance to have a house built for us, will want something big. When we're given the chance of, say, a bespoke kitchen, it suddenly takes on the guise of John Carbone's SUV – a showcase of our success, all gleaming chrome and granite worktops. Plans end up featuring a kitchen-diner with an 'island' the size of a billiard table, enough storage to house the food for a polar expedition, and a table that can comfortably accommodate three Last Suppers. Big kitchens, living rooms and bedrooms mean big houses. This means a lot more concrete, bricks, steel, and embodied energy. Bigger houses also take more lighting, heating and cooling. A climate-aware new build will therefore combine energy-efficient design and low embodied-energy construction to make a house that doesn't share its dimensions with an aircraft hangar.

The house we live in plays a big role in our climate impact throughout our lives. There's a chance to radically change this for better or for worse when the kids have finally left home, you've drunk your last office coffee and collected your carriage clock. It is at this stage that so many of us up sticks to move to the coast/closer to the grandchildren/further away from the kids. Like Grandma Carbone.

She's now moved into the retirement community apartment, which has a suite of rooms, including a small kitchen. As well as being close to the family it also has wonderful lawned gardens all around. Her decision to sell the old house and move into the apartment pays big climate dividends. The apartment makes great energy savings by being part of a larger building, her neighbours act like layers of the very best blue-rinse insulation. Just keeping the old house warm in winter and cool in summer used to get through almost four times the energy it now takes to keep her apartment the right temperature. Overall, her house move has meant a cut in her home energy use and related emissions by a whopping two-thirds.

Appliances in the average home are responsible for over 4 tonnes of greenhouse gas a year and threaten to overtake heating and cooling as the biggest source of home energy use. Simple message then: always buy the model with the highest efficiency rating. This isn't the whole story though. Rushing out this weekend to get a shiny new refrigerator to replace a slightly less energy-efficient one ignores that old enemy embodied energy.

Tonnes of plastic and metal go into making our appliances. Before switching a three-year-old dust-entombed fridge for a brand new, cobweb-free one, it's usually worth giving the thing a dust-off (just keeping the coils and door seals clean can cut 200 kg off its greenhouse emissions each year) and getting a few more years of use out of it. Sure, if we're fitting out a kitchen with the necessary appliances for the first time, then opting for the most energy-efficient version is a must climate-wise. But most of us already have a kitchen complete with glossy-fronted oven, refrigerator and washing machine. In this case, the longer your refrigerator or washing machine keeps going, the more it is effectively running down its embodied energy, eking it over more and more years. As a rule of thumb, if it's less than five years old and still working fine: keep it. With new appliances, as with designing that new house, the trap of 'bigger is better' is waiting for us again.

Kate Carbone is excited. The kitchen table is covered in glossy brochures and magazines filled with pictures of stunning kitchens invitingly lit by spring sunshine streaming through leaded windows. Other, rather less evocative pictures, show blinding white refrigerators and washing machines, along with sheet after sheet of specifications on why this model happens to be the biggest, fastest or whitest. The Carbones are having a kitchen overhaul with the cash saved from extending rather than moving. Their current kitchen hasn't changed much since they first moved in, though over the years various new appliances have come and gone, including their first washing machine, which took exception to a full load of nappies, threw itself across the kitchen floor and caught fire. Now, a combination of the Carbone dishwasher making the dishes marginally dirtier than before they were put in, Christmas coming up, and so many TV makeovers of kitchens, has galvanised them into action. For his part John Carbone is interested in how big an oven can be bought and how many hobs they will have, though in the finer points of the new kitchen design he is less enthusiastic.

The Carbones pay a visit to the kitchen design desk, set amongst a maze of show kitchens at the local mall. Within minutes, George and Henry are foot-stampingly bored, finding it difficult to get excited about brushed steel extractor hoods and Victorian filigree cupboard handles. After ten minutes of moaning they are packed off to the nearby Gamezone with strict instructions not to buy anything and to come back within half an hour. Kids despatched, the Carbones sit down with the fast-talking sales assistant who, after getting them to answer a series of questions, produces a set of plans and 'artists' impressions' of what their glorious new kitchen would look like. The picture even has a couple, just like the Carbones, apparently sipping wine as they admire the beauty of the work surfaces. The Carbone sons, though, seem to be absent.

Having talked at length about 'the magic kitchen triangle' and the best size of sink, they get on to the choice of appliances. The options on offer are dazzling: hobs with eight rings, ovens big enough for half a horse, let alone the Thanksgiving turkey, and computer-linked refrigerators able to keep track of its contents and let you know when a re-stock is required. The cost is equally impressive, with replacement of all the Carbones' appliances adding up to about three times the price of the kitchen makeover. In the end they head home promising to phone the salesperson at the first opportunity once they've had a chance to think about things. After prising George and Henry off the games console in the shop next door, the jaded family head back home loaded with yet more brochures, plans and specifications.

It is only when John and Kate finally slump down at the kitchen table with a steaming cup of strong coffee and stare once again at the pile of brochures that they start to voice their worries about the mass dumping of their not-so-old kitchen appliances. OK, the dishwasher may be misbehaving, but John is pretty sure that with a clean of the rotors it would be as good as new. As for the other appliances, they may not be as big or gleaming as the dozens they have looked at that morning, but they do the job. It may be fun to have a talking refrigerator – well, for the first five minutes anyway – but their current one is only three years old and is in perfect working order. The fleeting image of dumped refrigerators in hedgerows, a sight they are both sick of seeing when walking Molly in the local parkland, adds further weight to their feeling that such revolving door appliance buying is a bad idea. A giant oven and a hob the size of a table tennis table would certainly be good for those family feasts, but they've always managed in the past with their standard-sized oven and its four rings. Kate then confesses that she was only ever really interested in getting the rather beaten-up looking cupboard fronts and worktops replaced and that it seemed almost criminal to throw out what were perfectly good kitchen appliances to make room for another cutting-edge set which would remain at the cutting edge for all of a week.

That afternoon, with the help of a kebab skewer, John sorts out the dishwasher problem and, after a successful first run, the Carbones decide for definite that they'll keep all their current appliances and just revamp the doors and work surfaces. As John goes off to phone the shopping mall and break the bad news to the commission-hungry sales assistant, he can hear Kate explaining to a rather disappointed Henry why they really don't need a refrigerator that tells them when they need to buy more juice.

Given the Carbones' existing appliances aren't all that old and already have quite good energy ratings, the large new ones they were planning to buy actually come out as greater energy users than their older cousins. The big fridge, though at the cutting edge of technology, will produce three and a half tonnes of greenhouse gas over its lifetime, compared to just over two tonnes from the smaller, less talkative, Carbone fridge. This is in addition to the embodied energy penalty carried by the new appliances.

At some time, things do have to be replaced. Just one too many slices of jammy toast will get posted into the video recorder, the washing machine will rebel against having to spin-rinse enough beach towels to make a Bedouin tent, and the fridge will take umbrage at never being cleaned and start running at $-20\,°C$. This is where those energy efficiency ratings come into their own. Big energy-using appliances in our homes include boilers, refrigerators, washing machines and, for more and more of us, air-conditioning. With most of these, simply not having one is not really an option. Instead we are faced with the choice of model, make and size, all of which can have a substantial effect on the contribution our households make to global warming.

Energy advice labels appear on most new appliances. The benefits of going for the more efficient models can be big. The labels vary from country to country with a star rating (the more stars the better) in the USA and Australia, and a letter rating in the EU. For letter ratings, A is the most efficient, dropping to G (for godawful). All allow you to compare one model with another and so make an informed purchase. If you're the proud possessor of an A-rated washing machine you'll be cutting up to a third of a tonne off your annual greenhouse gas emissions compared to someone with a G-rated energy-guzzler. Even bigger savings are to be made with boilers. New generation condensing boilers have great fuel efficiencies (around 90%) and can take more than two tonnes off the greenhouse emissions from home heating. If everyone in the UK with gas central heating installed one it would save enough energy to heat 4 million homes, and cut greenhouse gas emissions by 17 and a half million tonnes.

Aside from the standard household appliances that are big individual energy users, there is a wealth of other less essential electrical appliances and gadgets common to most of our homes. Every one of these gizmos carries a cost to the climate, used or not (embodied energy again).

On the worktops in our kitchens, the shelves in our living rooms, and even the window sills in our bathroom, there's stuff. Lots and lots of stuff. As good members of a consumerist society we have bought into the idea that we must have more stuff, until we either need to put up more shelving, have a gigantic garage sale, or move to a bigger house. Countless tonnes of infrared binoculars, pasta-making machines ("Make your own fresh pasta in only five and a half hours") and nose-hair trimming sets ("Articulated arm reaches even the most hard to get to areas") now lie forgotten and unused in the houses and self-storage warehouses of the developed world.

Christmas is our bonanza time for sending and receiving these gadgets and novelty gifts. It is, after all, the time for giving, and what do you get those friends and relatives who already seem to have everything? With the shopping days until Christmas rapidly falling to single figures it's either an online shop to see if the executive toys website can deliver in time, or its back to the simmering mix of sweat, tears and *Jingle Bells* that is the shopping mall.

In the end, most of us are just glad that we managed to get the last Portable Walrus Cleaning Kit and it's warm smiles all round when the big day comes and we exchange our hard-won present for our very own Horse Grooming set, with fetlock volumiser. Clearly, demanding that all your friends and family refrain from buying you anything other than clearly specified items is something which gets increasingly difficult from the age of about 8 onwards. Each of us can, though, reduce the unwanted 'stuff' problem by buying presents for others with a much smaller climate price tag than the usual gadgets, such as a charity donation. Many people are already doing it. In 2004, for instance, Oxfam sold more than 30,000 Goat Gifts as Christmas presents – a card (and goat picture) for the 30,000 recipients and a potentially life-saving injection of aid to the developing world.

As before, when I began to write about our car use, I can feel myself slipping off down the road of open-toed ranting, call-ing for rebellion against capitalist values and the immediate incarceration of all shopping channel presenters. Turning our lifestyles back to the dark ages doesn't appeal though. I like TV (well, some of it) and I like having a video recorder and a computer (what a naughty consumer I am), but by avoiding all those extra gadgets we can have these things and still make meaningful reductions in our energy use. Christmas, and in particular the 'consume till we bust' side of it is in for some stick throughout this book – if I'm not destined to be Jacob Marley, then Ebenezer Scrooge certainly looks on the cards. I love Christmas, and I really do dream each year of a white one. It's hard to beat isn't it? The surge of excitement as you wake up on Christmas morning and know from the yellowish tinge to the light and the muffled sounds outside that it has snowed. Keep on with all those gadgets though, and we can all forget about white Christmases and just get used to wet ones.

If you're at home, listen for a minute. Quiet? Listen very carefully and you'll probably just about be able to hear a hum. I can hear it right now. Over on the stereo a little red light gives the game away – standby power. The waste of energy in our households through things being left on standby is a quietly growing monster. We see those little red lights on our TVs, VCRs, stereos and set-top boxes so often that it's all too easy to forget that they are slowly eating up energy (I've just turned the stereo off at the socket). Manufacturers must carry a good amount of the blame for this problem, for making it appear that things are turned off when in fact they are on standby, and for not providing easy ways of switching things off completely, other than pulling them out of the wall.

The spectre of standby power has been with us for many years now, but it is the booming market in household electrical appliances which has sent this source of household emissions soaring. Computers are a prime example. They can take over a minute to start up and so are often left on all the time, the words 'All work and no play makes Jack a dull boy' slowly turning against a backdrop of stars. Screensavers are not energy savers. Switch the monitor off while you're away and you'll halve the energy use of the PC. For always-on PCs the energy saving options can make quite difference. The sleep mode can cut greenhouse emissions by 80%.

Our complacency about background energy use has reached a stage where plug-in air fresheners are now bought in their millions. Together, those quietly humming appliances are eating up over 10% of the electricity used in most homes, just to sit in standby mode. For the average house, three-quarters of a tonne of greenhouse gas is emitted every year by this route. On a national scale the wastage of energy and emission of greenhouse gas from standby power is simply embarrassing. In Australia, standby power is responsible for over 5 million tonnes of greenhouse gas every year and in the USA the figure is closer to 30 million tonnes. All just to keep those red lights blinking.

The third biggest slice from our home-made emissions pie, and one we've touched on already, is water heating. It's not desperately exciting, but at up to 2 tonnes of greenhouse gas per household each year, it's too important to ignore. As with home heating, the big climate-saving actions with water heating are installing good insulation and an efficient boiler. Lagging the hot water pipes can cut the energy-related green-house emissions from your water heating by 120 kg a year. Fitting one of those puffer jackets to your hot water tank can cut its energy wastage by three-quarters and save up to half a tonne of greenhouse gas each year.

There's room again here for cuts in energy use through changes in our behaviour and, in particular, in our use of hot water. Visit your own government's Department of Energy (or equivalent) website and somewhere there'll be a page berating you for leaving the tap running while you brush your teeth, using too much hot water for washing up, and having too many baths. For every 15 litres of hot water coming from an electric heater about a kilogram of greenhouse gas is emitted – just fixing a dripping hot water tap can save more than 100 kg of greenhouse gas a year.

What actually powers all the space and water heating, appliances and gadgets in our homes plays a crucial role in determining how much they help drive global warming. Gas heating, for instance, produces about two-thirds less greenhouse emissions than standard electric heating. The electricity supplied to our homes tends to carry with it a rather hefty greenhouse penalty because of the leading role that coal-burning power stations play in its generation. If you're lucky, you'll be able to switch your energy supplier to one providing renewable energy, such as that from wind farms, and so slash the amount of greenhouse gas released for every unit of electricity you use by over 90%.

While we're on the subject of what provides the energy in our homes, and the benefits of using renewable energy, indulge me for a moment while I go a bit woolly-jumpered and look at home power generation. It may conjure up images of bearded woodsmen whittling clothes pegs on their solar panelled front porches, but the generation of renewable energy at home is more widespread than you might think. As well as being climate-friendly, it is less wasteful. It avoids the long-distance transmission of electricity from power stations, provides more energy security in times of high demand or blackouts, and can be cheaper. In terms of emissions, the level of cuts you achieve depends on the scale of action you take. Small solar panels, for example, can be used to charge batteries, provide garden lighting, or top up energy use in the home.

For those homeowners keen to generate a large proportion of their own electricity, an expanse of photovoltaic (PV) cells is the usual option. In sunny climates these can fulfil all the household's energy requirements for much of the year. Even at higher latitudes you can expect an average installation to provide between a third and half of your annual energy use. Most systems allow you to sell any excess power back to the grid, so making you a bit of money and allowing others to make use of your renewable energy.

Such solar systems tend to be expensive, even with government grants to help soften the blow. For a less than sun-drenched area like my own it would take around twenty years for the energy produced by a big set of panels to offset the initial costs of installing it – twice the guaranteed lifespan of the panels. Even leaving the money aspect aside, the energy which goes into producing these solar panels in the first place can be substantial, and take off much of their climate-friendly gloss. For sunny Scotland, I'm looking at between 8 and 12 years of running my very expensive panels before they've produced enough energy to cancel out the energy that went into making them.

The technology, though, is moving on apace, and in large areas of the USA, Australia and elsewhere it is a very real alternative to the greenhouse gas-heavy electricity currently coming down the wires. It's worth mentioning the cheaper, less well-known cousin of solar power generation: solar water heating. At a fraction of the price of the electricity-producing PV cells, and requiring much less energy to manufacture, these water-heating systems – essentially a network of water-filled tubes on your roof – can offset their embodied energy tag and begin saving energy within just 6 months of their installation. In temperate climes, such solar water heaters generally serve to take the edge off the coldness of the water before the heating boiler has to do its work, with a greenhouse gas saving of up to 1 tonne a year. In the sun-kissed suburbs of Sydney, though, such systems can meet the bulk of hot water demands and mean greenhouse gas reductions of more then two tonnes a year.

Wind and water power can also be harnessed to produce some or all of a home's energy needs through small scale turbines and a suitable location. Other options include biomass boilers which use wood chips for home and water heating, and ground source heat pumps which collect heat from the soil around a building and transfer it inside.

Enough, for now, of these home energy and heat-generating technologies. Let's get back to the sharp end of the problem – where we use, and lose, all that energy, renewably generated or not, in our homes. We've already looked at the big three: space heating, appliances and heating our water, so now let's turn to the simplest climate-saving action of all: changing a light bulb.

I can't even begin to write about home lighting without thinking of my father. When my brothers and I were growing up in the 1970s, hardly an evening passed without Dad coming in from work and getting cross at us for the house being lit up like 'Blackpool Illuminations'. This of course was long before the greenhouse effect was making the headlines, but our dad, never a man happy with waste, hated such profligate use of lights (and the resulting electricity bill).

Over the past few decades our lights have got more and more efficient and at the same time we've been using more and more of them. Overall, home lighting is hoovering up even more electricity than it was when my brothers and I were busy making a DIY Blackpool in our small corner of Lincolnshire.

In the top tips books on individual action, climate-friendly lighting always gets a big push. It's obvious why: it's so easy to do. This isn't about our abandoning the car for a bike, spend-

**Figure 8** The evolution of Edison.

ing thousands on solar panels, or even reading the labels of the food we buy. Low-energy bulbs are cheap, easy to get hold of, will save us money and will cut our emissions. Why isn't everyone using them already? Goodness knows. For an average house with, say, 12 lights, replacing old light bulbs with low-energy bulbs can cut almost a tonne off the annual household greenhouse emissions – a big result for standing on a chair a few times. Next time you're in that big blue shop of Swedish origin, and before you get side-tracked into 'Beowulf' drinks coasters or 'Hagrid' shelving units, stock up on some low-energy bulbs.

After lighting, the final sliver of the emissions pie is, rather fittingly, cooking. Over a year, using gas for cooking, rather than electricity, will save up to a quarter of a tonne of emissions. Other strategies, such as always putting lids on simmering pots – this uses a third less energy – and filling kettles only as full as required, can make small but effective dents in a household's power drain. If everyone in my home nation of tea drinkers stopped overfilling kettles the energy saved could power more than two-thirds of all UK street lighting.

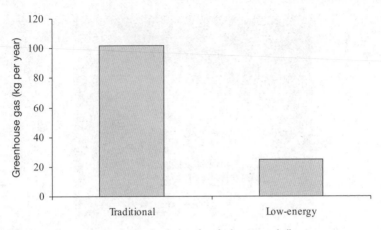

**Figure 9** The climate benefits of a low-energy bulb.

We've talked then, about the main areas of our home life that eat through our annual energy budgets and so generate greenhouse gas. Clearly, we can do a lot to make our home life more climate-friendly (Table 2). But there's another big emitter of greenhouse gas in our homes, and more specifically in our kitchens, which uses huge amounts of energy indirectly and whose contribution to global warming is growing fast: our food.

**Table 2** At-a-glance ways to cut greenhouse gas emissions from your home.

|  | Heating habits | Efficient appliances | No standby power | Efficient lighting | Better insulation |
|---|---|---|---|---|---|
| Greenhouse gas savings | 🌍 | 🌍 | 🌍 | 🌍 | 🌍 |
|  | Up to 30% | 10–20% | 5–10% | 5–10% | Up to 40% |

# 4

## flying strawberries

It's easy to see why wasting electricity in the home or driving a big car is bad for the climate. Though the carbon dioxide released is invisible, we know that doing these things burns fossil fuel and that, by doing them less, we can cut emissions. Things get less obvious when the emissions arising from our lifestyles are several steps removed from us. The whole embodied energy problem is a case in point. Who would have thought that the innocuous looking gnome in next door's garden carries a climate tag? Sitting there, fishing rod in hand, slowly growing a covering of lichen, its climate impact is hidden in the energy used to mine its materials, to manufacture its cement body and its paint, and finally to transport it from World of Gnomes to your neighbour's garden. Unless you are willing to spend an awfully long time reading some of the driest research papers in Christendom on 'The life cycle analysis of gnomes and their rods' every time you want to buy something then your climate-aware choices boil down to simply buying less stuff.

There is something, though, that we can't just stop buying, and which can carry much more of a hidden climate tag than our bearded fishing friend: our food.

As with the bricks in our walls, the appliances in our kitchen, or the ornaments in our garden, the chain of events which gets a pre-packed cheese and ham bagel onto the supermarket shelf can use a lot of energy. Like a rather tasty snowball rolling downhill toward us, our lunchtime bagel builds up ever more embodied energy, and so more greenhouse gas emissions, on its journey from field to food aisle. Before we expose the bagel for the climate pariah it is, before we get into the nitty-gritty of food miles and belching cows (you'll see), what about our two-way climate change street? If we're going to address the climate impact of our food, what about the impact of climate change on what we eat?

Just as northern hemisphere homes are gradually moving south climate-wise, so are farms. Over the next 20 years many farmers will be able to grow more crops previously the pre-serve of lower latitudes. The flip side of this of course is that the crops they are used to growing might not fare well in such warmer climes. All that extra carbon dioxide we're pumping into the atmosphere means that some crops will grow faster and bigger – so bumping up yields. For some farmers this will be of little comfort after their entire harvest has been destroyed by the more intense droughts, floods and storms we can expect along with the carbon dioxide-accelerated growth rates. Even this so-called carbon dioxide fertilisation effect is not necessarily a good thing. It can make weeds grow faster still, so lowering yields or requiring big increases in the use of herbicides. Overall, some crops will do better, some much worse. For staples like wheat, rice, maize and soybeans, the 2080s could see yields fall by up to 50%, global price hikes of up to 45%, and a 50% increase in the number of people at risk from hunger as a result.

The wine industry in California is worth $4 billion each year, and produces some cracking wines. As summers get hotter and drier over the 21st century, the grape harvest is likely to shrivel and the wine industry with it. Likewise, Californian dairy farming will probably suffer as more intense heatwaves and droughts mean poorer grazing, increased stress to the animals and an overall drop in production of up to 20% by 2100.

More frequent droughts, storms and flooding will disrupt food imports and exports, with increases in pests and diseases further exacerbating these problems. Climate change is going to have far-reaching effects on food in developed countries, but it is food production and supply in the developing world – so often the stalking ground of famine – that face the biggest threat.

In Africa in particular, the outlook for food security is grim. Already nearly 200 million people here are classed as under-nourished, and much farming is on the margins of what the climate will allow. As the century unfolds, the same intensification of droughts, floods and storms that threatens Californian wine growers could cost the lives of millions of Africans. Globally, we can expect around 80 million extra people to be at risk of famine due to climate change by 2080, up to 65 million of these will be in Africa. That's the equivalent of the entire population of Great Britain facing starvation as a direct consequence of the fossil fuels we are now burning. The very food we eat today may starve millions in Africa, Asia and South America tomorrow.

And so to the food in our cupboards, fridges and supermarkets: how exactly does it pick up such a big climate tag and how can we avoid this hidden strip of the grocery bill? It all starts down on the farm. Agriculture is to blame for almost half of all human-related methane emissions and three-quarters of our nitrous oxide emissions.

Take something as innocuous as a wheat field – once a woodland, drawing in and trapping carbon dioxide. Each year, after the harvest, the soil is ploughed. This exposes deeper, carbon-rich soil to the air and leads to a flush of carbon dioxide into the atmosphere. To get the next lot of wheat growing fast, farmers heap on tonnes of nitrogen fertiliser, increasing emissions of nitrous oxide. The same is true of just about every crop – add nitrogen fertiliser and you get nitrous oxide.

Then there's methane. The bugs that produce the gas like all things wet. If you've ever plunged your booted foot into a waterlogged bog and seen bubbles rushing up from the ooze, usually along with a smell of rotting vegetation and the creeping realisation that your boots aren't waterproof, then you've seen methane escaping. As with boot-eating bogs, the saturated soils of paddy fields house countless billions of methane-producing bacteria. These pump out around 60 million tonnes of the stuff a year.

As the consumers of these crops there's little we can do about such emissions (apart from avoiding wastage and growing our own). Governments around the world are already trying to limit how much nitrogen fertiliser goes on fields, not least to stop it getting into our drinking water when it gets washed off. Rice farmers too are increasingly encouraged to let flooded soils dry out a bit more often and so keep a lid on all that bubbling methane. Where food-related greenhouse emissions start to get really big, and where we do have some choice, is with meat.

Imagine your average cow (Figure 10). As well as eating lots of grain grown in the fertiliser-soaked, nitrous oxide-emitting fields, she also emits buckets of methane. As she trundles around the field this cow and all her bovine friends belch out methane, day in day out. In just one day your typical Daisy burps around 200 litres of methane into the atmosphere. Where you've got a lot of cows this adds up to a great deal of methane. In Australia for example, the climate impact of

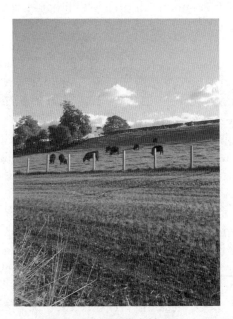

**Figure 10** Bucolic belching.

carbon dioxide is in danger of being overtaken by that of live-stock-burped methane – at a massive 3 million tonnes a year. Something similar is going on in New Zealand, in large part due to its 50 million or so sheep. Even in the USA, where energy use and transport dominate greenhouse emissions, methane from cattle tops 5 million tonnes a year. Cattle, the biggest of our methane-emitting farmyard friends, are not the only ones burping their way to a warmer world. Sheep weigh in with about 30 litres of methane per day each, while pigs emit about 8 litres.

Yes, some humans can also release large volumes of methane (and this time it's not belching we need worry about). Thankfully, the condition is quite rare. Whereas most of us let out just a few hundred millilitres in the privacy of our own bathrooms, some, probably quite lonely, souls emit as much as 3 litres of methane per day.

Meat, then, has often built up a big climate burden when the time comes for that one-way trip to the abattoir, thanks to the energy and emissions associated with feed and methane. Every beef steak results in around 15 times its own weight of green-house gas even before you add in transport. In the Nether-lands, a nation very fond of a bit of animal for breakfast, lunch and tea, meat contributes almost a third of all food-related emissions. Dairy products, incidentally, with their obvious requirement for more belching cows and grain, make up nearly a quarter of Dutch food-related emissions.

Even without the heavy greenhouse gas tag, meat's statistics are pretty sobering. Currently over 800 million people are either undernourished or lack a secure food supply; water is critical in getting these people the food they need. Much of that precious water goes into growing food for livestock. Producing a kilogramme of beef uses 15 cubic metres of water; a kilo of cereals needs less than 3 cubic metres. Meat uses up to seven times more land than crops of the same food-value.

Since the Second World War the amount of meat each of us in the West eats has soared to 100 kg a year. That's a steak per person per day.

I enjoy meat. No barbecue in my street would be the same without some charcoal sausages and my neighbour's wonderful spicy kebab. Where things have gone wrong is in the sheer volume of the stuff we now get through. Meat used to be a treat, something which cost quite a lot and wasn't always available. With intensive production methods, farmers and supermarkets have pushed the price of meat down to a level where a whole chicken costs less than a high street coffee. Now we feel that a meal isn't a meal unless a large chunk of animal flesh is involved. These low prices hide big social, environmental and medical costs, as flagged so articulately in Felicity Lawrence's recent book *Not on the Label*.

The fact remains that meat, no matter how well looked after, is bad for the climate – another moral fly in your oxtail soup. Cutting down on the amounts we chomp through can make a difference on several levels. If you long ago shunned meat on the grounds of your health or animal rights, you can congratulate yourself that at the same time you've also been cutting swathes through your emissions. If, like me, your mouth still waters at the thought of rare steak, then at least cut back a bit, with the added bonus that you'll be healthier as a result. Just two fewer beef burgers or steaks a month can slash your annual greenhouse gas output by a third of a tonne.

The research on food, its embodied energy and its contribution to global warming, is nothing if not thorough. I have before me papers listing the embodied energy of everything from unsalted nuts to block margarine, from wholemeal bread to fortified wine. A particularly diligent group in Sweden have calculated the energy which has gone into not just pork, but fresh pork, frozen pork, pork from Sweden, pork from Europe, pork stew and pork sausages.

For the whole life-cycle of a meal, from field to plate, the differences in the greenhouse gas emissions for vegetables compared to meat are stark. So let's take a trip to Sweden, land of saunas, home furnishing and, yes, ABBA. After a heady night of outrageously priced beer and a morning of groaning and sipping water, we make our way down to the hotel's restaurant for the buffet lunch.

On the menu today are five appetising options: roast pork, boiled carrots, fresh tomatoes, fried potatoes and beef stew. If each of these trays of food had its climate tag they'd be labelled as follows: 50 g of carbon dioxide for a serving of carrots, 330 g for some of those shiny tomatoes, a mere 17 g for those great smelling potatoes, but an appetite-quelling 610 g for a few slices of pork and a massive 1,500 g of greenhouse gas for a couple of scoops of beef stew.

The tomatoes, grown in Sweden but in heated greenhouses, have clocked up a big climate tag through the oil-powered heating systems used to keep the glasshouses balmy even while the snow is settling outside. Storage, and in particular refrigerated storage, eats up energy too. For the carrots, 60% of their total emissions arise through keeping them chilled until the supermarkets want them. And then there's the extra climate whammy of food transport.

Yes, some foods have already packed a big climate punch by the time they pass through the farm gates. For others the contribution to global warming really starts to build up as they set off on what is likely to be a very long journey, crossing borders and even continents.

Pick half a dozen food items at random from your cupboard or fridge and you'll probably have before you food which together has travelled thousands of kilometres – now dubbed food miles – to your kitchen. The six rather tasty fridge items in Figure 11 would together travel over 40,000 km in getting to my fridge in Scotland, were I not such a seasonal, local pro-

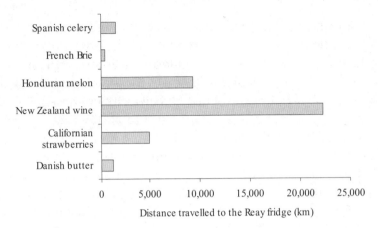

**Figure 11** Around the world in a fridge.

duce/grow your own evangelist. This long-distance transport of grub means the burning of a lot of fossil fuel and so the emission of a lot of greenhouse gas.

Our Swedish buffet was relatively food-mile-lite, much of it having been produced within Sweden. What about those luxury or out-of-season foods which have sailed the seven seas, been trucked the length and breadth of continents, or garnered enough air miles to qualify for a free Harley-Davidson? Their tags are big. A recent study found that one basket of 26 organic items clocked up over 240,000 km and 80 kg of greenhouse gas emissions before being pedalled home by a right-on shopper.

Take your lunch at work: it's rarely anything to write home about, more a fuel stop to get you through the next four hours of keyboard tapping. You pop out to the shop and grab that pre-packaged cheese and ham bagel, a drink and some fruit, paying handsomely for this collection of clear plastic containers. Back at your desk you rip open your bagel, stop to staunch the blood flow from your newly lacerated thumb, and munch down the chilled offering while typing 'packaging injury and litigation' into Google.

Producing the ham and cheese, as we've seen, results in lots of greenhouse emissions. Getting them into our bagel then racks up yet more emissions during processing, refrigerated storage and 1,000 km of travel. Add to these emissions those of the bread and butter surrounding them and you have a bagel with an overall climate tag of almost half a kilogram of greenhouse gas. That's one heavy snack, even before we start on all the plastic packaging, of which more later.

Feeling health-conscious you also bought a bunch of grapes and a bottle of mineral water. Now things take a real turn for the worse. The bottle of spring water, with its label showing a babbling brook in Canada, has travelled nearly 6,000 km by boat and truck to get to the supermarket, where it has since sat in a refrigerator. This one bottle, which, let's face it, contains an expensive version of what we get out of the taps, has clocked up nearly 300 g of greenhouse gas – truly heavy water.

The grapes are the killer. So far this lunchtime our food and drink has crossed oceans and international borders using boat, truck and van. The grapes bring us to air freight. It is preposterous that while worrying about exhausted oil reserves and the environmental damage caused by the rapid growth in air travel, we continue to fly tonnes of exotic fruit and vegetables around the world.

Your 200 g bunch of grapes has clocked up over 10,000 km on its way to your desk, most of that by jet. Its transport has added one and a half kilograms of greenhouse gas – six times its own weight in emissions and equivalent to leaving a climate-unfriendly light bulb on all weekend. If the mineral water is like a lead milkshake as far as global warming is concerned, then these grapes should sit in your stomach like a bag of ball bearings.

Air transport of food has reached ridiculous proportions. Every new and exotic ingredient used by the celebrity chef of the moment sparks a surge in demand for fresh tiger prawns or papaya, all flown in that same day. Felicity Lawrence tracked the life and times of a hand-tied bunch of chives which says it all. Though the chives started off in the UK and were destined to be bought and eaten in the UK, the little bunches were first flown to Kenya for the 'hand tying' before being flown straight back, thereby clocking up about 14,000 km and over a kilogram of greenhouse gas for every 20 g bunch.

All over the developed world the story is the same. A bunch of grapes at a Chicago market in 1972 would have travelled about 2,500 km; by 1989 Chile had become a major source of grapes and the average distance each bunch was travelling had almost doubled.

It would be daft to say that we should all consume *only* locally produced or home-grown food and spend our winters smeared in goose fat and sewn into our long-johns, eking out the last few shrivelled apples from the autumn. But simply sourcing some food locally can massively cut emissions. Apples, shrivelled or otherwise, are a good example. In the UK the supermarket shelves are dominated by imports; even during the British apple harvest most of the varieties on show are imported from New Zealand, Australia or South Africa. Buying local apples, instead of travellers from the Southern Hemisphere, can cut the related greenhouse gas by nearly 90%.

The icing on our well-travelled climate cake is shopping trips. The number of shopping journeys we make and their distance has grown in recent years – over 200 shopping trips a year on average. Strolling down the high street to the butchers, bakers or grocers clearly leads to lower emissions than getting in the car. Increasingly though, high street food shopping isn't an option – few of us have local stores anymore. Instead we have out of town malls like aircraft hangars with many kilometres of roaring tarmac between us and their hectares of parking lot. These barns, purveying everything from Bleu d'Auvergne to porcelain statuettes of Kermit the Frog, should mean we take fewer trips. They don't.

A 25 km shopping trip in the car equals emissions of 5 kg. Divided between all the items in your trolley this trip adds just 125 grams to the climate tag of each. It's the extra 'nip out' for a bag of mixed nuts that can dump a whole 5 kg of greenhouse gas on your nutty snack. Cutting out these extra trips by always making a list and resisting the temptation to grab the car keys every time you see an advert for a new flavour of nachos is a start.

Another, very 21st century, option harks back to the days of delivery boys on wobbly bikes: Internet shopping. One truck can deliver the weekly food shopping of dozens of families, preventing dozens of trips by car and reducing greenhouse gas emissions by between 20% and 90% (depending on how close together the drop-offs are).

Climate-aware food shopping is a prime example of the clash between 'doing your bit' and real life in the developed world. Food shopping is about keeping the family fed for the coming week on a limited budget, and getting out of the shop before your last strand of good humour snaps and the kids take to beating each other with bags of toilet tissue.

Even those unhurried 'ethical' shoppers with baskets full of expensive organic products and an air of smugness (they undoubtedly model for energy-saving pamphlets) can end up laden with greenhouse gas. Indeed, it's these shoppers who are most likely to buy hand-tied chives to serve at that night's dinner party with organic baby sweetcorn from South Africa, lamb chops from New Zealand and wine from Australia, while wringing their hands over the recent flooding.

We're bombarded with messages about our food all the time: eat less fat, eat less sugar, buy organic, buy fair trade. Adding to this list 'buy low food miles' is vital but difficult in practice. Labels tell you little about climate impact and supermarkets' range of local produce is often limited. If we knew which foods were global warming gremlins and which weren't, if labels carried the number of food miles for instance, we could make informed choices. This would put pressure on the supermarkets to sell more local produce.

One suggestion is ClimateWatchers, a greenhouse gas-aware version of WeightWatchers. The idea is that people will go to meetings with till receipts and be told how much weight (of greenhouse gas) they've gained or lost. It conjures images of 'Climate Slimmer of the Month' – a bearded man who has lived solely on nettle tea and boiled limpets for the past four weeks – but the idea is sound. Until branches of ClimateWatchers spring up in church halls we'll have to rely on Country of Origin stickers to help us eschew globe-trotting food and the threat to our climate it represents.

In the developed world the average person emits an extra tonne of greenhouse gas each year through the food they eat. A weekly trolley load of globe-trotting supermarket produce can push that to over 4 tonnes a year. With a climate-aware diet on the other hand – local produce, no flying food – annual food-related emissions can shrink to around a third of a tonne: a 90% cut (Table 3). Switching to a life of wild berry eating, interspersed with the occasional grub or roasted squirrel, isn't necessary.

**Table 3** Potential cuts in food-related greenhouse gas emissions.

| | Less meat and dairy | Fewer food miles | Fewer shopping trips | Food delivery | Home grown |
|---|---|---|---|---|---|
| Greenhouse gas savings | Up to 30% | Up to 90% | 5–10% | 5–10% | Up to 100% |

↔

Assuming we've cut back on steaks and sneered at the exotic fruit section for most of the year, there are surges in consumption, of food and everything else, that still lie in wait. Weeks when the idea of keeping an eye on the food miles, the amount of meat in the shopping basket, and our own waistlines tends to go out of the window: celebrations like Christmas and Thanksgiving.

Yes, it's Scrooge time. We're talking about food, and these festivals for most of us revolve around meals of gigantic proportions, so let's get out the humbugs.

It's Christmas Eve and the smell of pine needles is in the air, radio stations are stuck in a repeating loop of Bing Crosby, and the arguments about whose relatives should visit or be visited have been settled. For the Carbones, Christmas is a traditional affair. Grandma Carbone comes to stay and the kids work themselves up into a frenzy of over-excitement about the presents they hope to get. The tree is already standing in the front window, bedecked in bright fairy lights, miniature elves and slowly rotating baubles. The glitziness of the tree is nothing compared to the decorations outside. John Carbone, determined not be outdone by the neighbours, has really gone to town this year. The front hedge winks on and off under the power of a hundred bright white bulbs. Along the eaves glowing white 'icicles' are picked out by ripples of light travelling backwards and forwards in never-ending waves. On the roof a brightly lit Santa Claus waves to all who pass by, while resting against his gift-packed sleigh and four reindeer, themselves picked out in hundreds more brightly coloured bulbs. In the front garden the Carbones' one tree hasn't escaped: every branch is covered in closely packed fairy lights that appear and disappear at apparently random intervals.

John and Kate are scrumming down with, seemingly, the rest of humanity at the local mall. Having done half a dozen circuits of the car park and finally found a space, they trudge the half kilometre to the stores and hit the blazing lights and the wall of jingly sound that is the Christmas shopping experience. Their aim is to get the last few presents for the boys and buy enough food to last through to Boxing Day, all without losing the plot and attacking the nearest group of handbell ringers.

The presents for the boys are, without exception, electronic gadgets, so one shop meets all their needs. For George a new cell phone is a must, as is a new games console. For Henry a new laptop is his main present, with another new mobile to boot. John and Kate also take the opportunity to buy a big, new plasma screen TV – something John has been lusting after for several months.

Having run the gauntlet of the electrical goods store, tried 23 different cell phones, and plumped for 'Dictator: Crush and Control' as the game to go with George's new console, it's off to the food hall to do battle with the other 200 people over that last tub of fresh cranberries. Grabbing a trolley each, and consulting the long shopping list, they launch into the melée and begin to collect the food planned to satisfy the family over the coming days of over-indulgence.

Three hours later, and with the mad shopping experience over (at least for a couple of days), the Carbones make their way home to get the food put away and the presents wrapped before the boys' prying eyes seek them out. Grandma Carbone arrives just before supper-time and, as the Christmas Eve excitement builds, the Carbones sit down to the first of many blow-out meals.

Christmas Day dawns warm and wet, much to the disappointment of the whole family, who were hoping against hope for a white Christmas. It's been 20 years now since it snowed on Christmas Day. The sledges in the shed might get an outing come January, though even that's not a sure thing. With Christmas carols on the stereo competing with *It's a Wonderful Life* on the TV, everyone gathers for the gift opening. Paper is torn, novelty ties are put on, batteries are hunted down for new gadgets and dust jackets of new books are read. After a long session of present opening, the table is set with the best cutlery and glassware and it's 'all hands on deck' in the kitchen as a turkey the size of a small ostrich comes out of the oven, followed by trays of ham, stuffings, and mashed potato. Lashings of hard-won cranberry jelly are scooped into dishes and pints of sauces come off the hob. In the dining room the diners take up their positions for the feast ahead and, as the platters come through, the table groans under their weight. Just as it seems the table has reached its limit, out comes the champagne, the wine, the beer and the cola. Glasses are filled and raised all around and the feast begins. Some considerable time later, after the final spoonful of mash has been forced down and that slice of cherry pie has accounted for the last notch on John's belt, it's time to load the dishwasher and slump down in front of the new TV for the Christmas Day movie. With luck, when the time comes for another few plates of cold meat and pickles everyone's stomachs will have shrunk slightly and the bloated pain they are all suffering will have subsided. After some colourful swearing at useless instructions and missing connectors from John, George quickly takes over and gets the new plasma TV set up and running. The surround sound is soon joined by the combined snoring of Grandma and John.

Later, as the house lights dim due to John flicking the switch for the outdoor illuminations, the Carbones can reflect on another Christmas Day done. After another raid on the bowls of nuts and sweets, a new DVD, and an argument about who will go to the sales the next day and what food needs to be bought, it's off to bed for George and Henry, and a glass of eggnog all round.

The Carbones' Christmas Day food consumption is average for the developed world. Together, the bowls of nuts, boxes of sweets, and the stocking satsumas, the turkey and trimmings, lashings of wine and spirits, and chocolate, add up to emissions of well over 25 kg – double those of a normal day. For the Christmas holiday as a whole each household belches out about a quarter of tonne of greenhouse gas just from food. And it doesn't stop there.

There's the extra power use, in particular those Christmas lights. For the Carbone household, the hundreds of bulbs, not to mention the waving Santa, burn around 200 kilowatt hours of electricity during the Christmas period, leading to an extra 120 kg of greenhouse gas going up into the atmosphere and helping to ensure that next Christmas won't be a white one either. Across the USA, festive lights fritter away 2 billion kilowatt hours every year: enough energy to power 200,000 homes all year round.

A more lasting drain on electricity, and belcher of greenhouse gases, comes in the form of all those presents, each with its embodied energy tag. Most homes on a Christmas afternoon suffer from a new rash of blinking and buzzing gadgets, some eating their way through their first and last set of batteries before being relegated to a dusty cupboard. The more tenacious electronic devices soon take their place in the standby power hum and the three-quarters of a tonne of related greenhouse gas emissions.

Finally, there's the most conspicuous side of our rapacious Christmas consumption: rubbish. After the big day and all that present opening, most of us feel we need to drag ourselves out for a bit of fresh air to try to digest enough food in our stuffed stomachs to make room for the next round. The bins outside every house tell the story of just how much consumption has been going on inside. No bin is big enough for the onslaught of wrapping paper and packaging, discarded food and bottles. As the garbage collectors are usually at home creating their own mounds of trash, Christmas and Boxing Day are the few days each year when you really get an idea of how much stuff every house is throwing out. Street corners rapidly fill with bulging plastic sacks, Santa-covered paper peeking over their tops or blowing down the street. Another week and the Christmas trees start to appear, sad browning skeletons of their former bushy selves too big to get in the bin so leaning dejectedly against the wall until the next collection. All this waste means a lot of truck collections and some very rapid filling of landfill sites. Each Christmas the UK throws out an extra two and a quarter million tonnes of waste food, wrapping paper and packaging, plus about 6 million Christmas trees. In the USA the numbers are even more boggling: 33 million Christmas trees are dumped each New Year. This Yuletide bonanza for the landfill bugs means an extra 200 kg of greenhouse emissions per household.

An average Western Christmas – the food and the presents, the lighting and the waste – adds up to a badly wrapped present to the atmosphere of over half a tonne of greenhouse gas. The most direct way to reduce these emissions is to cut back on the amount of stuff consumed in the first place and direct those tonnes of wrapping paper, silly hats and old sprouts somewhere other than a landfill site. Which brings us neatly to our backyards – a potentially big source of planet-warming emissions, and a great place to slash them.

# 5

## in my backyard

Our backyards are increasingly extensions of our homes. Turn on daytime TV and there's certain to be some green-fingered presenter telling you how to make the garden an extra room of the house. Now, in even the most frigid corners of Europe and North America, you can find families out on the decking having a barbecue, year-round. It may get cold (though less so these days), but there's always the forest of patio heaters to keep us warm – the last word in climate control. With this deepening love affair with outdoor living has come a whole new industry: from those winsome TV gardeners, to garden centres selling everything from electronic chimes playing Slim Whitman hits to grass that glows when you walk on it. Yes, we love the great outdoors.

Climate change is set to spoil the party. The TV garden shows of 2050 will be less 'Hanging baskets and the need for threes' and more 'My lawn's dead and the kids have got ticks'. What's in store at the bottom of the garden? It's not *The Good Life*, that's for sure.

As you tentatively stick your nose out of the door, you might well encounter the  first impact of climate change in the very air: the smell of smoke. With the intense summer droughts forecast to result from global warming, forest and range land fires are also predicted to increase. Hot-weather smoke isn't just an annoyance if you've put your washing out to dry, it is bad for your health. When several major forest fires broke out in south-east Asia in 1997 their combined smoke darkened the skies for weeks and led to a tripling of respiratory disease cases and a drop in lung function in schoolchildren. The next year, raging fires in Florida doubled the number of people visiting the ER with asthma and bronchitis and upped the admissions due to chest pain by a third.

Studies have also linked baking summer weather to increased radon concentrations (a cause of lung cancer), increased ground-level ozone (causing respiratory problems), and health damage from a host of other air pollutants. Across Europe, more than 300,000 people already die prematurely each year because of air pollution.

If you haven't coughed from the smoke and other air pollutants you'll probably sneeze. Every hay fever sufferer knows that long periods of hot dry weather make going outside at all something which should only be attempted with an inhaler and swimming goggles. Tree pollen is likely to rise along with summer temperatures, and the carbon dioxide fertilisation effect will make weeds grow faster and produce more pollen. Experiments have already shown that a doubling in carbon dioxide concentrations leads to a quadrupling in ragweed pollen.

As we snuffle and hack down the garden path, the health threats continue. A changing climate will make our gardens home to a host of new pests and pathogens, as well as changing the numbers and behaviour of the ones we have already. In the early 1990s, following a period of exceptionally heavy rainfall in the USA, the mouse population exploded. Along with a rash of mouse dropping-covered cupboards came the first recorded US outbreak of Hantavirus Pulmonary Syndrome (this is one nasty disease: sufferers' lungs fill with fluid and over a third of those who contract it die). Warmer winters will spur other diseases, as will increased flooding. Extreme weather may damage health services and malnourishment will weaken immune systems. All in all a perfect recipe for epidemics. So far, climate change isn't thought to have directly caused the resurgence of any infectious diseases, but chances are that it will.

Topping the list of diseases threatening to spread to a garden near you is malaria. Forty per cent of the world's population are currently at risk from the disease; over two and half million people are now infected and it kills a million each year. A child dies from malaria every 30 seconds. It is on the rise across the globe, because of poor public health, pesticide-resistant mosquitoes, and increased human movement. Climate change is the last thing this deadly mix needs.

Malaria doesn't like it too hot, and where it's already living at really high temperatures – in some areas of Kenya, for example – further rises in temperature could kill it. For most of the world though, the mosquitoes and their malarial payload will lap up the heat, with even small rises massively boosting transmission rates. By 2080 malaria's global reach is expected to have extended to encompass an extra 300 million people. In South America, the range of the engagingly named malaria-carrying mosquito *Anopheles darlingi* is at the moment limited by temperature; climate change may see it extending further south into Argentina, exposing more people to the disease.

Much of the developed world got rid of malaria back in the 1950s and 60s. What we didn't do is get rid of the mosquitoes which carry malaria – something all too obvious on a warm still night when, as you tuck into your climate-friendly barbecued mushroom, you realise that half a dozen of the little beasts are tucking into you. Thanks to scattered reintroductions of malaria by sun-tanned neighbours returning from holiday with tales of great scenery but unexplained cold sweats, the potential for more frequent outbreaks is very real.

Assuming that our health services remain intact in the future we should be able to head off such invasions and limit the damage. More of a worry is when outbreaks occur in countries like Russia, where the medical infrastructure is more fragile and the disease could get out of control.

Of the other diseases more likely to visit our backyards, one of the most dangerous is dengue. Like malaria, dengue is on the rise, with more than half of the world's population now at risk. It too is transmitted by mosquitoes and there have been a growing number of imported cases and outbreaks in the USA and Australia in recent years – it's estimated that travellers introduce around 200 cases to the USA each year. Dengue causes fevers and, in its haemorrhagic form, kills 1 in 20 of those who contract it.

Probably the best-known mosquito-borne nasty on the march is West Nile Virus. This virus was first isolated from a woman in Uganda 1937 and until the 1990s it seemed the Western hemisphere was free of it. Then, as summer turned to autumn in 1999, unexplained cases of encephalitis – inflammation and swelling of the brain – started cropping up on the east coast of the USA. The outbreak centred on New York City and coincided with the sudden deaths of crows and other wild birds. From one of these dead crows a lab in Iowa isolated a virus, later identified as the same one causing the outbreak of encephalitis in humans. West Nile Virus, previously known in Africa and Asia, had arrived in the West. By the time winter came and the mosquitoes were hidden away awaiting spring's warmth West Nile Virus had caused 62 cases of encephalitis, seven of them fatal. In subsequent years the virus rolled out across the USA. By 2003 there were 9,800 confirmed cases in 46 states; 264 died. The true number of Americans infected may be a quarter of a million, as in most instances West Nile Virus causes no symptoms. It is in the elderly or weak that severe illness can ensue. There is no treatment for the disease and no vaccine to prevent it.

Meanwhile, in Southern Europe, leishmaniasis is on the move. Passed on by sandflies, this disease causes sores, fever and weight loss; untreated, it can kill. Other diseases whose ranges could expand include bilharzia (fevers and liver damage caused by parasitic worms); Chagas' disease (passed on by the Assassin Bug and already found in the southern USA); and that old chestnut plague – still absent from its old killing fields of Europe, for now.

Finally, much of the USA and Europe is set to be overrun by ticks. If you own a dog and live in the country you've probably already encountered these tenacious hitchhikers. They sit in the grass waiting for an unsuspecting sheep, deer or Labrador to pass; then they jump aboard and burrow down to the skin for a good meal of blood. Ticks are not averse to a bit of human too and can carry a host of diseases. During their bloody feasting they can pass on Lyme disease, which can cause fevers and fatigue; Tick-borne Encephalitis Virus, which can result in inflammation of the brain; and something called Rocky Mountain Spotted Fever, complete with vomiting and abdominal pain. Already tick numbers have soared in North America and Europe thanks to 20 years of warmer winters. Lyme disease cases in the USA jumped from 491 in 1982 to over 23,000 by 2002.

The advice from the US Department of the Interior is to keep skin covered when outside and to stay indoors around dusk and dawn. Those neighbourhood barbecues clearly have an additional danger to that of being given an undercooked chicken leg. And talking of undercooked chicken legs, food poisoning will also soar with rising temperatures. In the UK the prediction is that climate change will add about 10,000 extra cases of food poisoning each year by 2050 – not just because we'll be eating more dodgy barbecues, but because higher temperatures will mean shorter shelf lives for many consumables. For most, such food poisoning means spending two days within rushing distance of a toilet, but for the frail and elderly the consequences can be fatal.

With rat, fly, mozzy and tick-borne diseases waiting in the fields, parks and streams, those salmonella-garnished burgers crashing our barbecues, and the very air making us wheeze like a forty-a-day smoker, we'd be excused for staggering back indoors for a lie down. But while we can retreat to the air-conditioned cool, our gardens will take the full brunt of global warming. How are those beloved begonias going to cope?

In general, the story is the same as for crops. More carbon dioxide in the atmosphere will make many plants grow faster. Rose fans can expect more buds and earlier blooms. In Europe's milder, shorter winters we'll be able to sow seeds earlier and many of our plants will enjoy longer growing seasons. In the UK, spring already arrives between 2 and 6 days earlier per decade, while at the same time autumn is being pushed back a couple of days. Warmer conditions will alter the types of plant that can successfully grow in our gardens – swapping hostas for poppies and sprouts for kumquats. My Reay Rioja could actually be drinkable. Indeed, large-scale vineyards may spread as far north as Scotland by the middle of this century.

On the downside, soaring summer temperatures and warm damp winters will put an end to the herbaceous border and reduce the rockeries of heather and slow-growing Alpines common to many northern gardens to... well, rocks. Most of us can also resign ourselves to many more hours on hands and knees pulling out the weeds that have lapped up extra helpings of carbon dioxide. Even worse, the lawn may start needing a cut in late autumn or even during winter, assuming it survives that long. With water supplies stretched to breaking point during summer and hosepipe bans in place, the days for many of those precious green squares are numbered. An increasingly desperate battle of the brown patches will be waged across the south of England, home of striped lawns and garden parties. In a country that has always been able to rely on the summer rains and cool days so beloved of lawns, the hot dry summers of the 21st century will change the traditional garden irrevocably. Instead of cream tea on the grass, it'll be chilled water in the shade of the gazebo.

Assuming our plants weather the extended droughts and scorching temperatures, there are yet more unpleasant surprises in store for them. Longer growing seasons will give aphids, mites and thrips – already common garden pests – many more breeding cycles, enabling them to dominate plants from much earlier in the year. Milder winters will also allow larger numbers of these bugs to survive through to the following spring, when they will rampage through the first green shoots of the year. Take the cabbage aphid: for every 1 °C temperature rise they will be able to start their attacks two weeks earlier. For cabbage root fly, an increase of 2 °C will allow them to attack cabbage roots a whole month early (bad news all round for cabbages).

Some infestations currently confined to greenhouses will notice that, actually, it's now rather nice outside and make their escape. Fungus attacks are likely to soar, as the amount of lush vegetation increases, and winters become ever milder. Still more pests will extend their ranges into regions previously too cold. In Europe, termites are tramping north, already cropping up in the south of England. In the USA, trees are falling victim to attackers, such as spruce budworm, previously confined to the warmer south. Overall, our gardens can expect a whole new influx of exotic species, invited or not.

Climate change is coming and none of the standard 'Not In My Back Yard' protests will stop it. Do get out the 'Save Our Neighbourhood' signs and write angry letters to your MP or Senator, but she's probably at home nursing her family through a particularly severe bout of food poisoning, while occasionally sneaking out to break her own hosepipe ban. If you want real action, if the prospect of your garden becoming a parched health risk makes you angry, then it's down to you. In our backyards this action starts exactly where we left our food: in the bin.

There sitting outside the back door is that seemingly bottomless pit for the detritus of Western life. Time was that all that went in the trash was ash from the fire and a few food scraps, but as packaging and consumption have grown so have our bins. As the bins expand we throw more trash in them. Today's average bin will swallow up 230 litres of garbage – that's the equivalent of about three cleaning-obsessed old ladies. It's easy to chuck everything that you don't want into its gaping black maw and forget about it. This is no magic box though. Our trash may disappear from view but it has to go somewhere. Before we look at exactly where all this stuff ends up, let's get out there before the garbage collectors and take a look, like some sweaty paparazzo combing through your week's rubbish for the next big scoop.

An average wheelie bin gathers about 20 kg of trash every week. In other words, over a year, each of us ditches 10 times our own weight. If you were brave enough to push your arm in and pull it all out you'd find something like the breakdown shown in Figure 12.

The biggest part, and most likely the smelliest, is organic waste. This is the remains of last night's pizza, the leftover salad, and the contents of that cup at the back of the fridge which might once have been egg yolks but which now only DNA testing could identify for sure. Across the USA, 25 million tonnes of food are discarded each year. For many with gardens, organic waste also includes the grass clippings from the lawn and what's left of that dead plant bought on a whim from the garden centre. It's estimated that each of us produces between 50 and 125 kg of plant waste every year – nearly 30 million tonnes of yard trimmings in the USA alone.

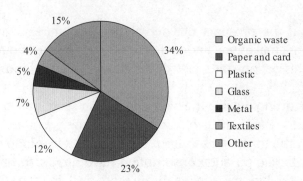

**Figure 12** Components of domestic waste in Europe.

All this organic waste, from teabags to banana skins, from apple cores to bindweed, produces that powerful greenhouse gas methane when trucked off to the landfill site. Here about 60% of all trash is compacted down and, when no more can be crammed in, is covered in a layer of soil and left. Down in the dark bacteria get digesting (these are the same bacteria that churn out methane from squelching bogs). Worldwide, landfills emit around 50 million tonnes of methane each year, much of it from the breakdown of kitchen and garden waste. In the USA about half of all landfill methane is now captured and used to power turbines, but the rest bleeds out into the atmosphere.

In short: throwing all those coffee grounds and hedge clippings in the bin is to be avoided. The simple way for a family to starve the methane-producing bugs involves something gardeners have been up to for generations: composting. The average household chucks out around 3.5 kg of food every day, more than two-thirds of which could instead go on a compost heap or into a worm farm (Figure 13), along with the majority of garden waste.

I'm rather a compost nut. The idea that I can throw rubbish from the kitchen and garden atop a heap, give it the occasional fork, and take buckets of crumbly nutritious 'black gold' from the bottom to fertilise the plants a month later never ceases to

**Figure 13** The author's composting worms busy making 'black gold'.

get me excited. (In West Lothian you have to get your kicks where you can.) Even better than the compost heap is the worm bin. This converts all the motley cabbage leaves, potato peelings and other organic waste from the kitchen into yet more black gold, and in double-quick time.

It's the ultimate in garden-friendly recycling. Not only do you avoid all the methane emissions, but, after a few weeks, your old carrot tops have become a top-grade soil dressing enabling you to grow even better carrots next year. For every kilogram of potato peelings, teabags or grass clippings that you compost rather than send off to landfill, you'll stop around twice that in greenhouse gas from going into the atmosphere. Over a year, the average household can shave almost a tonne off its emissions in this way. Not bad work for a few worms.

For the garden-less or worm-averse, centralised composting schemes are springing up in large towns and cities. By collecting your organic waste and then piling it onto giant-sized community compost heaps, rather than trucking it out for burial, local authorities end up with tonnes of free compost which they can then sell to garden centres. These huge heaps of collected organic waste are turned regularly to keep up the supply of oxygen and keep a check on the stinkier, methane-producing sections of microbial society. Such a scheme in Albuquerque composts nearly 10,000 tonnes of grass clippings and the like each year, preventing over 4,500 tonnes of greenhouse gas from being emitted.

Back to our eviscerated bin. Paper is the next biggest component in the pile of trash tipped across our pavement. Those spaghetti sauce-covered phone bills and till receipts may be the stuff of dreams for a bin-rifling paparazzo, but they also represent a large chunk of our waste's contribution to global warming. An average family throws out 8.5 kg of paper and card every week, half of this as newspapers and magazines. In the USA, around 85 million tonnes of paper and cardboard are chucked each year. More than 80% ends up wrapped around the TV dinner scraps in the dank depths of landfills. It's not quite as sumptuous a meal for methane-belching bacteria as banana skins with a teabag compote, but it is a welcome accompaniment – an appetiser before the main course, so to speak.

Recycling is an increasingly available alternative here. Not having to chop down and then process trees, with all the associated waste this creates, saves an awful lot of energy. In Australia, the greenhouse emissions arising from making paper total more than 12 million tonnes. Recycled paper takes a third to two-thirds less energy to make than the same amount of virgin paper. So every tonne of paper or card we recycle prevents up to two and a half tonnes of emissions. Every Sunday paper you put out to recycle, rather than heave into the bin, can therefore stop 2.5 kg of greenhouse gas – 150 kg's worth in a year's worth of Sundays.

The motto on every council leaflet about recycling and waste awareness website is 'Reduce, Reuse, Recycle'. It's estimated that for every tonne of bin-bound stuff another five tonnes of waste was produced during its manufacture, and a massive 20 tonnes of waste at the point of extraction. This takes into account all the resources dissipated, say, at the mine where the iron ore that went into making a baked bean can was extracted, or by the logging company that sliced its way through a forest to make the paper label on the tin.

Route one to reducing the amount of stuff thrown out in the first place is less packaging. It seems everything is wrapped and rewrapped as though it needs to survive re-entry from space. Some shops now sell single bananas in a heat-sealed moulded plastic sheath. Yes, a fruit you'd have thought already comes with a rather handy natural wrapper. Then there are the burger bars: you pay an hour's salary for more fat in one meal than is recommended for a week and, along with this heart-stopping culinary delight comes an avalanche of polystyrene containers, napkins, wrappers, bags, cups, lids and, if you're really lucky, novelty toys. I presume this all started out as a way to hide the fact that customers are paying a heap of hard-earned cash for what amounts to a greasy sandwich and 27 limp fries. The result has been that for miles around every fast food joint the bins overflow. Such excessive packaging might be explained away on the basis of health and safety – our burger and fries need to be wrapped in three layers of polystyrene to keep the bugs in – but it's product marketing rather than public safety that calls the super-size shots.

Almost a third of all US waste is packaging, around 70 million tonnes of the stuff at the last count, 20 million of which are plastics. In the UK, we produce over 9 million tonnes of waste packaging every year, with over half of all goods, from bread to bananas, being wrapped in plastic. Plastic doesn't grow on trees, though it may often festoon them on windy days. No, this plastic, the millions of tonnes of it keeping our bananas safe from air and lacerating office workers around the world, comes from that oh-so-finite fuel of the modern world: oil. About 4% of the world's oil is used as the raw material for plastics, with another 3–4% going into plastics manufacture. This is equivalent to the total annual oil production of Kuwait and Iraq.

If, like me and the Carbones, you do try to recycle your trash you've no doubt found plastics to be rather a tester. There may be kerbside collections for papers, bottles and cans, but plastics largely remain the ugly bath-time duckling in council schemes. Down at the supermarket there's a row of brightly coloured domes for your glass of every hue, and two huge metal skips with finger-snatching letter boxes for your newspapers and textiles, but plastics? You'll be looking for a long time in some countries. The recycling rate for plastics in the UK and USA is currently less than 5%, and that number doesn't look like shifting any time soon.

It comes back to just how cheap plastics are to produce, and to how varied and bulky they tend to be. While it's often cost-effective for councils and companies to recycle glass, metal and paper, plastic recycling just doesn't hold the same cash incentive. Sorting is a big problem: glass can be separated by colour, so it isn't too taxing. For cans, it's aluminium versus steel – a bit more tricky but if the label's still on or you have a handy magnet then no problem. For plastics it all gets very complicated. There are about fifty different types. The American Society of Plastic Industry, ASPI (Christmas parties there must be a hoot), has helpfully put these into seven groups. For one of the bigger categories, 'High density polyurethane' (shampoo bottles, for instance), every tonne recycled means a greenhouse gas saving of about 1.4 tonnes. But, with caps which can't be recycled on bottles that can, it's not surprising that most plastic ends up in the trash.

On the positive side, plastic collection and recycling is on the up. Today you can go online and order anything from a fleece made from recycled plastic bottles to a bag made out of their caps. Plastics can often fit the 'Reuse' category, in particular all those shopping bags. In the UK a staggering 8 billion bags are given out free each year – 130 for every man, woman and child. The kitchen drawers of the western world are home to many billions of the things, with yet more ending up swirling down streets and blocking drains. This isn't just unsightly: it can cost money and lives. In India, plastic bags have been banned in many areas because of their tendency to block sewers and so endanger health. Many animal species are also at risk. In the waters around Australia errant plastic bags kill turtles, whales, seals and birds who mistake them for food. In Ireland the imposition of a plastic bag tax has resulted in a 90% reduction, the few pence charge meaning most bags are now reused rather than binned.

Reuse of plastic, other than as carrier bags, has unfortunately made a rather stuttering start. The Body Shop, for example, offered refill services so that people could use the same bottles again and again for their beauty products. But only 1% of customers actually used this service and it was withdrawn in 2003.

And now to the things that really shouldn't make an appearance in anyone's bin: the glass and metals. An average Western family gets through about 500 glass jars and bottles each year. The UK as a whole uses around 2 million tonnes of glass packaging each year and recycles about a quarter. This is pretty poor compared to the rest of Europe where the average is over half, Switzerland managing a smashing 95%. Making glass uses lots of heat, and so lots of energy. Recycling cuts back greatly on this manufacturing energy, as well as saving on the extraction of all the raw materials. Every tonne of glass that gets recycled means 1.2 tonnes less raw materials and a reduction of 300 kg in greenhouse emissions.

For metals it's a similar story. Recycling steel packaging, usually in the form of cans, again removes the need for all those raw materials. A tonne and a half of iron-ore and half a tonne of coal is needed for every tonne of new steel, so recycling saves about 70% of the energy it would take to make the steel from scratch. Recycling aluminium holds even more climate benefits: every recycled kilogram saves over 14 times its weight in greenhouse gas from being emitted into the atmosphere – a cut in the energy use and emissions of over 90%.

Another 4% of household garbage is textiles. All those holey shorts, odd socks and itchy jumpers ("Honestly, Mum, I lost it when we moved house") add up to between a half and one million tonnes a year just in the UK. Recycling clothes avoids the manufacture, transport and use of new materials and dyes. And for natural fibres like cotton and wool it also robs the methane producers of yet another tasty, if tickly, snack.

Last of all, in the 'other' category, there are things like the computer keyboard that's had one too many cups of coffee spilled over it; the bits of wood left over from a failed attempt to put up a new shelf; and the commemorative 'Charles and Diana' mug that broke when said shelf fell off the wall. Some of this (the keyboard for example) can be recycled by specialists. Other bits, like the smashed Charles and Di mug, could provide a useful drainage layer at the bottom of a potted plant or might after all find a final resting place as the royal retreat of several thousand landfill bugs. There will always be some stuff that really is rubbish, but well over half of what most of us junk could have a different fate.

Our bin is noticeably lighter now. Through a combination of reduce (no single bananas in moulded plastic for us), reuse (the bursting carrier bag drawer in the kitchen now shuts), and recycle (1,000 composting worms are in the post), we've halved the greenhouse emissions of our trash from almost two tonnes to just one. Such action, multiplied across neighbourhoods, states and countries, can mean big emissions reductions.

Some governments have recognised this and are now taking a very proactive line on household recycling, providing free recycling bins, kerbside collection for a host of materials, local processing facilities and even free composters. In Germany they have taken things even further, imposing fines on those who don't recycle and obliging manufacturers to take back up to 70% of the packaging they produce. The potential is great. In the USA, increasing the current 30% level of trash recycling by just 5% would mean a cut in greenhouse emissions of around 36 million tonnes – more than 100 kg for every man, woman and child.

With the compost bin rather than the trash can overflowing, it's time to grow some food. Planting the kind of fruit and vegetables that you buy regularly and which would often be imported by air – soft fruit and salad for example – is a great way to get your backyard punching its weight in the fight against global warming.

Kate Carbone loves her garden. She cherishes its shifts in colour and texture with the onset of each new season. Her weekends and evenings are largely defined by weeding, digging, sowing and harvesting. When the Carbones first moved into the house the garden was a mess. The borders had merged with the lawns, the thistles and brambles were head-high and somewhere hidden at the back was a leaf-filled pond.

For the first year John and Kate left the garden to its own devices; there were a hundred and one other jobs to do inside before giving a thought to the outside. By the second spring, Kate had redecorated almost every room in the house and was heartily sick of wallpaper and soft furnishings. Having just finished the third coat of magnolia needed to hide what could only be described as the diarrhoea-yellow bathroom, she sat down on the back step for a coffee.

In front of her lay the jumble of brambles and grass, but amongst it, here and there, small flowers were emerging. A patch of what she had assumed was as wild and uncared for as all the rest, was sprouting into life. She plucked one of the new green shoots and breathed in fresh oregano. A quick search among the weeds and she had found sage, tarragon and thyme, plus some very happy looking mint sprouting from an old porcelain sink – Kate was hooked.

That year she, and John, when he could be persuaded, worked their way through the garden, weeding here, turning the soil there, all the time finding old gems to be kept and forming new plans of how to make the garden useable again. The big surprise came late that July when one of the apple trees at the bottom of the garden produced a great crop of 'Lyman's Large Summer', which proved not just edible, but delicious.

On paper the plans were straightforward: beat the borders into place, bring to life the small lawn, dredge the pond, cut back the brambles and open up the herb and adjacent vegetable patch. By the time the nights started drawing in and the frogs in the newly cleared pond had stopped singing, the Carbones still had a mountain of work to do, but they had already made big inroads and Kate now had a whole winter to plan next year's attack. The following year the first seeds went into the vegetable patch and later the Carbones tasted their first harvest. OK – it consisted of three oddly shaped carrots and some marrows so small that calling them zucchini would have been flattering, but they tasted so out of this world that the couple vowed to make next year's harvest bigger and better still.

So it was that order came to the borders and beds. The Saturday morning visit to the local garden centre became a feature of every weekend. When George and Henry came along it was also a great way to get a few minutes' quiet while the kids rammed cake into their mouths in the coffee shop. The big pile of weeds that built up at the bottom of the garden was tidied into a large compost bin which then produced nutritious organic matter to fork into the beds. John, though not quite as enamoured with the plant side of things, took to the role of chief composter with real energy. Each week he could be found checking it to see how much compost he was getting, feeding it with a mix of grass clippings, plant cuttings and the occasional shredded cardboard box, and wagging his finger at the kids when they chucked on indestructible weeds like bindweed or couch grass. One weekend at the garden centre he spotted a wormery and, a sucker for a new bit of kit, was unpacking worms-and-all at the kitchen table an hour later, much to Kate's dismay.

Each year the area of the vegetable patch increased in size, with the Carbones trying all sorts of different things. One year they (and their friends, neighbours and work colleagues) were rather overwhelmed by the pounds of runner beans the garden produced. Another year George and Henry had all but gone on hunger strike after a bigger than expected crop had meant carrot soup/curry/salad/stir fry for lunch for two whole weeks. As the Carbones' experience grew, and the amounts of useful food they produced leapt, Kate began to realise just how much this gardening could help the family out. Money, as always, was tight; hardly having to buy vegetables from the supermarket each week really helped the grocery bill, even if she did blow most of those savings at the weekend on her trips to the garden centre. Now, with the bump starting to kick each time she kneels to pull out another weed, John, Kate, George and Henry get through most of the summer and much of the autumn without having to buy vegetables at all. Though the Carbones today are better off, the thought of home-made apple purée for the new bundle of Carbone joy, rather than the mass-produced supermarket stuff, is a big added bonus. Indeed, Kate has plans afoot to make the garden work even harder.

This year she's going to turn over a section of herbaceous border to blackcurrant bushes and a pear tree. Her ultimate aim is to sail straight through both the fruit and vegetable aisles in the supermarket every week, something George and Henry have always wanted, but to do this without also condemning the family to scurvy. Meanwhile John plans to build a glasshouse. He already has dreams of growing the sweetest ever satsumas and chillies so hot that even Ted from next door will have to cry when he tastes John's chilli dip at the street barbecue. A glasshouse will also help the supply of cucumbers and tomatoes and give them salad leaves right into the depths of autumn, something they miss when dropping temperatures and day lengths mean they can no longer just nip into the back garden and fill a bowl for the dinner table.

Quite apart from the obvious benefits of the Carbones' garden – the exercise, enjoyment and assurance about the quality of the food they're eating – Kate's hobby-come-obsession makes big inroads into the family's greenhouse emissions. As we saw, our food often carries a big climate tag, especially if transported long distances. With an expanded vegetable patch, fruit trees and a glasshouse, the emissions savings will total almost a tonne.

Growing some food in the garden, as well as composting yard trimmings and kitchen scraps, makes a real dent in the family's contribution to global warming. To reduce the climate change-related dangers of spending time outdoors even further, there are several other possibilities. In some gardens emissions can be reduced by planting trees. Aside from the carbon dioxide that the trees suck out of the atmosphere as they grow (every cubic metre of wood locks up around 800 kg of carbon dioxide) they can shade the house in the summer and so help keep the air-conditioning quiet. More garden shade, along with more careful irrigation, less lawn and more drought-tolerant plants, can also minimise water use. Even here in rain-soaked Britain there are plans afoot to build an energy-hungry desalination plant to meet soaring demands for fresh water.

Finally in the garden, there's yet more stuff. As gardens have become 'extra rooms' they've also become prone to the same array of furniture, accessories, gadgets and toys as our homes. Buying less garden tat saves emissions in just the same way as does eschewing a pasta maker for your kitchen or nose hair trimmer for the bathroom. Less stuff equals less embodied energy. Even the choice of the more necessary garden gadgets matters: for those with gardens on the smaller side, changing the lawnmower from a powered to a 'push' model can reduce emissions by another 40 kg a year. Or, like car share, there's always the option of mower-sharing with a friendly neighbour. As for those patio heaters? For every artificially heated outdoor soirée these can belch over 10 kg of greenhouse gas into the sky. That's a third of a tonne for a year's worth of barbecues. Instead, put on another jumper before you go outside. If you need one just write to me: I have some lovely woolly numbers thanks to Nana Reay.

The incentives to curb the greenhouse emissions from our backyards, be it through more recycling and a lighter bin, or by planting herbs at the back door, are big. You may well do most of these things already; if not, maybe the threat of those malaria-swapping, carcinoma-inducing barbecues will spur you to action. If not, here's something that will spur even the most gadget-loving, gas-guzzling sceptic into action: money.

**Table 4** Potential for cuts in backyard greenhouse emissions (% of 2 tonnes per household per year).

|  | Reduce | Reuse | Recycle | Compost | Home-grown |
|---|---|---|---|---|---|
| Greenhouse gas savings | | | | | |
|  | Up to 70% | Up to 30% | Up to 30% | Up to 50% | Up to 100% |

# 6

## money matters

Get past the first page of any energy-saving booklet and, alongside the smug-looking faces, you'll see the financial benefits of energy efficiency writ large. Long ago, pamphlet writers and policy makers realised that our pockets are a great way to prod us into action. This carrot strategy – insulate your home and you'll save enough money in five years to buy a new car or a holiday in the Maldives – is rife. But, as you've probably spotted, there's a flaw. Less heat wastage in the home equals more money equals bigger car/more holidays/a new fetlock volumiser. It's effectively pollution swapping: exchanging the emissions of home heating for those of longer flights or more embodied energy in the form of stuff.

For every coin we earn, for every free moment in our lives, something has been produced on which to spend that cash and fill that moment. We work hard to be able to while away the weekend in the shopping mall buying stuff. But no matter how hard we work, however big our pay rises or credit extensions, there's always more to buy. The green movement is continually faced with this problem. They tell us to pare down our lifestyles, to reject the consumerism that defines our waking days and save the planet for future generations. But once we've got our composting toilet, introduced the perplexed Merino sheep to the back lawn and installed the hand loom in the spare bedroom, we want to know what else we can buy. Where can we get our retail therapy now?

The answer is for the government-sponsored booklet in the dentist's waiting room to make the wider connection. If we knew that the climate benefits of better home insulation would be wiped out by our buying a bigger car, then we'd more likely spend the money saved on something else. Sustainability is the watchword here and it is down this rocky road that money and climate change are pushing and pulling us with increasing urgency.

Say you improve your insulation. Within five years, you'll have saved back the cost. Or, looked at another way, you'll have saved enough to upgrade your train pass to first class, or to convert your car to dual fuel, or to spend more on local, seasonal food with fewer food miles. Save enough and you could make that down payment on the solar water heating, or even work fewer hours each month. Or, more prosaically, your 'climate dividend' could simply dent your overdraft.

The relationship between money and the climate doesn't stop at making some savings on electricity bills from using low-energy lights. The many and varied ways in which climate change will hit our lives will, in most cases, hit our pockets too. We face a future of paying extra to repair damage to property, cars, gardens and health. Plus there could be soaring taxes, aimed at reducing our emissions and helping governments cope with rising sea levels, failing crops, more severe storms and the rest.

Over in Alabama at Casa Carbone there are big changes afoot, not least the arrival of someone whose generation will be lumbered with the global heating bill we're busy running up. Kate Carbone, as so often, is in the garden. Her full-term cotton-covered bump is obscuring the weeds at her feet and her back is aching like hell. Slumping down on the back step Kate admires her thriving plot – the rows of carrots and swelling pumpkins that, mashed to an orangey pulp, will make perfect baby fodder. Such sunlit dreams of feeding time and carroty faces will have to wait though – the back ache's worse and these contractions have never heard of Braxton Hicks. Time to phone John and get panting.

Twelve hours and 16 high-stepping laps of the maternity ward later the Carbones have a very cross, but healthy, daughter. Grandma Carbone brings in George and Henry carrying, respectively, a bear four times the size of the baby and an activity centre with 'real train noises'. As the Carbones gather around the pale, smiling Kate and the well-wrapped baby, the question of the moment is "What's she called?". Suggestions range from Ruby (Grandma Carbone – "it was your Great Aunt's name"), through Belinda (George – "My rabbit's a girl too"), to Buffy (Henry – "I'm 8 and she's my hero"). John and Kate are already decided though: Lucy Carbone has arrived.

Lucy has been born into an affluent family in the richest and most powerful country on the planet. She has opportunities that babies in the developing world can only dream of. Nonetheless, she too faces a lifelong battle with intensifying and accelerating climate change and a powerful sense of disgust at the knowing profligacy of her elders. If kids ever needed an excuse to hate their parents then Lucy Carbone and her contemporaries have a cracker in global warming.

She doesn't know it yet, her thoughts currently being centred more on nipples than work, but Lucy is destined for a glittering career in banking. Cut to 28 years hence (apply wobbly time travel effect as appropriate) and we find our Lucy at work as a team leader in the PR section of a thriving multinational bank. At 28 years old Lucy is still surrounded by those who did the job when every week brought another trans-America trip to meet the San Francisco team or red-eye flight to liaise with the Zurich branch. Now, in response to soaring air travel costs and the ease of virtual conferencing, Lucy rarely steps on a plane, with weekly international meetings occurring from the comfort of her own desk.

Outside Lucy's office window the parking lot has changed almost beyond recognition. The cars are smaller than today's and there are fewer of them. The area for car parking has been pushed back towards the boundary fence; the space close to the building has been turned over to cycle racks. Bike-buying grants started rolling out over a decade ago and for those living too far away to cycle, the car-sharing scheme is a must – arrive alone in a car and the already steep parking charges are doubled.

Even the building Lucy works in is different. It looks just as shiny and utilitarian as the corporate office blocks of today, but beneath the surface its construction is in line with much higher energy efficiency standards. Walls and floors have top spec. insulating properties, windows are situated to maximise passive heating and cooling, and even the revolving front door is designed to keep the temperature stable. No crumpled recycling trays in the bins here. Now each office in Lucy's building must by law have a recycling and energy-saving policy. Every floor has an energy officer and faces a green audit as part of annual accounting. Thermostats and lighting levels are checked and optimised, electricity and paper-saving options on office equipment are set as defaults, and anyone repeatedly throwing recyclable stuff in the waste bin gets a caution.

As the days are crossed off a dozen calendars around the office and the talk around the low-energy water cooler becomes dominated by holiday plans, yet more transformations are apparent. Jet-setting holidays are now off the agenda for most people, as a combination of emissions taxes and increased concern about global warming boosts tourism at home. It's not only climate-awareness that has changed the global tourist map. Holidays, even before Lucy was born, were changing for the Carbones. By the time it's her turn to flick through the online brochures, some of the destinations we currently flock to have dropped off the tourist radar altogether, the remnants of their heyday now little more than fading postcards.

Just as Mexico – the destination of choice for millions of sun-seeking Americans – got too hot for the Carbones, so the European equivalents faced temperatures that forced the tourist lifeblood of the economy ever further north. Jet travel, initially seen as a boon for tourism, has for many become a curse. The very same jets that in the 20th century flew in millions of visitors were at the same time driving the climate change that now keeps the tourists away.

Coral reefs once lured millions to resorts in the Caribbean, Australia and south-east Asia each year, along with billions of tourist dollars. By the time Lucy fancies a holiday underwater, many of these reefs and their resorts have disappeared owing to rising sea temperatures, over-fishing and pollution.

Today, dive tourism brings $2 billion a year to the Caribbean. Add to this the value of the reefs to the fishing industry and as protection from the sea, and these crusty wildlife havens earn the area between $3 billion and $4.5 billion every year. By 2015 it's estimated that these revenues could be tumbling by almost a third of a billion dollars each year, as tourists bypass the Caribbean for less degraded beaches on which to strut their stuff.

Down under, the Great Barrier Reef currently earns the Australian tourist industry over AUS$4 billion. Here the same threats to the coral, its wildlife, and the livelihoods that depend on it are apparent. Some scientists predict that up to 95% of all living coral in the reef will have disappeared by the middle of this century. The economic costs of such a die-back have been estimated at AUS$8 billion dollars and 12,000 jobs by the year 2020.

In his book *Last Chance to See*, the late great Douglas Adams visited numerous animal species on the brink of extinction and highlighted the need for their protection. Such action is vital for ecosystems and endangered species, and for the people who depend upon them. Just as reefs bring tourists and their wallets, so too do the iguanas of the Galapagos, the kiwis of New Zealand and the orang-utans of Borneo. Concern over damage to many ecosystems and the disappearance of animal and plant species has spawned the whole new holidaying ethos of 'ecotourism'. Faster than you can say 'handmade dominos', ecotourism has grown into an industry worth billions of dollars a year. The basic premise is that those visiting rainforests, savannah and the like should ensure the protection of the ecosystem and of the local economy. You therefore return with photos and stories, rather than the more traditional lump of dyed coral, mass-produced orang-utan doll, or slowly decomposing elephant's foot stool.

Unfortunately, rapid rises in sea level, temperature and rainfall won't be stopped by all the locally produced didgeridoos or low-impact nature walks in the world. It has been estimated that climate change could push up to a third of all plant and animal species to extinction during the 21st century, from the gibbons whooping through the forest to the wriggling bugs they eat. Whole ecosystems will be undermined with unknown impacts up and down food chains, of which we are usually part. The millions of people who rely on the flow of tourist money brought in by local wildlife will see their livelihoods disappear along with the last lonely cry of that final gibbon.

No Borneo jungle or St Lucia diving holiday for Lucy then. How about a ski trip? If she goes high enough, or the resort has enough snow machines, no problem, but many resorts that people visited in droves when Lucy was born are long gone by the time she collects her first lift pass. In some places that once saw a reliable 40 inches a year, snow has quite literally become thin on the ground.

Each winter I spend a lot of time flicking from one weather forecast to another, trying to find one that predicts snow for West Lothian. Many are the nights I can be found peeking out between the curtains to see if the 5% chance of snow predicted has given me an excuse for a day at home, drinking hot chocolate and building snow forts. Invariably it hasn't. This may annoy me and my wife, who has to put up either with a cold-footed husband moaning about climate change or a half-demented husband dancing around in celebration of a few snowflakes. For many in Scotland though, the failure of winter to bring any reliable snow spells unemployment. The ski industry in Scotland was never massive, being worth around £30 million a year at its peak. But what there is is now shrinking at an alarming rate. During winter 2004 – another characterised by little snow and by midge bites in January – two of Scotland's five ski resorts finally gave up the battle against falling revenues and rising temperatures and put themselves up for sale. The situation for the other three resorts looks bleak too and the industry as a whole is unlikely to last another 20 years. For the hundreds of workers in the Scottish ski industry, job losses, like snow-free winters, seem inevitable.

Worldwide the picture for the ski industry is equally grim. In Austria the snow line may rise by more than 300 metres in the next 30 years. On the other side of the world in Australia it's likely that by 2070 none of the existing ski resorts will be viable. Between them they net around AUS$400 million a year. In Switzerland, home of the chocolate box chalet and après-ski bill large enough to bring on snow-blindness, over 60% of the 230 ski resorts could find their snowfall becoming unreliable. Over in Germany and Italy it's a similar story.

Of course, as long as we all still want to go on holiday, someone somewhere will reap our tourist dollars. If the reefs are allowed to degrade too badly in one area but are better protected in another then we'll switch. In 1997 the Alps had little or no snow on the slopes. Instead, Morocco saw a huge surge in visitors to its ski resorts. Scotland's ski industry is going rapidly downhill, but warmer summers coupled with the Mediterranean becoming uncomfortably hot may simply shift the tourist boom to the middle of the year.

The tourist industry is not the only one facing great uncertainty. Severe weather can ruin farmers within a matter of minutes. Ice storms, like those in the USA and Canada in 1998, may kill many hundreds of cattle. Drought, like that resulting from the 1997–98 El Niño, can wipe out entire harvests – in New Zealand alone it cost well over half a billion NZ dollars.

If working the sea, rather than the land, calls, then a career in sailing might well be a better option than fishing. There's no denying that systematic over-exploitation has caused many of the crashes in world fish stocks and attendant job losses. But in many instances, North Sea cod for instance, rising sea temperatures make such crashes more rapid, and potentially more permanent. Separating the effects of over-fishing and global warming is difficult. But together they have led cod stocks to fall from over 250,000 tonnes in the 1970s to less than one fifth of that amount today. In the UK, 15,000 fishermen face the prospect of cod becoming commercially extinct in the next five years.

Foresters too face an uncertain future. More carbon dioxide should help some trees grow more quickly, but will also bring more pests, sustained droughts and the potential loss of large areas of forest due to storm damage. An average temperature hike of 2 °C during this century would push the ideal range of many US forest species about 320 km north. Such shifts are fine when species have millennia to colonise the warming north and retreat from the baking south. Given less than 100 years they'd need to be migrating north at over 3 km a year – way beyond what many trees can manage.

Tree surgeons meanwhile will be turning work away. In its 'great storm' of 1987 the UK lost an estimated 15 million trees. Kent's famous village of Sevenoaks (one-time home of

'Bloomsbury Set' writer and garden designer Vita Sackville West) became 'Oneoak and some rather large logs', and the nation's tree surgeons got a year's worth of business overnight. Builders should also be in the money. There will be a lot more repair and construction work, from subsidence damage and buckling roads to new flood defences and energy efficiency improvements.

John Carbone's line – insurance – could be an extremely rocky one depending on the people and assets a company insures. At the moment, the average person in the USA spends over $2,500 each year on insurance premiums. Between the mid-1980s and the late 1990s, weather damage, from storms and floods to tornados and drought, cost an estimated $253 billion, with 40% of this being privately insured. These already huge costs are rising fast. Climate change is playing a part, but so is wealth. Each year there are more people with more stuff in the way of more severe weather. If insurers are essentially gamblers, then the odds are getting worse and worse. Given the high standard of living in the USA, and the vulnerability of many US citizens, the potential financial losses are huge. Add together the value of properties along the Gulf and Atlantic coasts, from the beach condos to the Taj Mahal wannabes, and you've got well over $3 trillion of real estate sitting next to a swelling sea.

In 1990 flooding hit 23,000 people along the coastlines of Europe. If we fail to take action, then by the 2080s we will see around 5 million people a year suffering the same fate. A 1 metre rise in sea level would flood the homes of over three and a half million people in the Netherlands – a quarter of the population. It would cost $186 billion and destroy over 200 square kilometres of land.

The insurance offices of the world are having an increasingly bad time as weather-related claims soar. Between 1969, and 1998, 650 US insurers went bankrupt, 50 of these as a direct result of natural disasters. Hurricane Andrew in 1992 and the ice storm of 1998 cost them dear and spurred efforts to better model disasters and plan the siting of buildings, abandon high-risk insurance, or hang up those pinstripe suits altogether.

The costs of the 1998 ice storm were huge. In the USA and Canada it led to over 800,000 insurance claims to a value of more than a billion dollars. There were 45 deaths, over 5 million people were left without power, and 17.5 million acres of US forest was damaged. Workers in Canada lost a billion dollars in wages, with the agricultural sector haemorrhaging a further $25 million in livestock and crop losses.

In Europe, the story is similar. Severe storms in the 1990s clocked up heavy insurance losses. 'Daria', in 1990, cost France, Germany and the UK almost $6 billion and killed 95 people; the very next month storm 'Vivian' crashed its way along the North Sea coast, costing $4 billion and killing 64. Floods too have taken a heavy toll: the 1996 Odra flood in central Europe killed over 100 people and caused $5 billion worth of damage. Global economic losses from catastrophic events rose ten-fold from the 1950s to the 1990s. A single heavy hailstorm that struck Sydney in 1999 cost around a billion dollars.

These severe events that keep insurers awake at night are set to become more frequent and more intense. In response, premiums have already increased, with some areas becoming uninsurable because of repeated flooding. Even householders in low-risk areas might soon face having to pay excess to get cover for extreme weather.

The terrible thing about rapid climate change for insurers is that it doesn't fit with how they've usually done business. It used to be enough to ask "How often do we have storms with hailstones the size of baseballs?" and set the premium for car windscreens accordingly. When formerly 1-in-50-year or 1-in-100-year events may start to occur every year, or in areas where they've never been seen before, it all gets rather trying for insurers clutching their historical event tables.

Governments are also footing big bills and so, through taxes, are we. The Canadian administration spent around $15 billion on disaster relief between 1982 and 1999, while in the USA such payments amounted to $119 billion between 1977 and 1993. Hurricane Andrew cost over $15 billion as it ripped through the south-eastern USA in 1992. The same hurricane today would cost double, with inflation adding to the fact that a lot more property and people would be in its path.

By the time Lucy is looking for her first home, her choice is led much more strongly by climate change than the first-time buyers of today. "Is it in a flood risk area?" is something she asks even before looking into the number of bedrooms. Her next questions are: How prone is the area to storms? How hot does it get in the summer? Is the area home to West Nile Virus/ Malaria/Chagas disease? For a property free of all these Lucy will pay handsomely.

Today, even homes in the safest locations face costly increases in buildings insurance. In the UK the creeping cracks of subsidence already cost over $600 million a year. The Association of British Insurers predicts that the figure will rise to $4 billion a year by the middle of this century. A real deal-breaker question for home-buyers of the future will be "How is it heated and lit?". With electricity, oil and gas prices at all-time highs, no first-time buyer will afford a house with poor insula-tion or inefficient heaters and lights. When Lucy goes looking, solar panels aren't some estate agent oddity, but a standard fix-ture akin to an *en suite* bathroom.

Several governments have already introduced grant schemes designed to encourage more climate-aware living. These include help with the upgrading of heating systems, insulation, solar power, dual-fuel car conversion and buying compost bins. In the future we are likely to see more subsidies for renewable energy use, low-waste households, public transport and bicycle use, and more energy-efficient white goods – some carrots to go with the many sticks.

The aisles of the local supermarket in 2030 will likely look very different. Hand-tied chives? Take a hike. Hopefully, the food miles of each item will be labelled. Increased taxes on air-freight will mean if you want fruit and vegetables out of season from the other side of the world you'll have to make do with ocean-shipped produce, and pay a premium for it. The plastic-sheathed bananas of today should have gone, along with the triple wrapping on meat and dairy produce.

At the checkout there's no rack of carrier bags. If Lucy doesn't bring her own she pays through the nose for decomposable bags (refund on return). And her grocery bill? The estimates for the impact of global warming on worldwide food production are, given the uncertainty involved, wide ranging. The broad consensus is that if we see a global temperature rise of 2.5 °C or more then, as well as a multitude of other problems, we can all expect the cost of food to rise, with cereal prices surging by up to 45%.

Back home, having eaten her food-mile-lite dinner, there's less trash on the worktops and no throwing what there is into the wheely bin. Lucy separates plastics, metals and paper for recycling and sorts her leftover food for composting or collection. Too much in the bin at the end of the week and a fine is taped to it the next day. In fact, this already happens in some parts of the USA and Europe. 'Pay As You Throw' households shell out for every bag of waste. These schemes, though in their infancy, typically increase recycling rates by 30 to 60%.

As climate change intensifies, the financial carrots and sticks it creates will alter our lifestyles and pound our pockets. What though, if we could bill people for their emissions? What if we could charge the owner of the SUV next door, or the jet-setting advertising executive down the road, for the extra burden they place on our climate?

Imagine, for a moment, their hallways. The post has been delivered and there, amongst the usual heap of junk mail, lies what is obviously a bill. This is no ordinary bill: it is a demand for the damage they've done, it's an invoice from countless people, most of whom they've never heard of, in countries they've never visited: this is their own personal emissions statement.

The widely accepted range (accepted because it's so wide) is that every tonne of greenhouse gas emitted causes damage costing between $2 and $80. This is not terribly precise. For argument's sake, let's take the midpoint of these extremes, and say that every tonne of greenhouse gas costs $40 through flood and storm damage, crop failures, increased health care and the rest. The Carbones are responsible for over 39 tonnes of greenhouse emissions annually. This adds up to around $1,500 of damage every year for this typical US family. Simply driving an SUV takes these so-called externalities (nothing to do with bumper stickers or hub-caps) up an extra $500 a year.

What then might the world's big corporations be liable for? Recent studies have made a direct connection between human greenhouse emissions and weather-related disasters, such as the 2003 heatwave in Europe. If, for instance, the more than 20,000 deaths that resulted from this scorching summer were linked to the global warming contribution of

**Table 5** The annual Carbone emissions bill (in $ worth of planet damage).

| | Cars | Air travel | Home energy | Food |
|---|---|---|---|---|
| Carbone emissions bill | | | | |
| $1,500 | $720 | $100 | $520 | $180 |

some of the world's largest greenhouse gas emitters, litigation lawyers everywhere would be totting up one hell of claim.

Using the estimate of $40 per tonne of greenhouse gas, the annual costs arising from the emissions of some corporations run into many millions, and in some cases billions, of dollars.

Who pays this bill at the moment? In most cases it's whoever's house is flooded, their insurer, or their frantic government and sea defence building programme. Some of these costs will come back to bite the SUV driver and the jet-setting executive through increased taxes. But the global nature of climate change means that the bill is likely to end up on the doormat of someone much poorer.

If the Carbones' emissions cause $1,500 worth of damage, should they be taxed accordingly? In recent years the idea of giving individuals emissions quotas has emerged. Though still mocked as impractical, ineffective or even communist, it is beginning to catch on. There are various versions of the idea in circulation, but essentially they boil down to the same thing: each of us – you, me, Kate and John Carbone, even Lucy – is given a climate-warming allowance, and every time we fill the petrol tank of our car, hike up the heating, or go on a far-flung holiday we use up some or all of that quota. The idea is that by setting such rations, taxing those who over-emit, and rewarding those who don't, our collective emissions will be driven down and some kind of global equity can be reached. Climate credit cards have been suggested, the price of each tank of petrol being debited from your bank and your climate account simultaneously. Need to go over quota? That's going to cost you – say $40 for every extra tonne of greenhouse gas. Keep under quota and you get to sell your unused climate credit and spend the money on a new hair shirt...

The idea's great in theory and I'd love to see it become reality. Getting developed-world governments to commit to such direct taxation of an individual's emissions seems a long way off though. If a handful of disgruntled lorry drivers can bring the UK to a standstill over high fuel duty, as they did in the autumn of 2000, then imagine the reaction in the USA to the news that, instead of 'No New Taxes', everyone will be getting carbon dioxide quotas. Under the ground-breaking Contraction and Convergence model, designed to reduce emissions by the magic 60% by the middle of this century, we would each be allowed to emit 400 kg of carbon a year. Just one long-haul flight would blow a year's allowance. Carbon quotas for individuals will have their day, but if they are to be effective, the truck drivers and everyone else will need to know exactly why they're being made to pay.

From a political perspective new taxes, and increases in existing ones, are inevitable as the effects of global warming begin to bite. Such carbon or climate taxes, designed to discourage energy wastage and fossil fuel use, are likely to be extended from business to include communities and individuals. From extra payments on air travel to charges for more than one sack of rubbish each week, the average family will be under more and more financial pressure to cut greenhouse gas-producing activities. But whereas individual climate-saving actions generally cost nothing or actually save us money, some national or international mitigation measures will be very expensive. The real poser for governments is whether the costs of the destruction that climate change will wreak tomorrow will outweigh the costs of cutting emissions today. For many countries it's obvious: Yes, cut them and fast.

Sea level rise could effectively bring the Netherlands, for example, to its knees. Without mitigating climate change the only other option, besides evolving gills, is for the Dutch to build massive sea defences. The cost of adaptation to such sea level rise is colossal, at over $12 billion. In England and Wales there are currently more than one and a half million properties at risk from flooding. If flooding goes unchecked, instead of the $2 billion currently lost each year, we'd be looking at 20 times this figure by the year 2080.

In Japan, a rich country characterised by cramped low-lying and coastal settlements, sea level rise has similarly devastating potential. A hike of a metre – something we may well face as the 21st century draws to a close – would put at risk over 2,000 square kilometres of this already space-starved nation, endangering over 4 million people and 109 trillion yen's worth of property. The list goes on, the numbers huge. For example, Egypt would face a $35 billion bill from lost tourism, land and property with a 50 cm rise, while Poland would lose $30 billion from a 1 m sea level rise. For Australia and New Zealand the current prediction is for a drop in GDP of between 1% and 4% with a doubling of carbon dioxide. Globally, a doubling of carbon dioxide in our atmosphere may cost over $300 billion a year by the middle of this century.

The Kyoto Protocol is the scarred battleground, where economics and science have been used to suit every interest. This protocol represents the first real step in joined-up international action on climate change. For rich countries with large emissions, the USA and Australia for instance, even the rather limited reductions set out in the protocol would mean some big spending.

Back in 2001 the USA withdrew from Kyoto citing the economic cost it represented as a key reason. The cost of achieving the Kyoto-sized cut that the USA rejected (7% of its emissions in 1990) comes in somewhere between $13 and $397 billion.

So how do the mitigation costs stack up against climate change-driven damage in the USA?

You'd assume that the former must be far in excess of the latter to sustain the US position. Not so. For a doubling of pre-industrial carbon dioxide concentrations, losses of almost $70 billion a year have been estimated for the USA of 2050, health costs alone topping $16 billion a year. If some of the more dire scenarios come to pass (a sea level rise of several metres due to collapse of the West Antarctic ice sheet for example), costs to the USA of many hundreds of billions of dollars are possible. Both action and inaction will therefore present a big bill. A recent study which weighed these two bills against each other concluded the net costs to the USA of complying with its Kyoto commitments would be insignificant (±1% of GDP).

The arcane world of climate change economics will undoubtedly continue to provide ammunition for politicians of every persuasion, especially given the huge ranges of the forecasts. Predictions will get better with time, the ranges will narrow and the financial arguments for action are likely to get ever stronger. Unfortunately, by the time economists have a precise figure on the cost of climate change the flood water will probably be lapping at politicians' doors. While they sit on their hands and wait for the worst, we can get on with tackling global warming in every area of our lives, without requiring international consensus or kow-towing to vested interests.

Can we show our politicians the way? The scientific community warns that a 60% cut in greenhouse emissions is required to avoid catastrophic effects, yet even with a properly working Kyoto Protocol, global emissions will fall by just a few per cent. How then do our own actions stack up alongside the 60% target? Over a lifetime, from how we travel to nursery school to the type of funeral we have, just how big is our own contribution to global warming and how big a dent will climate awareness make?

# 7

## a green inheritance

One of the most distressing things about climate change is its momentum. Much of the greenhouse gas we emit today will go on affecting our planet for centuries. Molecules of carbon dioxide from today's shopping trip or journey to work will still be knocking about in the atmosphere when our grandchildren's grandchildren first emerge into the warmer world of the 22nd century. To use a deliberately ironic metaphor, the effect of all the greenhouse gas we are adding to the atmosphere, day in, day out, is like never-ending snowfall at the top of a glacier. The more snow that falls, the bigger the glacier gets and the more far-reaching its impacts. So every kilogram of carbon dioxide, every extra jet flight or office light, is another flurry to join the world-changing glacier of global warming. The big difference, of course, is that most of the world's real glaciers are shrinking precisely because our greenhouse 'glacier' is growing.

Over a lifetime, each of us clocks up a lot of greenhouse gas, but some are responsible for an awful lot more than others. The sum of every car journey and jet flight, every air-freighted kiwi fruit or plastic wrapped banana, is the global warming legacy we bequeath to all those who come after. Cutting these lifetime emissions, this extra snow on the glacier, holds the key to leaving a greener inheritance.

Just as Lucy Carbone is starting life, with all the decisions about her own lifestyle still to make, Grandma Carbone is reaching the end of her days. Born between the two great wars she has seen the rise in car ownership, home energy use, food consumption and technology that have transformed our world. These same shifts have also been largely responsible for the rapid climate change her granddaughter's generation faces. Grandma Carbone can recall a time when cars were still a novelty, jet travel was yet to be invented, and when the only things that went into the trash after a meal were some well-chewed chicken bones if it was Sunday.

We can't simply go back to a pre-1950s way of living; indeed, few would want to. It's all too easy to don the rose-tinted spectacles and hanker after a time when life was simpler. But this would be to ignore the great leaps forward in technology, healthcare, diet and standard of living that we now enjoy across much of the developed world. On the other hand, the price of this breath-taking development has been a huge growth in greenhouse emissions.

Grandma Carbone was born into the pre-war America of 1932. For the first 18 years of her life she went to school, helped out at home and saw numerous men in her home town, including her own broad-shouldered older brother, leave to fight and never return. The war years were hard, emotionally and economically, for everyone. They were, however, marked by relatively low household energy consumption, lots of home-grown and locally produced food, and no family car. Hence her childhood emissions were very low: just a few hundred kilograms per year. On her 18th birthday Lucy's Grandma met the amiable Lt. Francis Carbone at a dance, fell in love, and within six months was married.

In the hot summer of 1950 the newly married Grandma Carbone moved with her husband into their new house. In their first car – a blue and white Lincoln Capri loaded with suitcases – they pulled into the weed-choked drive of a clapboard house, and so began over forty years of married life – years which, as elsewhere in the world, saw huge changes in travel, home energy use and emissions.

At first Grandma and Grandpa Carbone produced relatively little greenhouse gas. Their car was inefficient, but the average annual distance travelled in the 1950s was substantially less than today. Their Lincoln clocked up less than 6 tonnes of greenhouse gas per year, 3 tonnes for each Carbone. In this first decade of marriage there were no plane journeys; even on their honeymoon they took the train to the Rockies.

The house was draughty but for these 1950s sweethearts the 'more clothes' solution was accepted without a second thought. In Alabama's hot summers they did less work at midday and kept in the shade. Coal-fired heating represented their main source of greenhouse emissions, amounting to about 5 tonnes a year. Household electricity use back then was about a tenth of the average today.

Most of the Carbones' food was locally produced and, thanks to tight budgets and wartime attitudes to waste, their trash was about a third of today's average. Throughout the 1950s then, Grandma Carbone's emissions were low, at about 6 tonnes a year if we split the household equally between her and her husband.

By the end of the 1950s and into the 1960s, things were a-changing. Electricity started replacing coal and wood as the home energy source of choice in the USA. Mains electricity supplies spread out across the country, bringing electric lighting, heating and power for the washing machines, fridges and other white goods that began to appear in the windows of the town stores. With greater supply, low prices and soaring demand, total energy consumption went up and up.

By the mid-1960s energy use in US households had doubled from that when the Carbones first moved in together. Electricity use quadrupled over the same time. Into these heady days of technological progress and nightmarish Cold War threats John Carbone was born, adding his own, initially small, contribution to the greenhouse emissions of the Carbone household.

In the 1970s the energy revolution was in full swing. Household emissions across the developed world soared. By 1975 home energy use in the USA had leapt to three times that in 1950. The Lincoln Capri was traded-in for a more stylish family car with an engine even less efficient than the family's 1950s roadster; it did fewer than 14 miles per gallon.

With each passing year, the greenhouse emissions of Grandma Carbone kept on rising. Labour-saving devices appeared in her kitchen, as in others. The fridges and washing machines of the 1960s were just the first scouts in kitchens, leading the way for today's army of tumble dryers, dishwashers, and eventually bread makers and fondue sets. By the time in the late 1980s that John Carbone left his family home, it, like many US houses, had air-conditioning, a microwave, two refrigerators and three TV sets. All around the house little red standby lights had taken up residence, the tell-tale sign of this appliance-invasion steadily eating its way through kilowatt hour after kilowatt hour of electricity.

By this time Grandma Carbone and her husband were travelling a lot further by car, jetting to Mexico for holidays and buying more exotic food. Even their once-echoing rubbish bin was filling up fast.

When, in the late 1960s, the young John Carbone first escaped the watchful eye of his mother and slipped out of the front door into the quiet lane outside, seeing a car was still quite a big event. Across the country the number of car owners amounted to 70 million – a select club compared to the 200 million cars on US roads today.

Imagine a time-lapse camera set up outside the Carbone house, trained on that dusty track of the 1950s. Its first shot is the pink-cheeked Grandma Carbone and her husband drawing into the driveway, full of dreams of their married life to come. Now, speed through the years. To begin with, the road sees just the occasional flash of a car; then the surface goes from dirt track to tarmac and the flashes of cars come thicker and faster. By the 1980s, the cars on the road start to blur together – the road has been widened and the traffic roar is increasing. Once it was a lane to ride bikes along, whose puddles served as oceans for paper boats; today, even playing near the 'lane' is a no-no. Now the blur of cars continues into the night.

The same insidious change would be seen had we pointed our time-lapse camera into the sky. A clear blue canvas to begin with – the skies over Alabama home to just a handful of planes each day and, before the war, no jets at all. Then, as the years roll by, more and more streaks start criss-crossing the sky as air travel begins to boom. Speed our camera up and it looks as though a three-year-old has been let loose with a box of chalks. The rate of growth in air travel since the 1950s has been astounding. Today there are 19,000 airports in the USA alone; together they see 9 million departures every year, subjecting over half a billion passengers to looped in-flight movies and vacuum-packed trout à la crème.

The Carbones' main airport, Birmingham, is not exactly JFK. In 1931 it was headline news when the airport was visited by its first passenger plane. By the mid-1980s it had around 40 departures a day. Then came cheaper fares and flying as the norm for both work and holidays. By 2000, Birmingham airport was sending over 80 departures into the skies of Alabama every day. Globally, this kind of air-traffic growth has been repeated again and again: well over a billion passengers now zip about on the world's airlines each year (Figure 14).

Go to the quietest spot you know, somewhere a long way from the nearest roads, where nature still seems to hold complete dominion and the sheer wildness of it all sends a shudder down your spine. Now look up. Chances are you'll find you're not alone. High in the skies above there will be a jet packed with business people, holidaymakers or hand-tied chives, marking its route with a long white vapour trial, and laying out its greenhouse gas nets like it's the last day of the fishing season.

You get a real sense of just how many flights are passing overhead at any given moment from the effect that the terrorist

All flights for 09/03/01 for Hour 0 Above 25,000 ft.

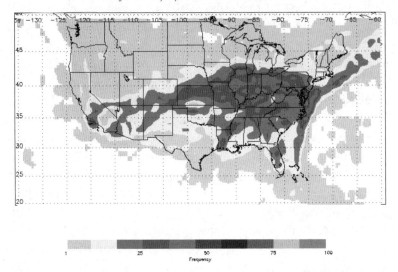

**Figure 14** Flight frequency over the USA, 3 September 2001 (Patrick Minnis, NASA Langley Cloud and Radiation Group, USA).

All flights for 09/11/01 for Hour 23 Above 25,000 ft.

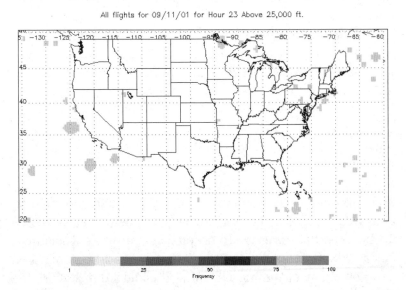

**Figure 15** Flight frequency over the USA, 11 September 2001 (Patrick Minnis, NASA Langley Cloud and Radiation Group, USA).

attacks of 11 September 2001 had on a satellite's view (Figure 15). The skies were suddenly emptied of the thousands of jets normally making their way across the USA. For a brief window, while all air traffic was grounded, the skies became clear and sombrely quiet.

Back to the climate impact of Grandma Carbone's life and the 1990s. She and her husband retired in 1992 and their emissions finally started to fall. No more trips to work meant a cut in their annual car travel. But they had more spending power and more time. Why have one jet-setting holiday a year when you can have three? Why have a small runabout when you can afford a Jaguar? More time at home also means more energy use there. Overall, the greenhouse emissions during retirement for Grandma Carbone and Grandpa Carbone remained large. Only after her husband died did emissions really start to drop back when Grandma Carbone swapped the gas-guzzler and draughty house for a nippy runabout and a well-insulated retirement flat.

For Grandma Carbone the picture is almost complete. After more than 70 years of life, most of it very happy and all of it in a fast-changing world, there is one final (and potentially big) addition to her lifetime's climate legacy.

The Carbones are in mourning. Two nights ago the phone rang and a softly spoken casualty nurse told them that Grandma Carbone had been rushed to hospital after a stroke. The ambulance crew had done everything, but she had been declared dead on arrival at the hospital. After the initial devastation, the Carbones are slowly coming to terms with her death and their minds are turning to arrangements. Already, John has contacted a local funeral director to discuss the service and burial, all the time fielding calls from friends and relatives.

Grandma Carbone had never talked about wanting a specific type of interment, though she regularly said that the last thing she wanted was a lot of fuss. In the end the family opts for a traditional send-off. They arrange for the so-called 'Presidential' option. This all-inclusive package comprises three limousines to take close relatives to and from the service, four pall bearers, a top-of-the-range coffin, and a steel-lined concrete vault, with a 50-year no-rust guarantee.

This final steel-clad send-off for Grandma Carbone sends one last large belch of greenhouse gas into the waiting skies, the final kilograms of a lifetime's climate bequest.

Given that death comes to all of us, opting for a climate-aware funeral is one way we can guarantee a greener inheritance. Our burial is the last chance any of us will have to either improve or worsen the climate we leave to those left behind. Funerals may not appear to be that big an issue climate-wise, but once you enter their velvet-curtained world, the huge amounts of material and energy used show just how important this final choice can be.

The Valley of the Kings has nothing on the sheer mass of material we bury each year. In the USA alone, over 1.5 million tonnes of concrete and 14,000 tonnes of steel is sunk into funeral vaults. A further 90,000 tonnes of steel goes into funeral caskets, along with nearly 3,000 tonnes of copper and bronze. Remember embodied energy? Burials in the USA produce over 1.5 million tonnes of greenhouse gas every year – equivalent to the emissions of about 200,000 big cars. All this comes atop the environmental damage resulting from the embalming fluid (800,000 gallons per year) and hardwood (30 million square feet) used in US burials each year.

In a world where success is often judged by the size and expense of the car someone drives, it was inevitable that more and more of us would demand the Rolls Royces of the hereafter. Casket makers haven't let us down. At some point most of us will be faced with a brochure detailing the ways in which we can give our loved ones the send-off they deserve and, in the small print, how this will bankrupt us. Glossy page after glossy page describes boxes with names like 'The Statesman' or 'Excelsior' with the blurb stating just how thick the brass plating is, what flowers are embroidered on the silk interior, and whether the things come with an air- and watertight seal as standard.

Let's push the boat out. What can we get that says to everyone else in the cemetery "My family thought so much of me they remortgaged their house just to pay for my funeral"? How about a 'Sultan'? A snip at $6,000, this solid bronze number is lined with crushed velvet, has a seal guaranteed against rust, water or air entry for 50 years, and even comes with a discount on the 'Cambridge' vault. The vault? Well, the 'Cambridge' offers true quality and peace of mind, it being earthquakeproof up to a Richter scale of 5.4. Its steel-reinforced concrete construction, over a tonne in weight, comes complete with name plate and water seals. Inside, it complements the polished bronze of the 'Sultan' beautifully with its own thick bronze lining, just $10,000 all-in.

And the climate tag: over a tonne of greenhouse gas.

If you really want to Rest In Peace there is a lot of weighing up to be done. Both the standard options – cremation and traditional burial – have positive and negative aspects, climate-wise. Cremation using natural gas uses about 20 gallons of gas, while that with fuel oil gets through about 30 gallons per person (the research for this chapter wasn't a barrel of laughs), leading to emissions equivalent to about 120 kg and 300 kg respectively. Added to this are the emissions arising from the burning of the body itself. The amounts are relatively small at around 120 kg of greenhouse gas per person. In total, having your body cremated is likely to result in about half a tonne of greenhouse gas. Not great, but still better than the 'bells and whistles' burial. But cremation has the big drawback of causing air pollution. Mercury and dioxins from crematoria are now strictly controlled in most countries.

Burial, on the other hand, avoids air pollution problems and can be the more climate-friendly option – if the embodied energy involved in elaborate caskets and chambers is side-stepped. 'Green' burials now account for a significant and growing percentage of funerals. These aim to reduce the over-all environmental damage, with the impacts on air, water and soil all being considered. For an alternative casket, options include biodegradable body bags, cardboard or bamboo cof-fins, and wooden caskets sourced from renewable forestry. Such burials turn the premise of hermetically sealed vaults on its head. Instead of entombing the casket inside a thick, con-crete-lined vault to prevent any soil-based decomposition for generations, green burials are designed to allow the straight-forward breakdown of both casket and body in the soil.

Grandma Carbone's life was one of rapidly increasing emis-sions as living standards and energy use across the developed world rose following the spartan years of the Second World War. Her lifetime and in-death emissions amount to almost 800 tonnes. This is a small hill next to the Everest of her son's gift to the climate, born as he as into a world where gases from trans-port, homes, food and waste were already high and climbing higher.

John Carbone has already amassed three times the emissions his parents had at the same age. But what of his new daughter?

Will her lifetime emissions be even higher than her father's? The Carbones are already helping to reduce Lucy's contribution. From Kate growing much of the baby food, to her mode of transport being a small car rather than the over-sized people carrier of former years, the Carbones are at least making a dent in the Lucy-related greenhouse emissions. They may even be taking some of the heat out of the teenage blame-fests they will face in the future.

What if Lucy were to take climate awareness through into her adult life? What if she lived a low-emissions life: driving a smaller car, avoiding energy wastage in the home, buying more local food, and the like? If we were to stack up such actions, nothing too hair-shirty – no composting toilets or dancing on hilltops with shrubbery in her hair – just choices that fitted with her everyday life, what's the bottom line?

Indulge me with the plotting of another graph (Figure 16; a handful of pie charts was never going to keep the inner scientist at bay). Compare a climate-aware Lucy with a climate-ignorant one: how the emissions build up for these two Alabama girls and how the climate impact they bequeath to the

**Figure 16** Lifetime emissions of (left) climate-ignorant Lucy and (right) climate-aware Lucy.

world diverges over a lifetime. Let's see where we may all be heading.

On the surface we have two identical Lucy Carbones: one our climate-aware Lucy, born into an increasingly environmentally friendly Carbone household. The other is a Lucy Carbone of climate ignorance. The latter Lucy grows up in the Carbone household where John never did get embarrassed about his big car, where recycling always remained something the left-wing neighbours did, and where Kate's garden was little more than a large patch of concrete and weeds. We'll assume that no magic bullets to tackle climate change have appeared, and that fossil fuels continue to dominate the lives of the two Lucys, just as they have dominated all of ours.

Over at the climate-ignorant Carbone household, things are already stacking up for the baby Lucy. Until she leaves home, many of her emissions are down to the decisions of her parents. Even before she emerged, red-faced and angry this Lucy already had had a raft of important choices made on her behalf. The newly decorated baby bedroom is crammed with enough electronic monitoring devices to put the FBI to shame. Stacked boxes along one wall hold an army of battery-operated activity centres, dolls and singing bears. Nothing, not one pair of baby booties nor one cloth picture book, is second-hand. Everything is brand-spanking new, with the full embodied energy penalty of all this stuff dumped straight onto the tiny shoulders of the ignorant Miss Carbone. This is just the beginning.

Once the Lucys reach 18 months it's straight into the nursery run. While the climate-aware Carbones opt to get to nursery by bike, the ignorant Carbones use their four-wheel drive for these short journeys, so producing an extra 200 kg of greenhouse gas each year. As the years click by, the 'Back to school' signs in the mall once again indicate that, for George, Henry and now Lucy, the days of summer are drawing to a close and it is time to shop for new shoes. With junior school comes the choice between school bus and more travel in the car. The climate-ignorant Carbones stick with the 'safety' of the gas-guzzler to ferry Lucy about, adding another 700 kg of greenhouse gas every year to her already ballooning emissions. Our climate-aware Lucy gets the bus.

School holidays? With her parents having no scruples about clocking up tonnes of emissions flying, jet-setting holidays are the norm for the ignorant Lucy. Though the trips in the early years are marked by some ear-shattering crying, hasty breast feeding in the security queue and, on one regrettable occasion, some projectile vomiting at 30,000 ft, the sky-high travel continues. Before she reaches 10 this Lucy has already clocked up 80,000 km and 12 tonnes of greenhouse emissions on jets. Over in the climate-aware Carbone house, their choice to holiday closer to home and avoid the stress and emissions of jet travel mean that the emission gap between the two Lucys has become a chasm.

For the first time, as the Lucys grow through the years at junior school, they become directly responsible for some of their greenhouse gas emissions. Until now our ignorant Lucy could justifiably throw her arms up in the air and flounce around the room at the injustice of being blamed for her high emissions, given that her choice in them has been minimal or nil. Now though, as she goes through junior school, her own choices start to make themselves felt on the climate, these choices reflecting those of her climate-ignorant family.

We're a predictable lot. Despite the rebellion that strikes in our teenage years, we're more than likely to end up voting for the same political party as our parents, eating a similar diet and sounding like them. The effect of our upbringing on our attitudes and behaviour as an adult is powerful, so it's not surprising that the Lucy in the climate-ignorant Carbone house has already begun to follow the example set by her parents and brothers. Initially this takes the form of leaving the television, video, and video games console on all the time. This extra energy adds up to an extra 120 kg of greenhouse each year.

Into high school and adolescence, and ignorant Lucy now likes to turn up the heating at home to a level bordering on that of a sauna. Added together, her boost to energy use in the climate-ignorant Carbone house is now equivalent to an extra tonne of greenhouse gas emissions every year.

Soon the two Lucys have made their roller-coaster way through high school. The time has come for the beanbag to be rammed into the car, the dog to be hugged, and the drive to college made. It's time for the Lucys to start college at New York State.

Having left their family homes, the girls now become much more responsible for their personal greenhouse emissions. One of the first and most important decisions they make is their form of transport. Climate-aware Lucy opts for her bike and public transport, while climate-ignorant Lucy chooses to buy and use a sporty black SUV – each year widening the emissions gap by another 6 tonnes. In their dorm rooms, though they may cover their walls in posters and burn enough incense to make the whole floor smell like an aromatherapy shop, their climate change choices remain limited. However, by setting her computer to sleep mode and by replacing the two light bulbs in her bedroom with energy-efficient ones, our climate-aware Lucy shaves another half a tonne off her annual emissions.

The college years fly. Final exams are duly passed and the graduation ball is preserved as a set of embarrassing photos, to be dusted off and examined only when a college-mate runs for president or is found in a clock tower with a sniper rifle. Having finished their studies, they both take on the responsibility of first jobs and homes. They are now directly responsible for the contribution they make to global warming.

We've seen how bad things can get; how, as salaries increase, they can buy bigger cars, take more jet-setting holidays, and eat through more and more electricity as the army of appli-ances around their house grows. We've also seen that it doesn't have to be like this. Our climate-aware Lucy can have the same standard of living as her ignorant counterpart: she can eat well, stay warm in winter and cool in summer, and travel with ease, all while having a fraction of the impact on our climate and without ever going near a bowl of muesli.

Our grown-up climate-aware Lucy has that small car, the low-mileage food and the efficient boiler. She separates her trash for recycling, avoids air travel and is the scourge of standby power. In those key facets of our lifestyles that affect our climate – our travel, our homes, our food and our back-yards – she has slashed her emissions through thinking about it and choosing to do so. Across the board, she meets and exceeds that magic 60% reduction. The cumulative effect across a lifetime? Huge.

By the time the presentation of an engraved carriage clock is made, and plastic cups of fizzy Scottish Chardonnay are passed around, the difference between the emissions glaciers of the two Lucys is stark. At 65 they've had nigh-on 40 years of full control over their emissions and, with each passing year, the extras of ignorant Lucy have mounted up. After a good long retirement of 25 years the two Lucys die and are buried, one in a calico bag, and the other in an airtight testament to conspic-uous consumption.

The lifetime impact of our Lucy, for 90 years of climate-aware life in a developed-world country: 595 tonnes of greenhouse gas. For climate-ignorant Lucy: a staggering 1,800 tonnes.

What these two women will have seen by the 2090s we can only imagine. By then, the planet is likely to be substantially warmer and the effects of this severe. Just how much warmer and just how bad the impacts will be depends on how many Lucys of each type there are.

The true graph though, if we could take a real climate audit over the next 90 years, would probably show an even bigger divergence. I've assumed the status quo: the adult climate-ignorant Lucy using energy in the home at the same average rate as her parents, the distances she drives and flies being the same as theirs. In fact, predictions for the year 2025 are for massive rises in average greenhouse emissions from home energy use, food, waste and, the really big one, transport. Emissions from energy use in US homes are predicted to increase by over 25% in the next 20 years, while on the roads we'll be belching out an extra 50% compared with today – over a billion tonnes more every year. For climate-ignorant Lucy therefore, the true story is likely to be much worse. Enough to make anyone turn in a bronze-lined grave.

Add together just some of the emissions-cutting strategies described in the preceding chapters and incorporate them into our lives, just as Lucy Carbone did, and the target of a 60% reduction can be not just hit, but shattered. That the 60% cut is truly a possibility for each of us – something we can do right now, without the pillars of civilisation falling around our ears – represents a fantastic opportunity. Such a reduction is exactly what we need to make if disastrous climate change is to be avoided.

Achieving this 60% cut, one that our politicians can currently only dream of, means that for every person taking action, many hundreds of tonnes of greenhouse gas can be kept out of the atmosphere. Multiply this up for your whole family, your friends, your street, or for all your work colleagues, and you can see exactly how such alterations could literally change the world.

It starts with you and me, at home, at the shops, in the garden and on the way to work. It doesn't have to stop there. Though homes and private transport both play leading roles in global emissions, we have the power to take our new-found awareness of climate change beyond these most personal facets of our lives: we can take it to work.

From what we do with our scrap paper, to whether or not we congratulate John Carbone on his new SUV, this big part of our lives provides a wealth of ways by which we can either ramp up greenhouse emissions or drastically cut them.

So, on to the gleaming corporate tower blocks, to the open-plan offices, the bins stuffed with reams of virgin paper and the lights burning through the day and the night. Let's see just how far-reaching the effects of climate-awareness can be – how one memo from the boss can cut through the energy squandering of dozens of staff, and how just one person in the office remembering to turn the lights out can change our future.

# 8
## lights out

Our climate concerns may be something we'd rather keep quiet about around the water cooler – an embarrassing hobby for the evenings and weekends. Tackling climate change, though, is not some unfashionable activity for people without a life.

Cutting energy wastage and greenhouse gas emissions at work takes us back to the smoking analogy. You've seen the light – smoking (or in this case greenhouse gas emission) is bad for you, for your family, for everyone. You've changed your life-style and kicked the habit, so to speak. You feel good about your enlightenment and want to spread the word. Then, the ultimate test: you go back to work. At 10.15 a.m. on the dot it's the usual cigarette break. Out comes the chocolate bar, the stress ball and the family photo. After a while the smell of smoke reaches your nostrils and, if all that detox worked, it turns your stomach. How can people be allowed to smoke in the same building as non-smokers, exposing you to their smoke and the potentially fatal consequences? You complain. If you're the boss you ban it there and then; if not then the union gets it banned.

In the same way, if you and your family are saving energy and cutting emissions by having low-energy bulbs at home, why should the office be lit like the set of *Ice Cold in Alex*? Why, when at home you pull on a sweater in winter and open the windows in summer, should your office get away with T-shirt tempera-tures even in the hardest winter snaps and feel like the inside of a refrigerator during the heat of summer? It's not right and, as a climate-aware employee, boss, or even client, by taking a stand against energy wastage in the workplace you can mag-nify the extent to which you mitigate climate change many-fold. Sure, we can make a big difference at home by being cli-mate-aware, but we can then take that awareness to work, when we go shopping, and maybe most crucially of all, when we step into the polling booth.

On the way home from work, those thousands of brightly lit office windows we pass every evening represent simply massive energy use and wastage. No matter how late at night, those windows will still be shining – and shaming. If you've ever worked in such offices you know just what overheated, overlit, humming computer-fests they are. As an insurance clerk, paid on an hourly rate and always strapped for cash, I'd often chug into the car park on my motorbike well before 7 a.m.

In the streets the traffic would still be a soft murmur compared with the roar of an hour later, and the night security guard on the front desk would be knocking back his eighth and final coffee of the shift. Through the big double doors into the foyer and I'd be hit by wilting heat (particularly in biking leathers) and a hum like an electricity substation.

Up to the open-plan office and the scene was always the same: all the lights on, the computers chuntering away to themselves, and the vending machines humming in unison. Around the room were the familiar array of novelty desk gonks, name cards on computers and photos of last year's office Christmas party. Like some 21st century *Marie Celeste*, the photocopier would be going through another systems check and the drinks machine would be heating up its coffee and cooling down its vat of limeade; again, the only thing missing were the people. From the outside you'd have imagined the building was bursting with activity – from every window on every floor, the lights burned.

Of course, no matter how early I got in there was always somebody in before me. That person in offices the world over – Gareth with the sunken eyes from Loss Assessment in my case – who is always the last to leave at night and the first to arrive in the morning. Maybe Gareth never did go home.

From gnome factories to schools, from butchers to candlestick makers, businesses account for around 40% of greenhouse gas emissions in developed world countries. Put this together with our own residential and transport emissions and you've got the bulk of all developed-world greenhouse gas emissions right there in front of you.

For every square foot of space at your work – about the space your waste bin takes up – the amount of greenhouse gas emitted can be big. At the bottom of our 'emissions at work' league come warehouses. Work in a warehouse and, on average, for every square foot, 4 kg of greenhouse gas will be emitted every year. The bulk of this goes on refrigeration for the stocks in the warehouse and heating, though it may not feel like it, for you and your work mates. A few kilograms of greenhouse gas per square foot may not sound all that much, and compared to some other workplaces, it isn't. But 4 kg per square foot for an average-sized warehouse of, say, 15,000 square feet means 60 tonnes of greenhouse gas a year.

Next come schools. With the heating and cooling of classrooms and halls, the lighting, and the fuel used to produce all those lovely school dinners, the greenhouse emissions rise to 5.5 kg per square foot. The sugar and tartrazine-heavy vending machines that inhabit most refectories can also play a big role, each one being responsible for around two tonnes of greenhouse gas a year, not to mention the dozens of hyperactive kids.

Pop down to the mall for some retail therapy and, from the blast of air-conditioning which greets you as you walk in to the rows of spotlights blazing down on the clothes racks, the retail sector goes up the climate-warming scale again. The lighting-related emissions shoot up to over a quarter of the total, with heating and cooling the other big two. For each square foot, shops emit over 9 kg of greenhouse gas a year: well over 100 kg a year for every rack of sweatshop-stitched tops in this world of dry heat and commercial radio.

Next up the scale come the offices (see Figure 17). Lighting, heating and cooling these big open-plan spaces is again the

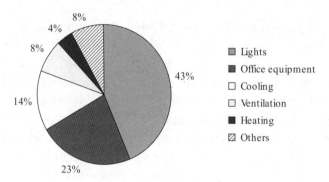

**Figure 17** Uses of electricity in the average office.

big draw on power, but all those PCs, photocopiers and vending machines really push things up. That square foot under the office waste bin generates 10 kg of greenhouse gas emissions each year. The office desk, along with its flaking skin of sticky notes, is emitting over 100 kg of greenhouse gas each year. Say you sit in an open-plan office with 19 others, all tucked behind *Dilbert*-style screens, sharing each other's phone calls and drinking stories. On a standard office floor of say 10,000 square feet, the emissions total around 100 tonnes a year. This is over 5 tonnes for you and every one of your colleagues, and equivalent to each of you driving two cars into work everyday instead of one.

I had hoped that the next workplace, my own, would be better. But as university offices and lecture theatres tend to suffer from the same 24 hour lighting, heating and appliance wastage as most offices, the emissions per square foot per year – the damning climate impact of every seat in every lecture theatre – goes up to over 11 kg. This is bad, but we're still only mid-table in the league of work-based warming.

Work in a health centre or hospital? Warm, isn't it? Heating and cooling use up more than half of all the electricity in these places, with all that lighting coming in a close third. Per square foot, the emissions total around 14 kg of greenhouse gas each year. It would be silly to argue that all the energy used in our hospitals is unnecessary. Some good lighting, I imagine, is fairly crucial in the operating theatres; all those machines that go ping also keep people alive; and sick people need to be kept warm. Nevertheless, as places which are likely to see more and more admissions due to climate change-driven heatwaves, disease outbreaks and storm damage, our hospitals are smack in the middle of the two-way street of global warming.

Now to the businesses with really big climate impacts. The next two take things to a whole new level. In second place, with soft lighting out front but a storm of energy use in the back, come restaurants. At over 26 kg of greenhouse gas per square foot, a table for two will clock up around 400 kg of greenhouse gas a year – the same as a year's servings of hand-tied chives. But topping the league for climate impact per square foot are the out-of-town food mile cathedrals that are our supermarkets. Space heating and cooling are pushed unceremoniously into third and fourth places by the huge amounts of energy needed to keep our Chilean grapes and Canadian spring water chilled – a massive 38% of total electricity use in this biggest of business energy users. Lighting for all those lovely packets of biscuits comes in as the second biggest drain on energy. In total, every square foot of your local grocery store accounts for over 30 kg of greenhouse gas. Walk down just one aisle and your trolley will have passed through an area responsible for 12 tonnes of greenhouse gas each year – as much as a large four-wheel drive.

Back when I was researching for the chapter on food and its greenhouse emissions, I volunteered to take myself and my daughter to the local supermarket, do the week's shopping and check out the array of food-mile-heavy produce on offer. This cunning plan went somewhat awry when said daughter took exception to my wanting to go down any aisle other than the one with cakes in it. My scribblings on the country of origin were therefore rather frantic. I did, though, manage to record the contents of one whole stand of luxury groceries. This stand was about 2.5 m long and 1 m deep, and on its shelves were a selection of plastic-packaged delights from all around the world, including runner beans from Thailand, baby carrots from South Africa and blueberries from New Zealand. But, sadly, nothing that could keep a two-year-old interested for more than the time it takes to ram a baby carrot up your nose.

My intention at the time was to calculate the contribution to global warming of this one short section of shelving. Having got carried away with hand-tied chives and lead grapes earlier, this somehow slipped by. Now, though, we've got the climate impact not only of the food miles, but also the shelves the food is sitting on.

Add together all the packets of blueberries, baby carrots and other jet-setting produce on this stand, assume just 20 packets of each type are bought every week, and the greenhouse gas emissions for this one stand take on mammoth proportions. The food mile emissions add up to over 40 tonnes a fortnight, and over 1,000 tonnes in a year. Combine these emissions with the energy used to keep all those pocket-sized packets brightly lit and cool, and in a year we've got emissions equivalent to driving 50 gas-guzzling SUVs all the way around the world.

To make real reductions in greenhouse emissions at your work-place can seem rather tricky. For one thing there's no clear monetary incentive for your colleagues, and for another, telling your boss she should turn down the heating and put on a sweater may go down about as well as when you try it with your teenage kids. Just as at home though, many of the smallest changes can have big effects.

Let's start with that over-lit insurance office of my biker days. The office has 20 big lighting units, each with four-lamp 4 ft fluorescent lights. They are on for 100 hours a week, 365 days a year. Now, before we start making Gareth sit in the dark or shut down the light show which is our office block at night, what if we just changed these fittings for more efficient bulbs?

By swapping over to more efficient bulbs we'd each year cut our office energy use by around 3,700 kilowatt hours, save the company over $1,000 dollars in energy costs and cut 2.3 tonnes off annual greenhouse gas emissions. We can go much further though. The current lights produce more than a third more light than that required for the work that's done, so, install enough energy-efficient lighting to hit the ideal lighting level for the office and we'd save almost 7,000 kilowatt hours – over 4 tonnes of greenhouse gas a year.

Always-in Gareth may not like it, but how about the lights being turned off when they're not needed? His frighteningly tidy area of the office aside, if the other lights were turned off outside of work hours then we'd go from 100 hours of lighting per week to just 50 hours, halving energy use and greenhouse gas emissions in a stroke.

Turning the lights out really gets to the crux of saving energy at work. So often the fact that it's not our own energy bill, and that someone else can always do it, means the lights in offices and factories are just left to burn. Aside from relying on you and me to break this cycle and flick that switch, there is the option of occupancy detectors. These mean that the lights go on when Gareth first skulks through the maze of desks at some ungodly hour in the morning, and turn themselves off again at night when he's finally had enough of trying to complete Minesweeper.

Imagine them as standard in schools, reacting to the con-
stant incoming and outgoing tide of classes throughout the
school day and so saving energy hand over fist. In the office
they'll save up to 50%, and in the bathrooms at work up to
75% (depending on how much coffee everyone drinks). The
same big cuts hold true for meeting and conference rooms (up
to 65%), corridors (40%) and in the cavernous space of a warehouse (up to 75%).

After lighting, one of the most conspicuous consumers of
energy at work is office equipment. And, just as for lighting, the
savings to be made simply through turning things off are big. The
desktop computer, that digital window we spend so many hours
staring at, is the biggest player here. PCs and their monitors have
become so ubiquitous that their always being on and draining
power is something that has become part of the background
scenery of every office. Offices across the world go through each
night to the hum of countless PCs, fans and hard-drives whirring
and clicking, 'The Matrix Has You' screensavers whirling around
their screens. Turn them off at night and for every PC without a
hum 675 kilowatt hours of electricity are avoided each year – over
400 kg of greenhouse gas emissions saved just for hitting that
switch. The photocopier over by the wall? Turn that monster off
each night and, as well as helping to prevent unsavoury photo-
copied body parts mysteriously appearing in the boss's in-tray,
you'll cut a buxom 4 tonnes off annual emissions.

While we're on the subject of turning things off, a brief mention of screensavers. These scrolling messages, virtual fish tanks
and *Star Trek* scenes might look rather jolly for the first two seconds they're in operation, but they do nothing for saving
energy. Instead, they keep the monitor and the PC eating
energy while you're off at lunch, rather than allowing them to
power down.

Just as some fridges can honk out much more greenhouse gas
than their more energy-efficient counterparts, so the printer you

have in your office, the photocopier you order for your floor, and the computers on all the desks, come in climate-friendly as well as unfriendly versions. Replacing defunct office equipment with Energy Star equipment together with turning those switches off at night, takes the greenhouse gas cuts possible up to almost 75% – around half a tonne of greenhouse gas for every PC and well over five tonnes for the copier. Want a new printer or fax machine for the office? Give laser printers a wide berth – these emit about half a tonne of greenhouse gas a year compared to just 20 kg for inkjets.

The same goes for the office fax, scanner and printer. Opt for energy-efficient versions and, during the times when the printer isn't spewing out a 100-page mobile phone user manual, and the fax machine isn't delivering offers of the ultimate in lard-only diets, they'll power down and so cut energy wastage and emissions by up to 50%.

With the average vending machine being responsible for around 2 tonnes of greenhouse gas a year, there are big savings to be made by opting for energy-efficient models. Using features such as proximity detectors – the vending machine only goes to full power when approached by caffeine- or chocolate-starved customers – can halve its emissions. In 2000 the schools of Moscow, Idaho, had 20 of their vending machines upgraded to increase energy efficiency. This was so successful that a further 250 vending machines in offices and public buildings throughout the community were also upgraded. The combined energy savings of these upgrades meant a cut of around 200 tonnes of greenhouse gas every year.

For the energy-intensive floor space in our supermarkets, restaurants and the like, having more energy-efficient appliances becomes even more important. As with vending machines, greenhouse gas emissions due to food store refrigerators and freezers can also be halved by opting for more energy-efficient models and keeping them well maintained.

Outside of direct energy use at work, there's one other major burden on the climate that's everywhere you look. Across our desks, filling the cabinets, in piles on shelves, and pouring out of the waste bins – paper.

Back in the early 1990s, as the Internet was just starting to spread its web across the world, personal computers like the one I'm using now were already eating their way through around 115 billion sheets of paper. Today, despite broadband connections and email as standard in most offices, paper use has reached staggering proportions. In the USA alone, laser printers are now getting through over a trillion pages each year and paper consumption continues to rise by 20% annually. Each of us uses an average of 100 sheets of paper a day, the bulk of this ending up in the bin. The paper used by a typical office worker over a year carries with it embodied energy equivalent to more than 100 kg of greenhouse gas. That's before it even gets to the landfill site.

While researching studies of paper use in offices and the effect of the Internet, what did I do? I used my PC, found some online papers and printed them out to read them (double-sided of course). Email, I had always assumed, was bound to have cut our paper use in the office. Surely, we don't send as many letters and memos as a result? I was wrong. On average, the use of email in an organisation actually increases paper use by 40 per cent.

The ways around having the equivalent of a finely sliced forest scattered around your workplace are many and, like flicking the light switch, take no more than a moment's thought. Need to make 500 copies of the interim report on expanding air-conditioning sales? Hit the double-sided copying button and save.

If you hold the precious keys to the stationery cupboard or have a hand in the paper that the office uses, providing recycled paper can make a real dent in the climate impact of your workplace. This doesn't mean a choice between grey and lumpy sheets and bleached-white paper. Much recycled paper can be impossible to distinguish from more energy-intensive virgin paper. Across a whole company the savings, energy-wise and climate-wise, of using it can be huge: the double-sided feature on the copier plus recycled paper saves two whole trees and a tonne of greenhouse gas for every 100 reams of paper used at work. To complete the recycling cycle, as it were, recycling office paper rather than sending it to the local landfill has the same straightforward climate benefits as we saw for our Sunday newspapers – around 2 kg of greenhouse gas saved for every kilogram recycled.

Providing recycling for cans, glass and the rest at work can also reap big dividends. Take the mass of aluminium cans resulting from a hundred desktop lunches every day, five days a week, 48 weeks a year in an office building – let's say a tonne of aluminium cans a year. To make these cans from virgin materials means the emission of about 20 tonnes of greenhouse gas; recycle this lot and next year's cans will be responsible for the emission of just 3 tonnes of greenhouse gas.

Our monster-size copying machine is a great example of somewhere that a range of energy savings and greenhouse gas cuts come together. Over its seven-year life span (barring buttock-related accidents), your standard copier will eat its way through electricity, paper and toner cartridges equivalent to 80 tonnes of greenhouse gas – the annual emissions of two average households for this one copier. A combination of an energy-efficient model, double-sided copying, and the use of recycled paper and toner cartridges means a cut of up to 75% in energy use, cost and greenhouse gas emissions, as well as avoiding the dicing up of 50 trees.

Work from home, like our tele-worker in his log cabin retreat, and the same sorts of savings apply. For an average home office with the standard printer, fax, small photocopier and PC, annual energy use will mean almost two tonnes of greenhouse gas emissions. Switch to energy-efficient equipment and settings and turn things off when they're not being used, and you'll get a cut in greenhouse gas emissions of 60% – over a tonne a year. Likewise with paper use at home: print on both sides and recycle the scrap stuff, and the annual greenhouse gas emissions will fall from about half a tonne to less than 50 kilograms.

One of the biggest energy hogs and greenhouse gas emitters at work tends to be heating and cooling. Before we touch the thermostat, simply opting for energy-efficient appliances can help a lot here too. Less wasted energy means less heat emitted, and so less need for the air-conditioning to be up full blast. For the average office, just having more energy-efficient equipment will cut the electricity needed by the air-conditioning by a third. After that, you can of course reach for the thermostat, but this is where our own control can often start to slip.

If your office is too hot you may be able to turn down the radiator, but in most offices the temperature is set by a control panel more jealously guarded than even the stationery cupboard key. So, rather than risk the wrath of Barbara, she of the poor circulation and undisputed Queen of the thermostat, we set up a forest of fans in our offices, blowing the over-heated air around the office, eating through yet more power and occasionally kicking up a virgin-paper storm. In open-plan work environments it's up the boss to ensure that the heating and cooling of the building isn't a non-stop fight between electric heating and cooling. If they do take such action – providing Barbara with her own heater and allowing everyone else to cool down a bit – the energy savings and emissions savings can be big. Exactly how big? Let's visit John Carbone one last time.

John's office is just like the dozens of others clustered around the south side of Greenville, Alabama. Today he's driving into work early with his fellow carpoolers to avoid the hundreds of other office workers who jam the roads leading into town each morning. He quickly finds a parking space amongst the acres of soon-to-be crammed car park, and heads towards his glass-fronted building. Even at this early hour it is ablaze with the lights of 200 offices. Within this hub of Alabama insurance there reside 200 PCs, 20 networked laser printers, five fax machines, five scanners and five giant-sized photocopiers, all munching through electricity round the clock. Determined to do something about the masses of energy he can see going to waste, and now, as Area Manager, being in a position to do something about it, John Carbone is set to slash energy use, costs and the greenhouse emissions of his workplace.

That same week, occupancy detectors are installed for the lighting system, immediately cutting the energy use for lighting by half and greenhouse gas emissions by 19 tonnes a year. Buoyed by the obvious savings in the next electricity bill, the process of ensuring that PCs, photocopiers and all the other energy-hungry devices are set to their energy-saving modes and turned off at night begins. With a few choice people on board, each known for their abilities in organising collections for leaving parties, John quickly succeeds in cutting energy waste from heating and office equipment by over 60% – over 100 tonnes of greenhouse gas emissions a year across the building. With this same team of office matriarchs, recycling becomes a matter of course on all floors. The bins are quickly transformed from their standard state – overflowing with virgin paper – to scrupulously managed recycling areas for paper, cans and bottles.

When it comes to renewing the lease on the 10 company cars, it's no more of those 3.5 litre gas-guzzling saloons for John Carbone and his staff. Instead, at a much reduced cost, the sales force now drive dual-fuel hatchbacks. This simple move cuts the fleet greenhouse gas emissions by over 50 tonnes a year. With new bike racks, shower facilities for the sweaty few who do brave the car-clogged roads, and a designated free parking zone for car pool users, John is well on his way to creating a truly climate-aware workplace.

Through his actions John has cut the greenhouse gas emissions of his office building by over 150 tonnes a year. This is the equivalent of taking a dozen cars off the road permanently, or of slicing over a tonne off the individual emissions of everyone working in the building. John Carbone's boss in the San Francisco head office will also be very pleased. He's cut the electricity bill by over $30,000 a year. Together with the fuel and hire savings on the company cars, and the reduction in paper costs around the office, John's earned the office a hefty Christmas bonus and set the standard for the other regional offices to follow.

As we go up the power ladder at work, the potential for such sweeping reductions in workplace emissions grows and grows. As well as promoting cycling to work and switching to more fuel-efficient company cars, options like choosing a renewable electricity supplier, providing financial support for office recycling schemes, even ensuring climate-aware building design, become possible.

The effects of such workplace energy initiatives are already being felt. In the USA, the Energy Star Programme has expanded to include more than 13,000 organisations and small businesses. Since its inception in 1992, it is estimated that Energy Star has helped save around 55 billion kilowatt hours of energy use by US businesses – the equivalent of over 30 million tonnes of greenhouse gas.

In the UK, my research funding body, the Natural Environment Research Council, now has a Green Audit each year, with the aim of reducing environmental damage across the board. Such organisation-wide greening, from cutting energy use to reducing paper wastage, is happening more and more frequently as a straight money-saving approach, through a wider concern for public image, or maybe even simple altruistic intentions (well, you never know).

*The Guardian* newspaper now has an annual audit by the Carbon Trust. Initially, this threw up some unpleasant facts. Its offices were producing 418 kg of greenhouse gas per square metre per year (even worse than a supermarket). It is now setting out to cut these emissions to the so-called Good Practice level of 95 kg per square metre. This will mean a cut for the newspaper as a whole of nearly 80% – 2,800 tonnes of greenhouse gas a year. This is all great news for a paper keen to reduce its damage to the environment, and for its bank balance. The potential energy cost savings amount to £120,000 a year.

Not to be left out, the World Wide Fund for Nature has got companies around the world to commit to cutting emissions through its Climate Saver Program. In short, from the first recycling trays appearing in our offices, right up to major corporations having green audits, climate change action is coming to work.

While we're on the subject of the ripple effect of awareness, it's worth mentioning how our attitudes can create changes right through to the very top. Politicians are all too aware of the need to either react to public opinion or face being out of power at the next election. So too are the owners of shopping malls, supermarkets, and appliance manufacturers. Get enough people complaining about digital TV boxes that can't be turned off and the manufacturers will soon start ensuring that there is an OFF switch as standard. If sales of high-efficiency light bulbs at that big blue shop from Sweden take off, then your local hardware store will suddenly sprout a special offer on these 'new' cost-saving bulbs.

Our bottom-up power to affect the decisions of everyone from supermarket chains to Presidents and Prime Ministers can't be overstated. These people of great power are still just that, people. They have homes, kids and friends who are just as threatened by climate change as we are. In the UK even the Queen recently opened a conference on climate change in Germany, expressing her concern over the issue and her intention to cut the Royal climate impact.

From a political perspective, the promotion and subsequent incorporation of individual-level cuts into national greenhouse gas budgets seems an obvious tack to take. Recent years have certainly seen increasing government interest in this area. The UK government is promoting domestic energy efficiency via better information, financial incentives and tighter regulations. The prediction is that implementation of these strategies will cut UK carbon emissions by around 5 million tonnes by 2010, all without having to upset any friends in big business. Other governments are even more proactive in the promotion of emissions cuts at the individual level. The Australian Greenhouse Office, for instance, funds Cool Communities, a programme which not only provides information on how individuals might reduce their emissions, but also provides grants for communities to implement these household greenhouse gas reduction strategies.

No definitive figures exist for the cost of reductions via the increased public awareness route, but there's little doubt that this option has huge potential in industrialised countries. For every million people with the old SUV-driving John Carbone lifestyle that switch to his new climate-aware lifestyle, the annual reduction in greenhouse gas emissions would be more than 10 million tonnes.

Over the next few years, each of us will be bombarded with energy-saving leaflets, recycling schemes and public awareness ads. There will be more climate tax carrots and sticks, more harrowing TV news coverage of the impacts of rapid climate change, and our kids will get increasingly cross with us. In the end though, it's our choice.

The greenhouse emissions from the smoky power station down the road can appear so great as to make our own actions seem meaningless. But much of the electricity it produces is then wasted on lighting empty offices, standby power in our homes and the rest. In the USA alone, energy wastage due to standby power requires the equivalent of 26 good-sized power stations, all just to keep the hum going. In fact, it's the energy and fossil fuel we use every day that dominates emissions and so represents the key to tackling human-made climate change.

About a quarter of all developed-world emissions come from our homes, another quarter from our transport, and most of the rest from our places of work (Figure 18). Now, imagine taking the chunks out of this emission pie that we've seen are possible: a 60% slice out of transport emissions; wiping away up to three-quarters of those residential emissions; and then going on to tackle the huge wedge that is the emissions from business. From the car we choose to drive to whether we turn the office PC off at night, it's these things which will decide the severity of climate change in the 21st century and beyond.

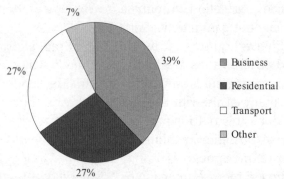

**Figure 18**  Carbon dioxide emissions by end user (UK, 2001).

If you combine this potential for emission cuts at an individual level with increased awareness, you've got to be optimistic. Our children and grandchildren don't *have* to face the full horrors of a high-emissions scenario. We don't *have* to go down as one of the most selfish and destructive generations in human history; this age of human control of the planet – this Anthropocene – doesn't have to consume itself and everything else.

I've talked aplenty about the magic 60% target – the reduction in emissions that the scientific community believes is necessary if we are to avoid the most devastating effects of climate change. But what, as far as the effects on our homes and holidays, our livelihoods and our health, will such cuts in our greenhouse gas emissions actually achieve?

Predictions of global warming rely on so-called Emissions Scenarios. These are the pathways humankind must choose between. Along each of these paths various changes in climate await. There are many scenarios, together covering the changes in population growth, economic development and greenhouse gas mitigation efforts that we may see over the next 100 years.

The most familiar of the paths ahead of us, the one that means, in theory, our lifestyles can go on relatively unchanged, leads to many of the most severe effects. In the world of climate science this path is part of the so-called A1 Story Line, a family of possible Emissions Scenarios sharing a future of rapid economic growth. The high-emissions scenario, called A1F1 (climate modelling doesn't go in for the most evocative names), represents a world where the high rate of international economic growth is driven by fossil fuel use. It's a world where stockbrokers, defence conglomerates and oil magnates remain the dominant powers, where the 'make money at all costs' ethic continues apace, doing wonders for the sales of red braces but pushing the rate of greenhouse gas emissions up and up. In the A1F1 story line we have the sleeping emissions giants of China and India developing in the same greenhouse gas-intensive way that we in the West have done during the 19th and 20th centuries.

In this chilling story, the world's population peaks by 2050 and then starts to decline. At the same time this scenario assumes the rapid development and use of more efficient technologies. Down this path, greenhouse gas emissions finally start to level off somewhere between 2050 and 2080. By this time though, carbon dioxide concentrations in the atmosphere will be more than double what they are today, and triple what they were before the Industrial Revolution – somewhere up around 800 parts per million (ppm). By following this long-burn path we will have loaded the climate change dice with over 2,000 billion tonnes of extra carbon, and so drastically shortened the odds on catastrophic climate change.

Round that first bend of the high-emissions path, only just out of sight for many of us, there lurks real danger. Under a high-emissions scenario, the UK, for example, faces an increase in the frequency of extreme sea levels, storm surges and flooding along the east coast of between 10 and 20 times what it is today. By opting for the high-emissions path, the brutally straightforward impact tables produced by the Intergovernmental Panel on Climate Change (IPCC) – their projections of disease, famine, flooding and death – are made flesh.

For the range of futures currently predicted, the IPCC has identified five Reasons for Concern categories (Figure 19). For each Concern there is a long box, at the left-hand end of which we have the situation today. As we look along to the right we

Figure 19 Reasons for Concern.

move into the future, ending up at 2100. As you'll have noticed, these five boxes all have one thing in common: they get darker as we move towards the right. With a high emissions scenario and a global temperature rise of 5 °C, we get the deepest of shadow – not good.

The top box is for 'Risks from future large-scale discontinuities' and goes from 'Very low' now, to the rather non-specific 'Higher'. This doesn't sound all that bad until you find out what it means. These are the risks of our greenhouse gas emissions having severe impacts right around the world: things like collapse of the West Antarctic ice sheet – something which would push up sea levels by around 6 metres and lead to death and destruction on a global scale. Then there's the shutdown of the North Atlantic circulation and the ushering in of Arctic conditions to huge swathes of North America and Europe.

Below this Hollywood-fodder box the Reasons for Concern may get less dramatic but the boxes quickly grow dark. First there are the boxes for the economic costs and geographical distribution of global warming. These go from today's situation, where we have 'Negative impacts for some regions' to the spread of impacts and financial costs to every nation, rich or poor, summed up as 'Negative for most regions' and 'Net negative in all metrics'. The bottom two boxes, those representing the 'Risks to unique and threatened systems' and of 'Risks from extreme climate events' are already shading given the warming we're experiencing today. Move to the right and through time, and a high-emissions scenario eats up more and more unique ecosystems and sees a large increase in the frequency of extreme climatic events.

The high-emissions scenario then, the A1F1 future of booming fossil fuel-fed economies and emissions, is a path paved with riches but leading to ruin. Thankfully, at the climate change crossroads at which we now find ourselves, there are other possibilities. Propping up the league of Emissions Scenarios used by the IPCC comes the Low Emissions family and its B1 Story Line. In this B1 future we have the world's population increasing up to the middle of the century, just as for the high-emissions story line, but in this future the world's population has a high level of environmental awareness. This is combined with a rapid change to a more information-based world economy, ensuring more sustainable development of expanding economies such as China. There's also a big and sustained drop in material intensity around the world – simply put, a big cut in the amount of stuff we make, use and throw away. Under the B1 scenario, carbon dioxide concentrations rise to 520 ppm by 2080 and global temperatures increase by about 2 °C. This 'best case scenario' may still represent a drastic increase in global temperature, but at least it keeps us out of the dark ends of the Reasons for Concern boxes.

Of all the Emissions Scenarios, none sees a cut in global emissions until the middle of this century and only one story line, good old B1, then sees a decrease to a level below that which we are emitting today. On the basis of these predictions then, all the paths open to us, from the high-emissions A1 scenario to the low-emissions B1, mean large-scale losses of jobs, homes and lives. At our climate crossroads though, there is one more path.

It's a path the climate modellers might be forgiven for over-looking. It doesn't rely on international climate change initiatives, on the development of 'silver bullet' zero-emission technologies, or even a falling global population, to cut global greenhouse gas emissions. Rather, the direction of this emissions path is nudged downwards by individual awareness and action – very tricky to predict but something with huge potential. The increased environmental awareness so important for the B1 scenario is expected to come from clear evidence of rapid climate change – our collective horror at the famines, floods and disease epidemics that climate change will bring. What though, would the future hold if we acted now? If, instead of waiting for climate change to hit us, we hit it?

This is no happy-clappy scenario of zero cars, planes or electric lighting. Rather, it's a real possibility. It's the sum of the world's Carbones doing their bit and more; it's Barbara and millions like her cutting energy use at the office; hell, it's even the world's Gareths turning off their PCs and cycling home from work. As individuals they are no more than grains of sand in the path of the climate change glacier; together they can radically change that path.

Extrapolate the cuts that we've seen are possible at an individual level to a global scale and the reduction in global greenhouse gas emissions would be like six Kyoto Protocols stacked on top of one another: no loopholes and backsliding, just real and significant cuts. If the emissions that each of us is responsible for, from our homes, transport and jobs, dive in this way, then we get a new scenario – let's stick with IPCC convention and call it 'C1'. This global future sees a carbon dioxide concentration in 2080 of below 500 ppm, avoids the 2 °C global temperature increase, and saves the world from the worst of the potential climate impacts.

This 'C1' path is our chance to make a real difference, a path open to us all. We're standing at this climate change crossroads right now.

Choose.

**Figure 20** Flooded sign.

# references and resources

## Chapter 1

Australian Greenhouse Office (2001) *Global Warming: Cool it!* http://www.greenhouse.gov.au/gwci/

Central Alabama Electric Cooperative. *Residential Energy Calculator.* http://touchstoneenergyhome.apogee.net/index.asp?id=centralal

Department of the Environment and Transport in the Regions (DETR). *Vehicle Certification Agency Emissions Database.* http://www.vcacarfueldata.org.uk/search_form_basic.asp

Energy Information Administration. Average Electricity Emission Factors by State and Region, USA. http://www.eia.doe.gov/oiaf/1605/e-factor.html

Friedland, A. J., Gerngross, T. U. and Howarth, R. B. (2003) Personal decisions and their impacts on energy use and the environment. *Environmental Science and Policy*, **6**, 175–9.

Greenhouse Gas Online. http://www.ghgonline.org/

Intergovernmental Panel on Climate Change (IPCC) (1999) *Air Transport Operations and Relation to Emissions. Aviation and Global Atmosphere.* Cambridge University Press, Cambridge.

Liverman, D. M. and O'Brien, K. L. (1991) Global warming and climate change in Mexico. *Global Environmental Change*, **1**(5), 351–64.

Reay, D. S. (2002) Costing climate change. *Philosophical Transactions of the Royal Society Series A*, **360**, 2947–61.

United Nations Convention on Climate Change (UNFCCC) (2003) *Caring for Climate: a Guide to the Climate Change Convention and the Kyoto Protocol.* http://unfccc.int/resource/docs/publications/caring_en.pdf

US Environmental Protection Agency. *Global warming.* http://yosemite.epa.gov/oar/globalwarming.nsf/content/index.html

US Environmental Protection Agency. *Greenhouse gas emissions from management of selected materials in municipal solid waste.* http://www.epa.gov/epaoswer/non-hw/muncpl/ghg/chapter4.pdf

US Environmental Protection Agency. *Solid waste management and greenhouse gases: a life-cycle assessment of emissions and sinks.* http://www.epa.gov/epaoswer/non-hw/muncpl/ghg/ghg.htm

WasteWatch. *WasteOnline: In depth information on waste.* http://www.wasteonline.org.uk/

# Chapter 2

Argonne National Laboratory. Center for Transportation Research http://www.transportation.anl.gov/

Australian Greenhouse Office. Fuel Consumption guide: 10 top tips for fuel efficient driving. http://www.greenhouse.gov.au/fuellabel/costs.html#tips

Bureau of Transportation Statistics, US (2003) *America on the Go.* National Household Travel Survey, USA. http://www.bts.gov/programs/national_household_travel_survey/

Caldwell, H. *et al.* (2002) Potential impacts of climate change on freight transport. *The Potential Impacts of Climate Change on Transportation Workshop 2002.* http://climate.volpe.dot.gov/workshop1002/caldwell.pdf

Cooper, J., Ryley, T., Smyth A. and Granzow, E. (2001) Energy use and transport correlation linking personal and travel related energy uses to the urban structure. *Environmental Science and Policy*, **4**, 307–18.

Elsasser, H. and Burki, R. (2002) Climate change as a threat to tourism in the Alps. *Climate Research*, **20**(3), 253–7.

Energy Information Administration, US (1996) *Alternatives to Traditional Transportation Fuels 1994.* Volume 2: *Greenhouse Gas Emissions.* http://www.eia.doe.gov/cneaf/pubs_html/attf94_v2/exec.html

European Environment Agency. *Vehicle Occupancy Rates.* http://themes.eea.eu.int/Sectors_and_activities/transport/indicators/technology/TERM29%2C2002/TERM_2002_29_EU_Occupancy_rates_of_passenger_vehicles.pdf

Fourth Virtual Conference on Genomics and Bioinformatics. 2004. http://www.virtualgenomics.org/conference_2004.htm

Friends of the Earth (FOE). *Why travelling by rail is better for the environment.* http://www.foe.co.uk/pubsinfo/briefings/html/20011012100132.html

FuelEconomy.gov. US Department of Energy. http://www.fueleconomy.gov/

Greene, D. L. and Schafer, A. (2003) *Reducing Greenhouse Gas Emissions from US Transportation.* Report for the Pew Center on Global Climate Change. http://www.pewclimate.org/global-warming-in-depth/all_reports/reduce_ghg_from_transportation/index.cfm

Intergovernmental Panel on Climate Change (IPCC) (2000) *Comparison of Carbon Dioxide Emissions from Different Forms of Passenger Transport. Aviation and the Global Atmosphere.* Cambridge University

Press, Cambridge. http://www.grida.no/climate/ipcc/aviation/126. htm

IRFD World Forum on Small Island Developing States. *Challenges, Prospects and International Cooperation for Sustainable Development.* http://irfd.org/events/wfsids/vc.htm

The Leading Edge: Second National Conference for the Stewardship and Conservation Community in Canada, 2003. http://www. stewardship2003.ca/

Lise, W. and Tol, R. S. J. (2002) Impact of climate on tourist demand. *Climatic Change,* **55**(4), 429–49.

Macedo, I. D. (1998) Greenhouse gas emissions and energy balances in bio-ethanol production and utilization in Brazil. *Biomass and Bioenergy,* **14**(1), 77–81.

Maddison, D. (2001) In search of warmer climates? The impact of climate change on flows of British tourists. *Climatic Change,* **49**(1–2), 193–208.

McCleese, D. L. and LaPuma, P. T. (2002) Using Monte Carlo simulation in life cycle assessment for electric and internal combustion vehicles. *International Journal of Life Cycle Assessment,* **7**(4), 230–6.

National Greenhouse Gas Inventory, Australia (2002) *Energy: Transport. 2002 Inventory and Trends.* http://www.greenhouse.gov.au/ inventory/2002/facts/pubs/02.pdf

Prodmore, A., Bristow, A., May, T. and Tight, M. (2003) Climate change, impacts, future scenarios and the role of transport. *Working Paper 33,* Tyndall Centre for Climate Change Research, UK. http://www.tyndall.ac.uk/publications/working_papers/wp33.pdf

Randall, F.J., Driscoll, W., Lee, E. and Lindsay, C. (1998) *Greenhouse gas emission factors for management of selected materials in municipal solid waste.* US Environmental Protection Agency. http://yosemite.epa.gov/OAR/globalwarming.nsf/UniqueKeyLookup/ SHSU5BVP7P/%24File/r99fina.pdf

Reay, D.S. (2003) Virtual solution to carbon cost of conferences. *Nature,* **424**, 251.

Reay, D.S. (2004) Flying in the face of the climate change convention. *Atmospheric Environment,* **38**, 793–4. http://www.ghgonline. org/flyingaea.pdf

Root, A., Boardman, B. and Fielding, W. J. (1996) *SMART: The Costs of Rural Travel.* Energy and Environment Programme, Environmental

Change Unit, University of Oxford, UK. http://www.eci.ox.ac.uk/pdfdownload/smartreport.pdf

Sausen, R. and Schumann, U. (2000) Estimates of the climate response to aircraft $CO_2$ and NOx emissions scenarios. *Climate Change*, **44**(1–2), 27–58.

Scott, B. M. and Plug, L. J. (2003) $CO_2$ emissions from air travel by AGU and ESA conference attendees. *EOS Transactions*, Fall 2003 Meeting of American Geophysical Union. http://surface.earthsciences.dal.ca/publications/abstracts/scottplug_agu2003.pdf

Shackley, S. *et al.* (2002) *Low carbon spaces area-based carbon emission reduction: a scoping study.* Sustainable Development Commission. http://www.tyndall.ac.uk/research/theme2/final_reports/sdc_final_report.pdf

Strategic Rail Authority, UK. *The way forward for Britain's railway: relative ($CO_2$) emissions for different modes of transport.* http://www.sra.gov.uk/publications/general/general_The_Strategic_Plan_2002/strategic_planthe_way_forward.pdf

Thomson, S. (2001) *The impacts of climate change: implications for the DETR.* Report for the Department of the Environment, Transport and the Regions by the In House Policy Consultancy Unit, UK. http://www.defra.gov.uk/environment/climatechange/impacts/pdf/impacts.pdf

Thomson, S. (2003) The impacts of climate change: Implications for Defra. Report for the Department of the Environment, Food and Rural Affairs by the In House Policy Consultancy Unit, UK. http://www.defra.gov.uk/environment/climatechange/impacts2/pdf/ccimpacts_defra.pdf

Toohey, R. (2001) *Travelling beyond boundaries? Catch a bus!: a rural perspective on public transport.* Conference Papers. Institute of Public Works Engineering, Australia. http://www.ipwea.org.au/papers/download/Royce%20Toohey.doc

Tyndall Centre for Climate Change Research. *Carbon emissions from transport: relative ($CO_2$) emissions for different modes of transport.* http://www.tyndall.ac.uk/research/info_for_researchers/emissions.pdf

UK Department for Transport. *Energy and environment: emissions for road vehicles (per vehicle kilometre) in urban conditions.* http://www.dft.gov.uk/stellent/groups/dft_transstats/documents/page/dft_transstats_032073.pdf

UK Department of Transport (2003) *GB National Travel Survey.* Personal travel factsheets. http://www.dft.gov.uk/stellent/groups/dft_control/documents/contentservertemplate/dft_index.hcst?n=7223&l=3

UK National Atmospheric Emissions Inventory. *Road Transport.* http://www.aeat.co.uk/netcen/airqual/naei/annreport/annrep98/app1_29.html

US Environmental Protection Agency. *On the Road.* http://yosemite.epa.gov/OAR/globalwarming.nsf/content/EmissionsIndividualOntheRoad.html

US National Biodiesel Board. http://www.biodiesel.org/

Vehicle Certification Agency (VCA). *Car fuel data.* UK Department of Transport. http://www.vcacarfueldata.org.uk/

Wang, M., Saricks, C. and Santini, D. (1999) *Effects of fuel ethanol use on fuel-cycle energy and greenhouse gas emissions.* Center for Transportation Research. Argonne National Laboratory. http://www.transportation.anl.gov/pdfs/TA/58.pdf

Wang, M., Saricks, C. and Wu, M. (1997) *Fuel-cycle fossil energy use and greenhouse gas emissions of fuel ethanol produced from US Midwest corn.* Report for Illinois Department of Commerce and Community Affairs. Center for Transportation Research. Argonne National Laboratory. http://www.transportation.anl.gov/pdfs/TA/141.pdf

Wasteline. WasteOnline UK. *End-of-life vehicles.* http://www.wasteonline.org.uk/resources/InformationSheets/vehicle.htm

Yang, M. (2002) *Climate change and GHGs from urban transport.* Asian Development Bank. Transport, Planning, Demand Management and Air Quality Workshop. Manila, Philippines. Document 10b. http://www.adb.org/Documents/Events/2002/RETA5937/Manila/downloads/cw_10B_mingyang.pdf

## Chapter 3

Australian Consumers' Association. *Standby Wattage – Standby Wastage.* http://www.choice.com.au/viewArticle.aspx?id=102226&catId=100447&tid=100008&p=1

Australian Greenhouse Office. *Embodied energy.* http://www.greenhouse.gov.au/yourhome/technical/fs31.htm

Australian Greenhouse Office. *Strategic study of household energy and greenhouse issues.* Prepared by Sustainable Solutions Pty Ltd, June 1998. http://www.greenhouse.gov.au/coolcommunities/strategic/

Australian Institute of Energy. *Energy value and greenhouse emission factor of selected fuels.* http://www.aie.org.au/melb/material/resource/fuels.htm

California Energy Commission. *Consumer tips for appliances.* http://www.consumerenergycenter.org/homeandwork/homes/inside/appliances/

Coley, D. A., Goodliffe, E. and Macdiarmid, J. (1998) The embodied energy of food: the role of diet. *Energy Policy*, **26**(6), 455–9.

Community Carbon Reduction Project (CRED), UK. http://www.cred-uk.org/index.aspx

Crawford, R. H. and Treloar, G.J. (2004) Net energy analysis of solar and conventional domestic hot water systems in Melbourne, Australia. *Solar Energy*, **76**(1–3), 159–63.

CSIRO Manufacturing & Infrastructure Technology. *Embodied Energy.* http://www.cmit.csiro.au/brochures/tech/embodied/

Durrenberger, G., Patzel, N. and Hartmann, C. (2001) Household energy consumption in Switzerland. *International Journal of Environment and Pollution*, **15**(2), 159–70.

Glover, J., White, D. O. and Langrish, T. A. G. (2002) Wood versus concrete and steel in house construction: a life cycle assessment. *Journal of Forestry*, **100**(8), 34–41.

Hashimoto, S., Nose, M., Obara, T. and Moriguchi, Y. (2002) Wood products: potential carbon sequestration and impact on net carbon emissions of industrialized countries. *Environmental Science and Policy*, **5**, 183–93.

Jungbluth, N., Tieje, O. and Scholz, R. W. (2000) Food purchases: impacts from the consumers' point of view investigated with a modular LCA. *International Journal of Life Cycle Analysis*, **5**(3), 134–42.

Kunkel, K. E., Pielke Jr, R. A. and Changnon, S.A. (1999) Temporal fluctuations in weather and climate extremes that cause economic and human health impacts: a review. *Bulletin of the American Meteorological Society*, **80**(6), 1077–98. http://sciencepolicy.colorado.edu/admin/publication_files/resourse-75-1999.11.pdf

Natural Resources Canada (2003) *Energy Use Data Handbook 1990 and 1995 to 2001: Canada's natural resources now and in the future.* http://oee.nrcan.gc.ca/corporate/statistics/neud/dpa/data_e/Handbook04/Datahandbook2004.pdf

National Assessment Synthesis Team, US Global Change Research Program (2000) *Climate Change Impacts in the United States: The Potential Consequences of Climate Variability and Change.* Cambridge University Press, Cambridge.

Office of Energy Efficiency, Canada. *Statistics and Analysis.* http://oee.nrcan.gc.ca/corporate/statistics/neud/dpa/home.cfm?text=N&printview=N

Parry, M., Arnell, N., Hulme, M., Nicholls, R., and Livermore, M. (1998) Adapting to the inevitable. *Nature*, **395**, 741.

Reddy, B. V. V. and Jagadish, K. S. (2003) Embodied energy and alternative building materials and technologies. *Energy and Buildings*, **35**(2), 129–37.

Rocky Mountain Institute. *Household Greenhouse Gas Emissions and Savings Measures.* http://www.rmi.org/sitepages/pid341.php

UK Energy Saving Trust. *My Home.* http://www.est.org.uk/myhome/

US Energy Information Administration. *Historical energy data for the US.* http://www.eia.doe.gov/neic/historic/hconsumption.htm

US Energy Information Administration. *Monthly energy review, US.* http://www.eia.doe.gov/emeu/mer/contents.html

US Energy Information Administration. *Residential energy consumption surveys, US.* http://www.eia.doe.gov/emeu/recs/contents.html

US Environmental Protection Agency and US Department of Energy. *Energy Star.* http://www.energystar.gov/

Wiel, S. and McMahon, J. E. (2003) Governments should implement energy-efficiency standards and labels – cautiously. *Energy Policy*, **31**, 1403–15.

Wilson, R. and Young, A. (1996) The embodied energy payback period of photovoltaic installations applied to buildings in the UK. *Building and Environment*, **31**(4), 299–305.

## Chapter 4

Carlsson-Kanyama, A. (1998) Climate change and dietary choices – how can emissions of greenhouse gases from food consumption be reduced? *Food Policy*, **23**(3/4), 277–93.

Carlsson-Kanyama, A. *et al.* (2003) Food and life cycle energy inputs: consequences of diet and ways to increase efficiency. *Ecological Economics*, **44**, 293–307.

Hora, M. and Tick, J. (2001) *From Farm to Table: Making the Connection in the Mid-Atlantic Food System*. Capital Area Food Bank of Washington DC report.

Jones, A. (2001). *Eating Oil: Food Supply in a Changing Climate*. Sustain and Elm Farm Research Centre.

Jones, A. (2002) An environmental assessment of food supply chains: a case study of dessert apples. *Environmental Management*, **30**(4), 560–76.

Kramer, K. J. *et al.* (1999) Greenhouse gas emissions related to Dutch food consumption. *Energy Policy*, **27**, 203–16.

Lawrence, F. (2004) *Not on the Label: What Really Goes into the Food on Your Plate*. Penguin, London.

Parry, M., Rosenzweig, C., Iglesias, A., Fischer, G. and Livermore, M. (1999). *Global Environmental Change – Human and Policy Dimensions*, **9**: S51–S67 Supplement S.

Pirog, R., Van Plet, T., Enshayan, K. and Cook, E. (2001) Report for Leopold Center for Sustainable Agriculture, Iowa, US. http://www.leopold.iastate.edu/pubs/staff/papers.htm

Siikavirta, H. *et al.* (2003) Effects of e-commerce on greenhouse gas emissions: a case study of grocery home delivery in Finland. *Journal of Industrial Ecology*, **6**(2), 83–97.

Subak, S. (1999) Global environmental costs of beef production. *Ecological Economics*, **30**(1), 79–91.

## Chapter 5

Australian Department of the Environment and Health (2001) *Independent assessment of kerbside recycling in Australia*, Volume 1. NOLAN-ITU Pty Ltd and Sinclair Knight Merz. Manly, NSW. http://www.deh.gov.au/industry/waste/covenant/kerbside.html

Bentham, G. (2002) Food poisoning and climate change. In Department of Health report – *Health Effects of Climate Change in the UK*, 4.2, pp. 81–98.

Bisgrove, R. and Hadley, P. (2002) *Gardening in the Global Greenhouse: The Impacts of Climate Change on Gardens in the UK*. Technical Report, UKCIP, Oxford.

Centre for Disease Control and Prevention. US Department of Health and Human Services. http://www.cdc.gov/

Environment Canada. *Canada's Greenhouse Gas Inventory 1990-2000.* Greenhouse Gas Division, Environment Canada. http://www.ec.gc.ca/pdb/ghg/1990_00_report/appa_e.cfm

Fehr, M. Cacado, M. D. R. and Romao, D. C. (2002) The basis of a policy for minimizing and recycling food waste. *Environmental Science and Policy,* **5**, 247–53.

Hayhoe, K. *et al.* (2004) Emissions pathways, climate change, and impacts on California. *Proceedings of the National Academy of Sciences of the United States of America,* **101**(34), 12422–7.

Hulme, M. (2003) Abrupt climate change: can society cope? *Philosophical Transactions of the Royal Society Series A,* **361**(1810), 2001–19.

NASA. Earth Observatory. http://earthobservatory.nasa.gov/

Parfitt, J. (2002) *Analysis of Household Waste Composition and the Factors Driving Waste Increases.* Strategy Unit, UK Government. http://www.number-10.gov.uk/su/waste/report/downloads/composition.pdf

Parliamentary Office of Science and Technology (2004) UK health impacts of climate change. *POSTnote* Number 232.

Pickin, J. G., Yuen, S. T. S. and Hennings, H. (2002) Waste management options to reduce greenhouse gas emissions from paper in Australia. *Atmospheric Environment,* **36**(4), 741–52.

Reay, D. S. (2003) Sinking methane. *Biologist,* **50**(1), 15–19.

UK Department of Trade and Industry (2002) *Environmental Life Cycle Assessment and Financial Life Cycle Analysis of the WEEE Directive and its Implications for the UK.* Report prepared by PriceWaterhouseCoopers. http://www.dti.gov.uk/support/dtiweeeupdate.pdf

US Energy Information Administration (2003) *Emissions of Greenhouse Gases in the United States 2003: Methane Emissions.* http://www.eia.doe.gov/oiaf/1605/ggrpt/methane.html

US Environmental Protection Agency. *Greenhouse Gas Emissions from Management of Selected Materials in Municipal Solid Waste.* Washington, DC. http://www.epa.gov/epaoswer/non-hw/muncpl/ghg/chapter4.pdf

US Environmental Protection Agency. *WasteWise: Changing with Climate.* Washington, DC.

US Environmental Protection Agency (2003) *Municipal Solid Waste in the United States: 2001 Facts and Figures.* Office of Solid Waste and Emergency Response. Washington, DC.

WasteWatch. *WasteOnline: In Depth Information on Waste.* http://www.wasteonline.org.uk/

Weitz, K. A., Thorneloe, S. E., Nishtala, S. R., Yarosky, S. and Zannes, M. (2002) The impact of municipal solid waste management on greenhouse gas emission in the United States. *Journal of the Air and Waste Management Association*, **52**(9), 1000–11.

Williams, I. D. and Kelly, J. (2003) Green waste collection and the public's recycling behaviour in the Borough of Wyre, England. *Resources, Conservation and Recycling*, **38**, 139–59.

## Chapter 6

Adams, D. and Carwardine, M. (1991) *Last Chance to See.* Pan Macmillan, London.

Allen, M.R. (2004) The Blame Game: Who will pay for the damaging consequences of climate change? *Nature* **432**, 551–2

Anderson, K. and Starkey, R. (2004) *Domestic Tradable Quotas: a policy instrument for the reduction of greenhouse gas emissions.* An Interim Report to the Tyndall Centre for Climate Change Research. Tyndall North, Manchester.

Australian Greenhouse Office (2002) *Living With Climate Change – An Overview of Potential Climate Change Impacts on Australia.* http://www.greenhouse.gov.au/impacts/overview/

Barker, T. and Ekins, P. (2004) The costs of Kyoto for the US economy. *Energy Journal*, **25**(3), 53–71.

Broadmeadow, M. (2000) Climate change – implications for forestry in Britain. *Forestry Commission Bulletin*, 125. Forestry Commission UK.

Burke, L. and Maidens, J. (2004) *Reefs at Risk in the Caribbean.* World Resources Institute. http://pdf.wri.org/reefs_caribbean_full.pdf

Clarkson, R. and Deyes, K. (2002) *Estimating the social cost of carbon emissions.* Government Economic Service Working Paper 140. http://www.hm-treasury.gov.uk/media/209/60/SCC.pdf

DeLeo, G. A., Rizzi, L., Caizzi, A. and Gatto, M. (2001) The economic benefits of the Kyoto Protocol. *Nature*, **413**, 478–9.

Dresner S. and Ekins, P. (2004) *Economic Instruments for a Socially Neutral National Home Energy Efficiency Programme.* Policy Studies Institute Research Discussion Paper 18. http://www.psi.org.uk/docs/rdp/rdp18-dresner-ekins-energy.pdf

Dresner, S. and Ekins, P. (2004) *The Distribution Impacts of Economic Instruments to Limit Greenhouse Gas Emissions from Transport*. Policy Studies Institute Research Discussion Paper 19. http://www.psi.org.uk/docs/rdp/rdp19-dresner-ekins-transport.pdf

Dresner S. and Ekins, P. (2004) *Charging for Domestic Waste: Combining Environment and Equity Considerations*. Policy Studies Institute Research Discussion Paper 20. http://www.psi.org.uk/docs/rdp/rdp20-dresner-ekins-waste.pdf

Insure.com (2002) *10 Years Later, Hurricane Andrew Would Cost Twice as Much*. http://info.insure.com/home/disaster/andrewtoday/

Howarth, R. B. (2001) Intertemporal social choice and climate stabilization. *International Journal of Environment and Pollution*, **15**(4), 386–405.

Kamal, W. A. (1997) Improving energy efficiency – the cost-effective way to mitigate global warming. *Energy Conversion and Management*, **38**(1), 39–59.

Ogden, J. M., Williams, R. H. and Larson, E. D. (2004) Societal lifecycle costs of cars with alternative fuels/engines. *Energy Policy*, **32**(1), 7–27.

O'Hara, M. (2004) Homeowners face a rising tide. Jobs and Money, *The Guardian*, 14 February, p. 9.

Stott, P. A., Stone, D. A. and Allen, M. R. (2004) Human contribution to the European heatwave of 2003. *Nature*, **432**, 610–14.

Thomas, C. D. *et al.* (2004) Extinction risk from climate change. *Nature*, **427**, 145–8.

Tol, R. S. J. and Verheyen, R. (2004) State responsibility and compensation for climate change damages – a legal and economic assessment. *Energy Policy*, **32**(9), 1109–30.

US Energy Information Administration (1998) *Impacts of the Kyoto Protocol on US Energy Markets and Economic Activity*. US Department of Energy, Washington, DC. http://www.eia.doe.gov/oiaf/kyoto/pdf/sroiaf9803.pdf

US Environmental Protection Agency (2003) *Pay-As-You-Throw: A Cooling Effect On Climate Change*. http://www.epa.gov/mswclimate/

Yohe, G., Neumann, J., Marshall, P. and Ameden, H. (1996) The economic cost of greenhouse-induced sea-level rise for developed property in the United States. *Climatic Change*, **32**(4), 387–410.

# Chapter 7

Clark, T. *Greening Your Final Arrangements*. Jewish-Funerals.org http:/
/www.jewish-funerals.org/greeningfinal.htm

Clean Air – Cool Planet. http://www.cleanair-coolplanet.org/

Linderhof, V. G. M. (2001) Household demand for energy, water and
the collection of waste: a microeconometric analysis. *PhD Thesis*,
Rijksuniversiteit, Groningen. Labyprint Publication, Holland.

Lyman, F. (2003) Green graves give back to nature: eco-friendly
funerals break new ground. *MSNBC News*. http://msnbc.msn.com/
id/3076642/

Rosen, K. B. and Meier, A. K. (1999) *Energy use of televisions and video-
cassette recorders in the US*. US Department of Energy. http://
eetd.lbl.gov/EA/Reports/42393/42393.pdf

US Energy Information Administration. *Historical End-Use Consumption Data*. http://www.eia.doe.gov/neic/historic/hconsumption.
htm

US Energy Information Administration. *Environment: Energy Related
Emissions Data, Forecasts and Analyses*. http://www.eia.doe.gov/
environment.html

US Energy Information Administration (2005) *Annual Energy Outlook
2005 with Projections to 2025*. Report #: DOE/EIA-0383(2005).
http://www.eia.doe.gov/oiaf/aeo/

Worrell, E., Price, L., Martin, N., Hendriks, C. and Meida, L. O. (2001)
Carbon dioxide emissions from the global cement industry. *Annual
Review of Energy and the Environment*, **26**, 303–29.

# Chapter 8

Australian Greenhouse Office (2005) *Buildings and Energy: Office
Building Energy Use*. http://www.greenhouse.gov.au/lgmodules/
wep/buildings/training/training4.html

Australian Greenhouse Office. *National Energy Star*. http://
www.energystar.gov.au/

Climate Ark. http://www.climateark.org/

Community for Environmental Engineering and Technology in Australia. http://www.comeeta.org/

Envirowise and the UK Environment Agency. *Green Officiency:
Running a Cost-Effective, Environmentally Aware Office*. GG256.
Envirowise, Oxfordshire.

Adams, D. and Carwardine, M. (1991) *Last Chance to See*. Pan Macmillan, London.

Bunting, M. (2004) *Willing Slaves: How the Overwork Culture is Ruling Our Lives*. HarperCollins, London.

Dauncey, G. and Mazza, P. (2001) *Stormy Weather: 101 Solutions to Global Climate Change*. New Society Publishers, Canada.

Diamond, J. (2005) *Collapse: How Societies Choose to Fail or Survive*. Allen Lane-Penguin, London.

Hilman, M. and Fawcett, T. (2004) *How We Can Save the Planet*. Penguin, London.

Houghton, J. (1997) *Global Warming: The Complete Briefing*. Cambridge University Press, Cambridge.

Intergovernmental Panel on Climate Change (IPCC). (2000) *Aviation and the Global Atmosphere*. Cambridge University Press, Cambridge.

Intergovernmental Panel on Climate Change (IPCC) (2001) *Climate Change 2001: The Scientific Basis*. Cambridge University Press, Cambridge.

Intergovernmental Panel on Climate Change (IPCC) (2001) *Climate Change 2001: Impacts, Adaptation, and Vulnerability*. Cambridge University Press, Cambridge.

Intergovernmental Panel on Climate Change (IPCC) (2001) *Climate Change 2001: Mitigation*. Cambridge University Press, Cambridge.

Jones, A. (2001) *Eating Oil: Food Supply in a Changing Climate*. Sustain and Elm Farm Research Centre, London.

Langholz, J. and Turner, K. (2003) *You Can Prevent Global Warming (and Save Money)*. Andrews McMeel Publishing, Kansas City.

Lawrence, F. (2004) *Not on the Label: What Really Goes into the Food on Your Plate*. Penguin, London.

Lynas, M. (2004) *High Tide: News from a Warming World*. Flamingo, London.

Meyer, A. (2000) *Contraction & Convergence: The Global Solution to Climate Change*. Schumacher Briefings, Green Books, Devon.

Monbiot, G. (2004) *The Age of Consent: A Manifesto for a New World Order*. HarperCollins, London.

National Assessment Synthesis Team, US Global Change Research Program (2000) *Climate Change Impacts in the United States: The Potential Consequences of Climate Variability and Change*. Cambridge University Press, Cambridge.

Smith, A. and Baird, N. (2005) *Save Cash & Save the Planet*. HarperCollins, London.

# index

h
insु
E
ri
U
Inte

IPC

jour

kitcl
Kyo
U
U

lanc
m
pi
leish
lifes
lifes
di
light
lo
Lon
Lym

mala
mea
cc
qu
meta
metl
Au
frc
gr
frc
frc
pa
so
metl

A1F1    175, 178
Adams, Douglas    126
air fresheners, plug-in    75
air pollution    101
air travel    47–8
    11 September 2001    146
    changing destinations    49
    growth of    144
    long-haul    49
    short-haul    49
    US business trips    51
    USA    144
    weather and    48
air-conditioning    12, 14, 59–60
    cars    43
aircraft    25
    greenhouse gas emissions    47,
        49
apples    91

basket of six    18
biofuel    40, 42
    greenhouse gas emissions    40

boilers    72, 75

car pool    36
car travel
    effects of climate change on
        29–30
    increasing cost of    30
carbon dioxide
    fertilisation effect    83
    increasing levels of    17
    UK emissions    174
carbon dioxide emissions,
        comparison    47
Carbone, George    7–8
Carbone, Grandma    9–10, 141
    death    146
    greenhouse gas emissions    141,
        143, 146, 149
    marriage    141
    retirement    146
    retirement apartment    68
Carbone, Henry    8
Carbone, John    6–7

public transport   33
  inconvenience of   33–4
  need to improve   31
  reduction in emissions   33
  short journeys   43
  subsidies needed   33
  USA   32

radon   100
Reasons for Concern   176–7
recycling   114, 170
  cans   168
  government initiatives   115
  reduce, reuse, recycle   110, 114
renewable energy
  home   76–7
resources, used by West   21
retirement   68
roads, effects of climate change on
    30
Rolling Stones, The   51

schools   160
scientific consensus   20
  dissenting scientists   20–1
screensavers   165
sea level rise   12–13, 15, 57, 130,
    136–7
  Japan   137
  Netherlands   136
SF6 see sulphur hexafluoride
shopping   91–2
  Christmas   95
  Internet   92
shops, greenhouse gas emissions
    160, 162–3
single-living   61
ski resorts, decline of   128
smoke   100
smoking analogy   32, 158
solar energy
  cost   77
  home   76

water heating   77
solar power, cars   41
speed, reducing   43
standby power   74–5, 174
subsidence   58
sulphur hexafluoride   18
sustainability   122

taxes, global warming-related   136
temperature rise
  UK   57
  USA   57
termites   106
textiles   114
Thanksgiving   94
ticks   103
timber, building construction   66
tourism   126–7
trash bins   107
travelling, avoiding   45
trees
  Christmas   98
  planting in gardens   119
  planting to offset emissions   51
  storm damage   129

UN Framework Convention on
    Climate Change   19
UNFCC see UN Framework
    Convention on Climate
    Change
universities, greenhouse gas
    emissions   161

vending machines   166

warehouses   160
waste   26
  glass   113
  metal   113
  organic   107–8
  packaging   111
  paper   110

plastic 112–13
textiles 114
wartime 142
water
  contamination 13–14
  food production 86
  for livestock 86
  minimising garden use 119
  shortages 2, 15
water heating 75–6
  solar energy 77
water vapour 18
weather
  extreme 15, 57, 128
    governments and 131
    USA 130
West Nile Virus 103
wind energy, home 78

wine industry, California 83
work, future 124–5
working from home 46–7
  drawbacks 46–7
workplace
  cooling 169
  energy wastage 159
  greenhouse gas emissions 159–62
  heating 169
  lighting 158–9, 164
  office equipment 165
  overheating 158–9
  reducing emissions 163–72
  shops 160
World Solar Challenge 41
worm bin 109

# THE WHOLE STORY

ALTERNATIVE
MEDICINE
ON TRIAL?

## TOBY MURCOTT

**THE WHOLE STORY**
**ALTERNATIVE MEDICINE ON TRIAL?**
by Toby Murcott
MACMILLAN; ISBN: 1–4039–4500–4; £16.99/$24.95; HARDCOVER
ISBN: 0–230–00753–8; £8.99/$14.95; PAPERBACK

"Essential reading. A balanced, sympathetic and long overdue look at the relationship between science and complementary medicine." *Focus Magazine*

"This book should be prescribed for bigots on both sides, to be taken thoughtfully, all the way to the last page." *Guardian*

order now from www.macmillanscience.com